DEFENSE AND CONSENSUS

There is today clear recognition that Western security policy cannot be formulated without due regard for the public opinion and the domestic political context of the countries concerned. To an extent that has always been true but, as the articles assembled here demonstrate, the need to establish and maintain a broad domestic consensus is now very much more pressing than it has ever been before. How that consensus can be established through effective public communication is one aspect of the problem but clear explanation and consistent political leadership is not the sole need; here another is for governments to formulate policies which carry conviction and are broadly acceptable to our peoples; a third is the increasing relative cost of defense and the impact of that cost on social programs in a period of recession; and finally there is the increasingly contentious issue of the extent to which minority groups holding strong views can or should be accommodated within the democratic process.

This book addresses these important questions. The authors analyze and describe current trends and political forces and they argue cogently that governments have tended in the past to ignore their publics when, either singly or in combination, they have developed their security policies. The contributors represent a wide cross-section of international opinion and were drawn deliberately from different sides of the security debate. Contained in the book are many suggestions as to what governments should and should not do if they wish to establish a domestic consensus on security policy, given that the issues are now more rather than less complex and increasingly difficult to explain in terms which carry conviction to the growing sceptical and alert publics.

The editor
Cristoph Bertram

The other contributors
Kurt Biedenkopf
Harold Brown
David Calleo
Sir Frank Cooper
Joseph Fromm
Johan Jørgen Holst
Michael Howard
Samuel P. Huntington
Lawrence Kaagan
Dominique Moïsi
Masashi Nishihara
Adam Roberts
Lothar Ruehl
Rudolf Wildenmann

Also from St. Martin's Press:

Studies in International Security

James Cable: GUNBOAT DIPLOMACY, 1919–1979
Lawrence Freedman: THE EVOLUTION OF NUCLEAR
  STRATEGY
Gwyn Harries-Jenkins (*editor*): ARMED FORCES AND THE
  WELFARE SOCIETIES: CHALLENGES IN THE 1980s

International Institute for Strategic Studies conference papers

Christoph Bertram (*editor*):
  AMERICA'S SECURITY IN THE 1980s

DEFENSE AND CONSENSUS

The Domestic Aspects of Western Security

Edited by

CHRISTOPH BERTRAM

St. Martin's Press   New York

© The International Institute for Strategic Studies 1983

All rights reserved. For information, write:
St. Martin's Press, Inc., 175 Fifth Avenue, New York, NY 10010
Printed in Great Britain
Published in the United Kingdom by The Macmillan Press Ltd
First published in the United States of America in 1983

ISBN 0–312–19098–0

Library of Congress Cataloging in Publication Data
Main entry under title:

Defense and consensus.

  Includes index.
  1. Europe—Military policy—Addresses, essays,
lectures. 2. United States—Military policy—Addresses,
essays, lectures. 3. Europe—Politics and government—
1945—   —Addresses, essays, lectures. 4. United
States—Politics and government—1981–   —Addresses,
essays, lectures. 5. Japan—Military policy—Addresses,
essays, lectures. 6. Japan—Politics and government—
1945–   —Addresses, essays, lectures. I. Bertram,
Christoph, 1937–
UA646.D45 1983   355′.0335′4   83–40182
ISBN 0–312–19098–0

11-14-84

CONTENTS

Introduction

CHRISTOPH BERTRAM

The Papers presented in these volumes were presented at the 24th Annual Conference of the International Institute of Strategic Studies in September 1982. It was a conference devoted to one of the most ambiguous, imprecise and elusive aspects of security: that of the domestic political factors influencing defence policies, doctrines and burdens. This is one reason why the subject has generally been unexplored in traditional strategic studies. The other is that, as long as domestic consensus on these matters existed, there was no real pressure to address them; that idyllic state of affairs no longer exists.

An important part of the public in our societies is no longer willing to trust governments or experts or even the media on matters of defence policy.

The Decline of Consensus
Many reasons can be advanced for the decline of political consensus. On a general level, our societies have become more sceptical, more half-informed, and hence more prone to doubt and question than to accept and agree. The *élites* have, as Rudolf Wildenmann and David Calleo point out, been in the forefront of this process, not mass public opinion. Moreover in all our countries, domestic priorities have acquired greater weight precisely at a time when the financial means of the state to provide a horizon of expectation have become tight, with the result that national consensus has been undermined, political forces have become fragmented, and frictions have been brought forth which in more affluent times could be lubricated away. For Kurt Biedenkopf, consensus on matters of defence and security can no longer be expected simply to derive from trust in political and military institutions. Indeed, the placing of trust in governments – with the notable exception of Japan – seems to have suffered a major setback.

But this has been a gradual, not an abrupt, evolution and cannot therefore alone explain why the decline of consensus has been a feature particularly of the past few years, or indeed why that decline has been partial, directed primarily against the nuclear dimension of Western defence. No such questioning and doubt has as yet affected conventional military efforts, although there are signs that this, too, might be drawn into the fray of controversy before too long.

There can be no doubt that nuclear issues have become more controversial, that there is now a widespread, if unjustified, fear of nuclear war, and that the beginning of the expression of this fear can be dated with some precision: to the 1979 NATO decision on introducing new medium-range missiles in Europe if negotiations for mutual limitations should fail, and the advent of the Reagan Administration in the United States. Lawrence Kaagan's Paper underlines that this is not merely a European phenomenon but an American one as well, although in the US this seems to lie more with President Reagan's bellicose rhetoric than with specific weapons decisions which have triggered public awareness and concern. There can be little doubt on this point: if nuclear deterrence is unaccompanied by a serious search for arms control, and presented in terms that suggest that governments are willing to engage in fighting rather than deterring nuclear conflict, while at the same time there is a marked deterioration in Soviet-American relations, this cannot but provoke public anxiety and fear. It may well be true that part of this anxiety follows from the decline in American power, as Samuel Huntington suggests. But even here, developments have been gradual, not abrupt: nuclear parity has been a fact of life for over a decade, and it has generally been viewed with greater calm in Europe than in the United States. In democratic societies, the way that govern-

1

ments and experts talk about nuclear weapons determines public acceptability; recent talk about nuclear weapons, starting – as Harold Brown admitted – before the Reagan Administration with the presentation of PD 59 in 1980, could not but erode that acceptability. This came at a time when public sensibilities had already been strained by the 'neutron bomb' affair two years earlier, by the NATO decision in 1979 and by the seemingly esoteric discussion over the MX missile and its elusive basing concept. Perhaps the true explanation for the outburst of concern lies here: the system was overloaded, and sensitive management of the issues involved was woefully absent.

Presentation or Substance?

It is probably no longer enough just to rely on better presentation: the substance of nuclear deterrence itself will have to be re-examined and adjusted to be acceptable for the public opinion of the 1980s. The problem will not go away. The peace and freeze movements will not disappear.

How to make nuclear deterrence more rational, more dependable and – so the assumption runs – more acceptable? There can be no real doubt that nuclear deterrence will remain essential to Western security. Nuclear weapons, just like the concerns they raise, are here to stay.

The remedies proposed remain, instead, within the system of deterrence; they involve adjustment and not radical departures. There can be no return to the sole reliance on a doctrine of mutual assured destruction, however tempting this might at times seem to America's allies. This is because it is precisely their need for protection under the American nuclear umbrella that requires the creation of options involving less than all-out nuclear strikes. Yet it is the practical translation of extended deterrence into strategic planning that has raised the concern on both sides of the Atlantic: in Europe of a limitation of conflict to the European territory; in the US of staking one's survival on a less than essential threat. Proposals for a more rational posture and doctrine must thus address these issues.

Michael Howard's call for reassurance through greater reliance on European conventional military efforts provides a coherent rationale for an Alliance less dependent on the threat of the use of nuclear weapons. Johan Holst's proposal of a posture of 'assured reflection', which emphasizes the survivability of command and control and of delivery systems rather than counter-force capability, has not only the merit of a more benign designation than that customary in strategic language, but also that of directing strategic thinking away from a fascination with the multitude of conceivable scenarios to the central task of imposing a barrier between the outbreak of war and the use of nuclear weapons. The apparent consensus that battlefield nuclear weapons could and should be scaled down is both politically attractive and in the interest of increasing control and delaying the nuclear decision in a crisis. Whether or not there should be a formal NATO declaration not to use nuclear weapons first remains an issue to be debated. But on balance the argument that there is little to gain in terms of political support, and something useful to lose in terms of the deterrence value of ambiguity and uncertainty seems to be difficult to dispute. After all, NATO finds itself today in a *de facto* 'no-first-use' situation given the potential consequences likely to follow from *any* firing of a nuclear weapon. Moreover, Soviet military planners cannot count on no first nuclear use by the West in times of war, however emphatically it is declared beforehand, while Soviet diplomacy could use such a declaration to interfere with Western nuclear decisions in peacetime.

A more rational nuclear posture is not necessarily identical with a more acceptable one. Even if the West were to decide tomorrow to adopt the Howard model, or a doctrine of 'assured reflection', if it were to do away with short-range battlefield nuclear forces, or if it renounced the first use of nuclear weapons, the basic uneasiness would remain: deterrence cannot be discussed as if it were disembodied from war and fighting, and the question what happens if deterrence should fail is not answered in these proposals.

The basic dilemma remains: deterrence has to be credible in order to deter, and that requires thinking and planning beyond the point where deterrence might fail. The present school of strategic thought which emphasizes the need for discreet countervailing deterrence at every level would seem to be misguided since it is essentially open-ended and seeks to refine what is basically non-refinable, namely the crude and primitive threat of using nuclear weapons once vital interests are threatened by an aggressor. But these are, in the final analysis, differences of degree, not fundamental alternatives of how to assure deterrence through nuclear weapons. Even Michael Howard's concept of deterrence depends on 'the distinct possibility that the conflict might escalate to nuclear war'. If public opinion is worried about the possible use of nuclear weapons, no policy based on threatening their use, even *in extremis*, can reassure them. Nuclear forces, in Dominique Moïsi's phrase, tend to atomize the spirit of defence. Correcting some of the excesses of present nuclear doctrines in isolation will not, by itself, re-establish the lost consensus.

The other challenge to domestic consensus lies in the economic costs of defence. The continued willingness of all European NATO members – and, Lawrence Kaagan's poll results suggest, not only theirs – to find the money to sustain the apparatus for deterrence and defence as at present conceived and organized must be very much in doubt. This is essentially for two reasons. First, the cost pressures within the defence sector push against the ceiling of realistically obtained increases in funding. Second, governments in the West are no longer willing to incur the large deficits in public expenditure which they accepted in the past and through which they were able to avoid the tough choice between allocating resources for internal welfare and external protection.

The political consequences of these two factors are gradually emerging. In the United States, as David Calleo points out, a budgetary freeze risks a backlash not only against the expanded military budget but against the NATO commitment itself. While the Mansfield Resolutions in the 1970s for bringing American forces home were motivated by concern over America's over-extension, similar requests may soon be pushed by the concern over the overall budget deficit and the sacrifices in welfare spending that ambitious defence pro-

grammes suggest. If public opinion in practically all Western countries is today supporting present defence expenditure in the non-nuclear field, this cannot, therefore, be taken for granted in the near future. The pressures are clearly mounting. Today, the issue of nuclear weapons is in the forefront of the public doubts over the wisdom of established security policies; tomorrow it may well be the issue of defence spending as such.

This gives particular importance both to the utmost rationalization in the defence sector, and to efforts to cut costs. Sir Frank Cooper addresses these possibilities in his Paper but he does not hide the limitations. There is a need for more effective long-range planning, since rational spending becomes easier if you know how much you have to spend. Perhaps there might be ways if not to standardize equipment at least to standardize specialized military education. Much promise was seen in the concept of multi-purpose platforms, implying a basic vehicle, aircraft or ship to which specialized missions could then be attached. The lessons of the Falklands War point to the option of making much greater use of the non-military, commercial capabilities that are available in the total arsenal of the Western countries, but no major breakthrough is apparent that would reduce the costs of sustaining the apparatus of defence *as at present conceived and organized.*

It may be necessary, therefore, to go beyond defence as presently conceived and organized. This may mean, as Sir Frank Cooper emphasizes, looking at output of military effectiveness rather than input of money; examining and reorganizing existing military structures and organizations; and making a stronger assault on the 'defence culture', which at present tends to reproduce its judgments and fossilize its positions and thus to control choice by inertia. But this is a task made even more difficult by the economic recession, when the vested interests in the armed forces and the defence bureaucracies tend to dig in, preferring to consolidate rather than to risk being cut down by politicians under pressure.

Re-establishing the Context
But can greater rationality in the economic, as in the nuclear sector, do more than satisfy the

expert? Can it convince a sceptical, and perhaps increasingly sceptical, public? Can the remedies be applied, the arguments won, in isolation?

One central aspect of this question is how public arguments are shaped. This is examined in three Papers dealing with the media, their influence on defence policy, and their influence on the image of policy in the United States, in Japan, and in Western Europe. All of them, particularly those written by professional journalists, conclude that the impact of the press is fairly marginal: in the United States the press is the conveyor belt for government; in Europe and Japan it follows the fashions.

With the possible exception of the 'neutron bomb' affair of a few years ago, when one particular press story defined the public debate, no single decision on defence policy seems to have been taken or not taken because of press reporting. Yet the former journalist Lothar Ruehl, who has assumed high office in Government, was very much concerned about the quality of the press and the impact it has had on policy, not in deciding specific issues, but in narrowing options and giving respectability to opposition arguments.

There was general agreement on the limitations of the press. There is in the US an editorial system which discourages specialization and focuses instead on news stories, with editors not sufficiently concerned and informed about the issues of defence and security, and reporters keen to provide scoops rather than insights. European newsmen fared somewhat better in this *critique* than their American counterparts, for reasons that Joseph Fromm so vividly describes in his Paper.

There has been repeated concern over the impact of television. As Joseph Fromm quotes a prominent TV commentator: 'Will democracy which has uncensored TV in every home ever be able to fight a war, however just?' The electronic medium is probably unhelpful in informing the public, and this has raised questions whether some kind of censorship should not be applied to the visible media in war, as was the case in the Falklands conflict.

There is no question that an informed medium is better than the uninformed one,

but consensus is unlikely to be built on co-ordination in the media. Rather, its role should remain that of raising issues for the debate, to articulate moods. In a crisis, special consideration will have to apply, but whether the handling of the press over the Falkland crisis can serve as a model must remain in doubt. It worked because the British action was crowned by success, but what if it had fallen short of that, requiring public knowledge to sustain, in adversity, public support in Britain?

Even with a more informed, expert or responsible press the problem of regenerating consensus will not be solved. The media reflects; it rarely creates events and policies. To encourage consensus, therefore, the policies must be right, and they must be convincingly defended.

A Context for Expectations

The central question, therefore, is how to achieve this. To tailor policies to what is acceptable to, or – in Michael Howard's useful term – what reassures, public opinion is as tempting as it is inadequate, for the simple reason that acceptability and reassurance, if tied to specific military programmes, are not an enduring yardstick. It is, after all, only a few years ago, as Harold Brown reminds those who have forgotten, that European governments insisted that *greater* nuclear involvement by the United States was needed to reassure them, and indeed reassurance of sceptical allies was precisely one major reason for the US to embark on the now so controversial NATO programme of nuclear modernization.

This suggests that merely to adjust specific military efforts and doctrines to become more acceptable to public opinion will not be successful. Indeed any answer given in isolation is likely to be inadequate. Rudolf Wildenmann points in his Paper to the way in which the dissent over defence and nuclear matters that arose in the 1950s was overcome and a new consensus created not by arguing in isolation the merits of weapons and missiles, but by putting the problem *in the context of European unification*. The post-war generation of the 1950s 'swallowed the frog' of German rearmament because 'it was linked to a concept of politics which put an end to wars in

Western Europe, by creating new European perspectives'.

This same theme is implicit in most of the Papers in this volume. To rebuild the consensus, so Harold Brown tells us, we need a clearer picture of what Western policy *should* be toward the Soviet Union – in military, economic and political terms. We are in a substantive crisis in the Alliance because of unsolved substantive problems rather than because of sociological phenomena, writes David Calleo. We must not see defence in isolation, writes Sir Frank Cooper. The lack of a persuasive vision of a better future for international relations is as disturbing as it is striking, according to Adam Roberts.

Indeed, the Alliance seemed in better shape, and defence expenditures and even nuclear weapons were less controversial at the time of East–West detente than they are today; it is the breakdown of that contextual framework which has brought forth the new concerns. Nuclear weapons and even defence spending for non-nuclear weapons are not in themselves sustainable by public opinion; they need to be put into a context of expectations. Only a consensus on that context will make the specific military efforts acceptable and reassuring.

If this is true, then the fight for the consensus has been badly conducted. It has only, at best, concentrated on specific issues – the number of Soviet missiles and the technical characteristics of Western missiles. It has not addressed the context for which deterrence and defence are worth having.

This inability, as Rudolf Wildenmann and David Calleo point out, is attributable to a failure of the Western elites, the results of their doubts and fashions, rather than that of public opinion at large. The public continues to believe in the Western Alliance. It is impressive – and surprising – to note the massive US support for the continuation of the European security link in Mr Kaagan's data, despite the frictions between the Allies. But, because the elites lack the confidence of a framework, they tend to narrow the debate to specific aspects which cannot alone justify the effort they demand. In isolation, consensus cannot be built on nuclear weapons, defence, the Alliance or much else.

To regenerate the consensus in the Alliance, more is needed than rational nuclear doctrines or transparent defence decisions. That is helpful, but not enough – particularly once the genie of popular doubt and anxiety has left the bottle. It also needs more than merely indulgence in the futile attempt to define defence policy by what is acceptable alone. Governments, as Johan Holst rightly reminds us, have to persuade and to listen. They are paid to lead, not to follow. They have failed in both in recent years. Leadership means the setting of the framework, of the context of security, in which destructive weapons can make sense. They will not make sense by themselves.

5

Domestic Consensus, Security and the Western Alliance

KURT BIEDENKOPF

In an article entitled 'NATO Myths' (*Foreign Policy*, Winter 1981/82) Lawrence Freedman observes: 'Whether a strategic doctrine is acceptable to the people for whom it has been developed is as important in an alliance of democratic societies as the doctrine's ability to impress the enemy'. Democracy, in Freedman's view, is crucial to defence 'because in a real crisis public pressure will affect the implementation and success of any doctrine'.

Democratic governments, whose mandates for foreign and defence policy are derived, as those for any other area of policy, from majorities determined by general elections, have always had to give heed to domestic consensus as providing the political basis for governmental actions in the security field. Recent history is crowded with examples of the efforts that may be required to produce such a consensus or what the lack of it can do to the execution of strategies and the pursuit of political objectives which those holding public office may have considered to be important or which seem to be demanded by the national interest or to be indispensable to repel imminent dangers to one's country.

Even though the subject is thus familiar to democracies, it has recently acquired new urgency. Two factors have contributed to this change: first the absence of economic growth from which additional defence needs could be satisfied without impediment to other important political objectives; and second the special aspects of nuclear strategy. Both factors, although not necessarily related, have appeared at about the same time, and have added new dimensions to the more familiar aspects of domestic consensus in defence policy.

Economics and Defence Consensus
With the lack of economic growth, it has become necessary for governments and legislators to make choices between defence appropriations and the earmarking of public funds for other, primarily domestic, economic and social programmes. Those who are asked to approve defence spending in elections today are asked to do so at the expense of social benefits or other transferral payments which they might otherwise have received. Thus defence outlays must be justified in ways that were not previously necessary to an increasingly well-informed general public.

In an alliance such as NATO the matter is further complicated by comparisons of the relative burdens placed upon the populations of member countries. If he is asked to explain the need for certain defence expenditures to his constituency, Senator Roth observed recently, the task will become next to impossible to achieve if the relative burdens placed on his voters and on the voters of his German counterpart do not approximate to their relative income or buying power. Or, to put it differently, if the Ford worker in Detroit is asked to approve of a defence burden of 6% of GNP, his willingness to do so will drastically decline if he learns that his counterpart at Ford Cologne can get away with approving only 3% of GNP for defence although his family income may enable him to travel extensively and his country's legislation gives him protection against social and personal risks which his American fellow-worker is asked to bear personally.

Consensus and the Nuclear Question
Apart from economic considerations and a new look at long-established priorities, the growing awareness of the special dangers and risks of nuclear strategy have clouded domestic consensus with respect to defence and security matters. Before he died, President Eisenhower is said to have predicted that, in

view of the menace of nuclear war, people would one day rise up and demand an end to this madness. Recently indications that this might indeed happen have appeared both in Europe and in the United States. Although differing in motives and objectives as well as organization, the so-called Peace Movements have succeeded in drawing general attention to the paradox of the policy of nuclear deterrence. The double-track decision of NATO, passed in the Autumn of 1979 and calling for the deployment of *Pershing* II and cruise missiles in 1983, if negotiations between the US and the Soviet Union in Geneva are not successful, has become a sort of catalyst for the movement in Germany and also in other European countries. In the US it has focused on demands to freeze nuclear armament in both the West and the East.

It goes without saying that such developments must affect the Alliance. As an organization for mutual defence, it is not based on an international treaty alone, which, once ratified by parliaments, is then executed by governments without further public control. The Alliance's real foundation is the support given to its objectives and strategies by the majorities of the peoples making up the Alliance.

The Nature of Consensus

As a consequence the Alliance has always been looked upon as a community of nations sharing common values and basic political objectives, united in the love for freedom and the determination to protect it. They are NATO's real charter. They have lent the Alliance its special character and cohesion. Overriding all national differences within the Atlantic Community, they have in the past successfully served as pillars on which the basic common interests rest. Most important of all they are the foundation for domestic consensus within the member countries. Freedom, democracy and human rights as common heritage and political beliefs were able to unite nations in common action that had been allies or enemies during the long course of European history.

More recently, however, this community of values and objectives seems to have weakened. Behind the political rhetoric, articulated as recently as on President Reagan's visit to Europe, more basic differences within the Alliance appear. They seem to change the nature and importance of the consensus still required in the light of the Alliance's overriding commitment to peace and the defence of freedom in Europe. Younger generations, unaware of NATO's charter experience and the continuing threats of totalitarian systems to human rights and freedom, are demanding new policies and are willing to apply new and as yet untested methods to secure peace. National interests are being restated and security priorities are being pitted against the community's interests. Apprehension is growing that the fabric of common objectives might grow weaker and no longer prove strong enough to absorb the shocks and pressures of the special interests pursued by member nations. Differences between the US and their European Allies on the strategic merits of trade sanctions imposed on the Soviet Union and the acceptability of extraterritorial effects of US administrative actions are seen by many as a rather fundamental conflict which might, if permitted to continue, threaten the very basis of the defence alliance.

NATO has certainly undergone times of crisis before. It has come through each one without permanent damage. It has adjusted to change and has proved more flexible than could ordinarily have been expected, given the rigidity of international organizations. The present developments might therefore not give cause for undue concern.

Yet a thorough re-examination of the conditions for consensus within the Alliance seems necessary. The passage of time and the arrival of new generations to shape public opinion and policy together with the sheer success of NATO in securing peace in Europe for more than three decades has not left the old consensus unaffected. What everybody has become accustomed to and learned to accept will increasingly be taken for granted. Confronted with the burden of new conflict the consensus might prove to be less stable and reliable than generally expected. A revitalization of the old consensus is therefore important but that is not enough. In addition the character and conditions of a new consensus must be developed.

If we want to reaffirm the democratic consensus as to our defence policies or to establish a new one, it is helpful to enquire how this consensus is made up and how it is brought into being. A consensus on any question of political relevance to society can be based on agreement on a policy or on support for a policy. If based on agreement, those forming the consensus agree on the substance of the policy in question. They will have studied the matter and have convinced themselves both that the recommended objectives and that the methods of accomplishing these objectives are sensible and that they can agree to them. Or they may firmly believe in the political objectives in question and therefore agree to carry them out. In either case the consensus is based on direct access to the substance of the political matter in question. People, as the saying goes, know what they are talking about. The consensus can be based either on knowledge or on basic beliefs or on common sense.

Obviously today's questions of defence strategies are not of a kind readily accessible even to the educated mind. They are the preserve of highly-trained specialists who have developed a language of their own. The rationale of their thinking and arguments is not easily understood. Indeed it is increasingly removed from those matters of political life which can be verified by personal experience.

Democratic consensus by agreement over substance is therefore rather unlikely to occur in defence matters. It can, however, still be based on public support for those who formulate defence policy, who define its objectives and requirements and who execute it. This kind of consensus is easier to establish. It does not require full knowledge and comprehension of all the intricacies of defence strategy by those who are asked to supply the political mandate for the policy. Rather consensus can be established and maintained if those voting *trust* those formulating policy to do the right things or if the majority considers the policy *plausible* in rather general terms or both. These might be described as *consensus based on trust* and *consensus based on plausibility*.

Trust
For most of the life of NATO, the defence consensus both in Europe and in the United

States has been based on trust. The objectives of our common defence efforts were obvious as were the dimensions of the threat. Progress has been the password and the specialists and experts were seen as the guardians of progress. Governments were expected to assemble the best experts in the fields to master the task of formulating defence policy and were trusted to be able to do so. Matters of cost and quantity seemed relatively easy to comprehend. Basically it was enough simply to point to the dangers posed by the Soviet Union and the Communist Bloc and their holdings of men and arms in order to ensure public support for an expansion of defence outlays or such other actions as were recommended by those in authority. This willingness to trust those in authority, both politically and militarily, has however diminished. To-day it is reasonable to say that defence policies can no longer rely for their political support on consensus based on trust. This is by no means exclusively or even primarily the result of misuse of the trust previously granted. The change that we can observe has been brought about by different developments. Disappointment with the specialization is one of them but it is not the only reason why the willingness to accept formal authority as a substitute for substantial explanation has all but disappeared in most of our Western democracies.

What has basically changed since NATO was founded in 1948 are the educational standards of the population, its level of and access to information and its vastly increased sophistication in all matters of politics. What has often been described as a revolutionary change of public information through the electronic media must obviously have consequences for the establishment and maintenance of public consensus in all public matters, let alone in matters of defence. The influence of an informed public on defence and security policies during the Vietnam War revealed the extent of the change.

As a consequence, consensus on matters of defence and security can no longer be expected to arise simply from trust in political and military institutions. The policies for which consensus is asked must be *plausible*. It must make sense to a well-educated public which time and again has had occasion to doubt the wisdom of specialists and which is supported in its quest for plausibility by the academic community and the media.

Plausibility

If plausibility of defence policy is required to bring about and maintain public consensus, then that policy must be explained. It is this need for explanation and what explanation requires that must be addressed next.

Obviously *any* defence policy only makes sense if there is a perceived need for defence. To the majority of our populations, both in Europe and in the United States, this need seems rather obvious. Even though the plausibility of the threat posed by the Soviet Union and her satellite countries may not be as strong today as it once was and may even have been reduced further during the 1970s by detente, it still prevails. In addition Soviet aggression in Afghanistan and Soviet support for martial law in Poland have helped to remove whatever doubts there may have been about the threat. But establishing a consensus on the basis of the need for defence is not enough. What is also required is public support for whatever answer to this threat is proposed. Defence policy *as such* must be plausible. It must therefore be explained also to those who share the view that it is necessary to be prepared to defend one's freedom and one's way of life.

This in turn means that some basic questions must be answered. One of them relates to the cost of defence. The cost argument has always been important. As long as there was substantial growth in the economy on which to draw, the conflicting demands on public budgets were not as incompatible as they seem today. It was possible then to satisfy both sets of demands and still avoid mounting public debts. We all know that these happy times of easy access to additional defence appropriations have passed. Today if we are to establish a consensus with respect to defence we must explain why certain additional outlays for military purposes are so important that other expectations or political objectives must give way to them.

I do not consider the competition for public funds, resulting from this development to be basically detrimental for the consensus on de-

fence policy but it will demand more explanation and substantial rethinking within the military and the political institutions that have to make decisions. For some time many of us have wondered whether ever more sophisticated weapons systems and technologies, integrating an ever increasing variety of functions and capabilities, are really necessary to do the job that we expect the defence system to accomplish. Large organizations that are permitted to grow rapidly without meeting competitive or other resistance tend to develop waste and their cost-effectiveness declines. This is true for monopoly enterprises. It is basically true also for defence enterprises.

Even though cost-effectiveness might be more difficult to determine in the case of defence, this does not mean that it can be ignored. By being forced to compete for funds, Defence Ministries will come under increasing scrutiny both in their operation and in their bidding for funds. It follows that, although the public may be in no position to judge the merits of particular choices, they are at least assured that political control of defence expenditure is being exercised. This may in the end lead to an increase in plausibility of defence spending and thus strengthen the consensus rather than weaken it.

However this will only be true if two requirements are met: first that the military and defence establishments really accept the competitive process as an expression of political control over the military; and, second, if genuine co-operation develops between defence and those segments of the body politic that are concerned with economic and social matters.

What many see as a coming danger for both social peace and the defence consensus is the conflict between social justice and military security, developing as a result of limited resources. This can be avoided provided that both are recognized as indispensable to the existence and viability of a free society. If this is the case, no basic objection can or should be made to a competition in which defence must argue its case for modern weapon systems or more men and against the need for additional transfer payments in the social area, while those representing the social interest must state their case for additional governmental action and question the wisdom of new defence outlays. Carried on in a constructive manner, this competition may both benefit and educate the general public for it is the general public which must ultimately approve.

Although an indispensable prerequisite, the establishment of the need for adequate defence expenditure is obviously not enough by itself to establish consensus. Apart from the cost, what is bought must be acceptable to the majority. In this context two questions arise which are relevant to the issue of consensus: are the means of our defence adequate to the purpose? are they acceptable as a matter of principal, that is on ethical or moral grounds? The first question is simply a statement of the old question 'How much is enough?' and thus leads to the ever present argument that we must do more because the other side does more. With few interruptions the history of NATO has been a history of the arms competition with the East for the purpose of establishing or maintaining equilibrium. The longer this process continues, the more problematic it will become in terms of establishing consensus. It is one thing to support defence spending and a defence strategy in order to maintain security. It is another to find oneself continuously frustrated by the argument that more is necessary if we are not to fall behind.

This is not only a problem of the nuclear arms competition although the issue is raised primarily in that context. It can also develop into a more general problem of acceptance, especially if we are setting out to strengthen our conventional defences in order to reduce the risk of nuclear war by raising the nuclear threshold.

In any case the plausibility of our defence strategy will be determined by the way we define equilibrium (or balance of potential) in this connection. If I read public debate and argument in my country (West Germany) correctly, we will find it increasingly difficult to maintain our defence consensus if we continue to match arms increases against arms increases and fail to find more independent standards by which to judge what is fundamental to adequate defence and what may be desirable as a marginal addition to safety.

Furthermore equilibrium (or balance) will be seen increasingly as including other factors besides the purely military. One such factor will be the *will* to defend freedom. Even the most sophisticated weapons system cannot substitute for popular will. Without it, a durable consensus on defence is impossible. If the will exists, however, and can be forcefully demonstrated to a potential adversary, it may very well have a substantial deterring effect of its own.

Another factor determining equilibrium will be the degree of consensus and internal support and control which the potential adversary can count on in case of conflict. The internal control of the armies and populations by the Soviet Union and her satellite regimes may have to be re-examined in the light of recent experience in Poland. If a totalitarian government obviously fails to keep even the children and the old women from openly demonstrating their opposition, it is difficult to assume that it would be in unquestioned control and find popular support in the case of armed conflict brought about by its own aggression.

I am fully aware of the complex issues that have to be considered in the calculations of balance. Their obvious relevance, however, demands such inclusion. The possibility of consensus will certainly be affected by the way they are evaluated.

Moral and Ethical Questions
Next to the issue of the budget, the consensus with respect to defence today is most notably threatened by the question of the moral and ethical acceptability of nuclear deterrence. Since Western security as maintained through NATO rests basically if not almost exclusively on the deterrent effect of nuclear arms, to question this defence strategy on ethical and moral grounds obviously goes to the very core of our defence consensus. Much has been said and written about this subject. The balance of terror, as Churchill called it in the 1950s, has always been seen by thoughtful students of the subject as difficult to explain. However, it seemed to have the substantial advantage of being relatively inexpensive to maintain and of avoiding the political and economic burdens connected with the conventional defence

of Europe. Today for all practical purposes we rely on nuclear weapons for defence. The conventional defence of Europe is such that military leaders consider that it provides no more than a 'delaying trip-wire' which, in case of an attack in Central Europe, will give them no more than a week or two to decide whether – in the words General Rogers, the Supreme Allied Commander, Europe – to go nuclear or to capitulate.

It is this situation that determines the fundamental importance of the nuclear debate for the consensus with which we are concerned. To avoid this debate would be foolish. To structure it properly and guide it to a conclusion that is both politically responsible and capable of achieving consensus is the real task before us. The following points seem to me essential:

– We must accept in principle that there is a relevant moral and ethical issue singular to the strategy of nuclear deterrence which cannot be compared with the issues involved in any other form of military defence, however devastating it may be.
– We must accept that all efforts aimed at minimizing the unique risks connected with nuclear deterrence by concepts of flexible nuclear response will not be plausible in the long run. The single most important reason for this contention is that no-one can make reasonable predictions about the possibility of controlling the process of nuclear exchange and curtailing it once it is set into motion.
– We know that we cannot maintain security through NATO for the forseeable future without reliance on the nuclear deterrent. At the same time, however, we must recognize that continued reliance on nuclear weapons for deterrence poses special problems for the consensus. The willingness to support the nuclear deterrent as a permanent basis for peace and security in Europe is diminishing. Both the Protestant and Catholic churches have declared that nuclear deterrence is only acceptable as a 'hardly bearable condition' if all efforts are undertaken to reduce nuclear arms by arms-reduction talks and to develop alternatives to nuclear defence.

– Efforts must therefore be made to develop and execute defence strategies which, while continuing to incorporate nuclear deterrence, tend to reduce the risk of nuclear exchange or the unacceptable alternative described by General Rogers. Obviously this must involve the reduction or elimination of tactical nuclear weapons and an adequate and compensatory increase in conventional defence capability. Just as obviously this also requires that real efforts be made to secure at least a semblance of civil defence in those European countries which are most exposed to possible military conflict.

I am convinced that if argued properly, and if full use is made of the moral and ethical dimensions of the issue, the development of NATO strategy in this direction and its implementation is possible. That is to say, I am convinced that it can be made plausible and thus capable of providing the basis for consensus.

Consensus and Alliance
What has been said so far about the conditions for consensus on defence policy is in principal applicable to the policies of all NATO member states. The practical conclusions that must be drawn for the policy of individual governments are largely determined by the political conditions under which these governments operate and these conditions obviously vary. Differences of considerable magnitude exist not only between the United States and their European allies. They also exist between the European members of NATO. The possession of nuclear arms or the refusal ever to exercise national control over them is one such difference. The relative proximity to possible theatres of conflict is another. Differences in the sizes of populations or in area, in historical backgrounds, in language or in orientation must also be taken into account and contribute to the plurality of conditions within the Alliance.

A defence community, however, is only viable if it is capable of defining and executing a common defence policy. If, as in the case of NATO, this community looks upon itself as a broad community of military and political interests, its defence policy must be defined in such a way as to include at least some basic common strategies in the fields of international trade, relations with the Third World and the like.

Viewed against the issue of consensus, this means that, as a *community of nations*, held together by a common political and cultural heritage, by common economic interests and by common defence purposes, NATO will have a tendency broadly to define the totality of its common interests. Made up as it is of individual democratic nations with individual sovereign governments, periodically facing elections, the consensus with respect to this community's common interests must be established within each member nation. Even if one assumes that, in defining the common policies of NATO, *national* consensus must be established, there will remain an important area of policy centering around defence and security which, because we are considering a *defence* community, must remain an area of common policy. Community policy must be supported by each national consensus.

Because the political conditions for establishing consensus on the common defence policies and strategies differ, the real challenge is to harmonize these two prerequisites of a successful defence community: the definition of a plausible defence strategy, with all its economic, political and strategic implications; and the establishment of the necessary consensus within the member states on a national basis. Since defence is one of the most important (if not the most important) expression of sovereignty and the formation of democratic consensus on defence is a kind of underpinning of democratic government, what is called for is nothing less than the harmonization of fundamental expressions of government and national existence and the foundations of the Atlantic Alliance.

It is important to realize that the plurality of interests within a community of democratic nations determines in part the level of consensus that can be attained. If consensus is to be based primarily on plausibility, whatever is defined as a political objective of the defence community must therefore be plausible also in terms of national consensus.

As long as such objectives relate to the fundamental conditions of the community, they will be plausible. This is obviously true for the commonly shared assumption that there is a need for defence or that there should be a common defence organization as long as there is to be a defence community.

As objectives become more concrete, however, their plausibility is increasingly determined by regional or national political conditions. To include them in the consensus therefore requires that they are defined in such a way as to allow room for regional or national differences. Obviously people who live close to the border dividing Germany will view certain elements of our common defence strategy differently from US citizens living in California or Canadians in Vancouver. The relative proximity to possible conventional conflict will naturally influence one's willingness to defend oneself. It will have relevance too for the support of political efforts at avoiding conflict with the possible adversary. The desirability and extent of political and economic relations with the Soviet Union will therefore tend to be viewed differently, depending on the political conditions and circumstances of the national consensuses under which alternative strategies are evaluated. This means that a durable consensus on a common defence policy can only be maintained within the defence community if this policy takes account of both the interests of the defence community itself and of regional or national conditions and particularities under which that consensus must be established and maintained. Or, to put it differently the Atlantic Alliance as a defence community based on national consensus is viable only if it succeeds in harmonizing the community's interests and the plurality of regional and national political conditions.

One way to do this is to accept the plurality of political conditions and faculties of member states as given and to use this plurality to develop the different functions of the Alliance. Plurality therefore need not be an expression of weakness with centrifugal forces harming the cohesion of the Alliance. Rather, if properly understood, it can serve to strengthen the strategic and tactical means of the defence community. It can broaden the community's scope of action and increase its plausibility at the same time.

If accepted as an opportunity, plurality can thus permit us to define the different contributions made by individual member states to the common objectives of the Alliance as being of equal significance. This can be very important when trying to overcome the problems of determining comparative burdens and the appropriate contributions that each should make to the Alliance. It would, for instance, allow us to accept that maintaining defence consensus in the immediate face of the enemy and the acceptance – under such circumstances – of the stationing of nuclear arms over which one has no control on one's own territory could be regarded as an assumption of a special political burden, to be recognized when enquiring into the equality of burden sharing.

If we are prepared to recognize the plurality of political conditions and regional interests within the community as relevant for the maintenance of consensus, we pay tribute to the fact that an Alliance of democracies is possible only to the extent that its members are capable of establishing the requisite national consensus. At first sight this may seem to be an inherent disadvantage of an alliance of democratic nations when compared to a totalitarian alliance. Indeed there has always been a tendency within NATO to view Western plurality in this way and this is especially true for the military side of the Alliance. More than once have the military leadership of the Alliance felt restrained in the execution of what seemed plausible in military terms by the need to establish plausibility in political terms.

Yet plurality properly applied can be a distinct advantage for the Alliance. Not only does it widen the scope of the tactical and strategic activities of the Alliance but it also increases its flexibility and thus its ability to adapt to meet new challenges and opportunities. If properly correlated with the common objectives of the Alliance, plurality can also broaden the consensus on which the Alliance is based. If individual countries within the Alliance find their own political identities represented in the pursuit of common objectives, the plausibility of consensus is increased. Consensus on defence policies within the defence community can thus be assured if the structural characteristics of the Alliance of democratic nations are properly recognized. This requires that no individual country tries to define its own interests as community interests.

Disregard for this structural condition of the Atlantic Alliance is at the heart of the present dispute between the United States and her European allies on the gas pipeline issue. It is not so much the controversy on the feasibility of sanctions that threatens to divide the Alliance, but rather the way that the United States seems to be trying to impose on the Alliance as a community interest what must appear to the other member states as a national interest of one member. The notion that what is good for General Motors is good for the United States has never been accepted in America. Within the Alliance the same may be true for the relationship between the leading member and its European Allies. What is good for the US may not be good for NATO as a whole.

European consensus on the objectives of the Alliance will thus be determined by, among other things, our readiness to respect and make constructive use of the plurality which exists within the Alliance. If we act properly, all will benefit from whatever increased plausibility and thus political strength the Alliance will gain as a consequence.

Public Opinion and the Defence Effort: Trends and Lessons

The United States

LAWRENCE KAAGAN

By the middle of 1982 it was possible to describe three salient themes which underlay American public opinion with regard to defence and foreign affairs. Deriving from these themes were a wide range of attitudes regarding allies and adversaries, support for and opposition to specific policy initiatives, and the presumed foreign policy mandate which the public has (or has not) offered the Reagan Government. The themes, stated most broadly, are:

- The American public, buffeted by domestic and international events which have shaken presumptions of hegemony, eminence and even potency in world affairs, have been rudely awakened to a world in which the United States can neither dictate nor dominate, and perhaps not even arbitrate. Yet no coherent set of principles has been offered by any recent Administration which would help the public to shape its expectations under these new circumstances. In a variety of situations, bombast has filled in where consistent policy was absent, and the inadvertent result over the period of the last six years is a public mood which is alternately assertive and angry, or disappointed and sullen. There is an inherent instability in a public whose psychology is simultaneously apprehensive and extrovert.
- The American public, starting at its fringes but working quite rapidly through the heart of the body politic, is having new thoughts about the definition of the phrase 'national security'. The decade-long trend, with a brief diversion during the Vietnam War, was to equate higher levels of military spending with higher levels of national security. This trend was accelerated by several traumatic events of 1979 and 1980, principally the taking of diplomatic hostages in Iran, the aborted raid in an attempt to rescue those hostages, and the Soviet invasion of Afghanistan. But since 1981 there has been evidence of second thoughts in the public mind concerning this equation. These second thoughts were prompted by two separate but related developments. The first has been the deep recession afflicting the American economy, and the sharp focus on economic policy during the first half of the Reagan Presidency, including the trade-offs between defence build-up and other national goals brought to light during that time. The second has been an almost uncharacteristic questioning of the premise that 'more is better'. While anxious to have the 'best defence that money can buy', Americans are now less than certain that current or anticipated outlays are in fact buying the 'best', or that throwing money at an arms race is any more likely to buy national security than the same behaviour directed at social welfare programmes is likely to produce 'the Great Society'.
- The third broad theme is closely connected to the first two, but contains such enormous psychological and political potential that it must be isolated and identified in its own right. For the first time, we are seeing the breakdown of what had been a hitherto unexplored popular assumption of American strategic invulnerability. While there is not yet any credible, stable measurement of the proportion of the American public which accepts President Reagan's assertion of Soviet nuclear superiority, his state-

ment, and those of others, have at least awakened a dormant public to the reality of nuclear parity. By a curious logic, the doctrine of Mutual Assured Destruction (MAD), for the years it lasted, was soothing to the national psyche. The all-or-nothing character of the doctrine seemed to dictate that, so long as maniacs were kept away from the button, the world lay suspended between the options of total annihilation and heavily-armed peace, with the latter choice the only reasonable one for both sides. However, since 1981, the American public (and the world public) have been confronted by official statements emanating from Washington which contained talk of nuclear 'warning shots', 'limited' nuclear war, a European nuclear battlefield, and 'winnable' extended exchanges. These concepts have absolutely no credibility with the American public, and have unleashed deep fears where only a short time ago there were complacent assumptions of vague threat. In short order, the invincibility of nuclear hegemony disappeared, the stable protection of MAD disappeared, and for better or worse, the strategic dialogue solely among expert 'mandarins' has disappeared as well. This changed consciousness rippling through the American public is of such magnitude that it is likely to remain until the issues are addressed in a manner the public understands and accepts – not an easy task.

Related to these three themes are a number of other observations about stability and change in US public opinion on international and defence issues. The connection between military budgets and domestic economics, the willingness to apply American force of arms in various circumstances, and the public opinion context of efforts to control and reduce nuclear arms, have all evolved separately but all should be seen in the light of the above mentioned themes.

Public Support for Defence Spending

For the first peacetime period in the nuclear age, the American people are really thinking about the economic impact of large-scale defence spending. Surveys show us several swings in mood from tempered isolationism to what Lloyd Free has recently called 'moderate extrovert internationalism'. And we have seen pre- and post-Vietnam fluctuations in what was considered 'morally' appropriate levels of defence spending. There has been a resurgence of support for a conscripted army and for bilateral reductions in nuclear weapons. Nevertheless, the phrase 'guns versus butter' has clearly taken on new meaning in the arena of American public opinion.

Post-war changes in public support for defence budgets have proved to be among the most dramatic indicators of attitudes towards a US posture in foreign affairs. In 1971, with the war in Vietnam still weighing heavily on the national mood, only an 11% minority of the public said they thought the Pentagon had too little to spend. A decade later in 1981, after becoming disenchanted with a period of detente which seemed to benefit only the Soviet Union, a 51% majority said that the American government spent too little on military and defence needs (see Table 1).

Table 1: Opinion of Defence Spending

In its spending on defence and military purposes the government in Washington spends:

	1982	1981	1976	1973	1971	1969	1960	1953
Too little	19%	51%	22%	13%	11%	8%	21%	22%
Too much	36	15	36	46	50	52	18	20
About the right amount	36	22	32	30	31	31	45	45
No opinion	9	12	10	11	8	9	16	13

Source: Gallup Poll Index 199, 1982

15

Table 2: Orientations Toward Defence

The US Government's emphasis on defence is:

	1982	1981	1980	1979	1978	1977	1976	1975
Too great	25%	11%	12%	17%	17%	12%	20%	29%
About right	48	35	33	47	41	51	41	41
Too little	22	47	47	30	35	31	32	21
Don't know/no answer	5	7	8	6	7	6	7	9

Source: Yankelovich, Skelly and White Surveys, 1982

Table 3: Defence Spending

Given all the international, defence and economic considerations, there should be:

	1982	1981	1980	1979
A reduction in defence spending	40%	17%	23%	40%
An increase in defence spending	51	76	65	50
Don't know/no answer	9	7	12	10

Source: Yankelovich, Skelly and White Surveys, 1982

Table 4: Defence Trade-Offs

A.   Solution: *More government spending on defence.*
     Sacrifice: *Some social welfare programmes may have to be cut.*

	1982	1981
Acceptance	23%	42%
Rejection	40	22
Net	−17	+20

B.   Solution: *More emphasis on defence programmes.*
     Sacrifice: *Less resources to rebuild American industry.*

	1982	1981
Acceptance	20%	29%
Rejection	45	25
Net	−24	+ 4

C.   Solution: *More government spending for defence.*
     Sacrifice: *Higher taxes, inflation.*

	1982	1981
Acceptance	15%	26%
Rejection	57	34
Net	−42	− 8

Source: Yankelovich, Skelly and White Surveys, 1982

But in the trend studies by the Gallup Organization, from which these data are taken, support for expanded defence spending has recently collapsed. In Gallup's most recent 1982 reading, only 19% felt that Washington spends too little on defence, a 32% decline – the most precipitous one-year change with respect to this issue since the Korean War.

The nature of this change is reflected in responses given to trade-offs, or sacrifice-versus-solution questions. Public sentiment is coming to regard military expenditures in a nuclear age not merely as a requirement of a super-power, or at least as an uncomfortable necessity without which national and international security might be threatened, but as a threat in its own right, and as an unacceptable economic hardship as well. The perception of the threat is demonstrated in a survey conducted for *Time* magazine in March 1982, in which the public split down the middle on whether further spending on nuclear weapons weakens the national security (45%) or strengthens it (48%).

In particular, the juxtaposition by the Reagan Administration of proposals for massive increases in defence spending and for broad reductions in spending on social programmes has had a sharp impact on public opinion regarding the acceptability of military budgets (see Table 4). In early 1981, when the Reagan proposals were simply the translation of a candidate's promise into a budgetary realignment, a 2 to 1 margin of the public (42% to 22%) accepted the proposition that some social welfare programmes might have to be cut in order to increase spending on defence. A year later, after absorbing the first of widely reported human costs of social welfare reductions in the midst of a recession, there was a 2 to 1 public margin (40% to 23%) *rejecting* the trade-off. Similarly, in 1981 a narrow majority accepted the idea that a renewed emphasis on defence programmes might diminish resources available to rebuild American industry. In 1982, a 2 to 1 margin rejected this trade-off as well.

Responding to what Americans saw as a long string of post-Vietnam humiliations, infringements and threatening developments, public opinion measurements recorded a virtual surge in approval for enlarged defence expenditures. Analyzing public opinion changes in their book *State of the Nation III*, William Watts and Lloyd Free called public support for defence spending in 1976 'little short of phenomenal'. That intensity continued to grow through 1980, and the assertive mood it represented helped to propel Ronald Reagan into the White House.

What we see now, however, is the fragmenting of consensus on defence spending that is almost equally phenomenal. And while the growth in public consensus was in large part tied to developments in the international arena, its fragmentation is attributable in an impressive degree to the traumas associated with a faltering domestic economy.

Episodes in American Involvement and Aversion

Over the past decade, a short inventory of events and episodes has helped to shape the current climate of US public opinion on international and security issues. The climate thus created became itself an interpretive filter through which the public viewed other events which drew the US into the world arena.

The first category of episodes are those which elicited from the American public a desire to be assertive and involved. This desire, which did not find a satisfying outlet in each instance, drew upon a wide range of civic emotions, including sympathy and altruism, patriotism bordering on jingoism, righteous wrath, stifled rage and frustrated impotence. Among the incidents falling into this category are:

– *The Panama Canal Treaties.* Despite nearly a decade of bi-partisan negotiations and support from most of the nation's military and diplomatic community, public response to the signing of the Panama Canal Treaties in September 1977 was ambivalent at best, hostile at worst. A significant part of public opposition to the Treaties was based on an incomplete knowledge of the purposes or contents of the agreements. (See 'Farewell to "President Knows Best"', *Foreign Affairs*, Vol. 57 No. 3, 1979). A vigorous campaign by the Carter Administration succeeded in gaining Senate ratification of the Treaties and in correcting widespread public misconceptions, but an equally large, or perhaps larger, ingredient in public opposition was the matter of national pride. A majority of Americans said they did not want to 'give away' something that 'rightfully' belonged to the US; and the logic of 'we built it, we own it' was strongly endorsed (65% in an October 1977 Harris survey) right up until the time of ratification. Even though there has been little polling of public attitudes on the Canal Treaties in the past few years, and the issue remains salient only to the most extreme conservatives, there is almost certainly a residue of dormant public resentment concerning this episode in which many Americans felt their country had been 'pushed around'.

– *The Overthrow of the Shah and the Rise of The Mullahs.* Americans had been conditioned to see the Peacock Throne as an important locus of American influence – if not power – in the Middle East. The Shah's regime had received considerable support from successive American Governments and, despite some public qualms about the human rights record in Iran, the modernizing, Westernizing rule of the Shah was viewed as a positive force. The overthrow of the Shah, and his replacement by the vehemently anti-modern Muslim clergy, devoted to the image of Uncle Sam as the devil incarnate, was a profound shock to the American people.

– *The Hostages.* The shock of the Shah's fall paled in comparison to the American public's response to the seizing of 52 US diplomatic hostages by Iranian militants in the American Embassy in Tehran. This event, as no other, riveted public attention to the vulnerability of Americans overseas, to the nuances of Middle East political affairs of which Americans had little knowledge and over which the US had no control and, with each passing week, to the impotence of the American military and diplomatic efforts to free the hostages. Concern for the welfare of the hostages barely suppressed the humiliation and outrage of the American public and, while there was little public clarity at any time during the crisis as to what measures should actually be taken, survey respondents agreed that the episode had diminished US prestige abroad and consolidated the sentiments of Americans at home.

– *The Rescue Raid.* The public anguish over the hostage episode only deepened the longer it continued, and became a gaping wound when, in April 1980, the raid intended to release the captives was aborted after a series of calamities. An already troubled national psyche was further troubled by the loss of the services of a respected diplomat when Secretary of State Vance resigned in disagreement over plans for the raid, and by the double trauma of a military mission failing in its purpose and of equipment and personnel appearing not to have been sufficiently co-ordinated to avoid catastrophe.

– *Afghanistan.* Coming in the wake of these developments in Iran was the Soviet incursion into Afghanistan. If President Carter was surprised by the boldness of the Soviet move, the American public seemed less so. Afghanistan proved to be the catalyst for a trend in public opinion which had for several years been growing more suspicious of Soviet behaviour under detente and, along with the Iranian situation, crystallized public sentiment for a tougher stance generally in world affairs. Military action was foresworn by both the Carter Administration and the NATO Allies, and economic sanctions had little impact except on American farmers. Public opinion reacted again with gnawing frustration as the US seemed impotent to counter Soviet aggression with anything but denunciations but support for higher levels of defence spending spurted after the invasion, as did support for the reinstatement of military conscription.

– *Cuba.* In the past few years, Americans have felt tricked, embarrassed and abused by a small island ninety miles off their coast. In 1979 the disclosure of the presence of Soviet combat units in Cuba caused more of a flurry of press coverage than of genuine strategic concern, but the public was once again forced to ponder whether the US was powerless to do anything about provocative Soviet acts, even within sailing distance of American shores. But somehow more galling to the public than the tenure of Soviet troops in Cuba was the arrival of 100,000 Cubans in Florida in May 1980. What was first seen as a 'boat lift to freedom' soon took on the aspect of a humiliating example of strategic 'people dumping'. The majority of Americans came to see the arrival of Cuban refugees as a successful attempt by Fidel Castro 'to make us look foolish', and to burden the US with an additional economic millstone when the nation could least afford it.

– *Poland.* The sympathies of the American public are with the people of Poland and Americans are convinced that the Poles are waging an heroic struggle against Soviet-enforced oppression. The public would also like to believe that some action, taken by the US alone or in concert with Western Allies, would have the desired effect of easing that oppression and restoring some measure of self-determination to the Polish people. However the pipeline issue did not engage public attention to any serious extent, and there is a sense in the public that, in this episode too, the US was in no way effective, either with threat of force or with the weight of economics, in affecting Soviet behaviour.

On the other side of the ledger are what might be called 'negative' episodes, those which draw most prominently on the 'lessons of Vietnam' on the American public's suspicions of bad management by its own Government, and on latent or overt fears of the consequences of precipitous actions in the internal sphere. These are situations in which, either convulsively or on some reflection, the public has shown some concern for taking a definition of 'the national interest' into its own hands.

– *Vietnam.* The most significant single imprint on the national psyche remains the experience of the Vietnam War, for it was in that morass that the American public first came to grips with the limits of super-power status. From the Vietnam experience, Americans took a series of lessons about US strategic interests and no-end-in-sight involvements, some of which continue to influence popular responses to a proposed American role in trouble spots around the world.

– *Angola.* When the Soviet Union and their Cuban surrogates began their most visible activity in Angola, the American people were in the early spasms of post-Vietnam self-doubt and apprehensiveness. Angola bore the stamp of the Vietnam *débâcle*, and neither popular nor congressional support for countering Soviet adventurism was forthcoming. The very idea of deploying American troops into what appeared to be a civil war on alien terrain was just too much for the American public in 1974 and 1975.

– *El Salvador.* Despite obvious hemispheric considerations to the contrary, El Salvador loomed in 1981 and 1982 as the first 'prospective Vietnam' for the Reagan Administration. The American public suspected that in El Salvador President Reagan had chosen his arena to 'get tough', regardless of the strength or weakness of El Salvador's claim to be a dispute which engaged vital American interests. The public rejected the claim, though there were, and are, abiding qconcerns about the stability of the Latin American region. So adamant were public sentiments against direct American intervention in El Salvador that, in one particular survey, a majority (51%) announced support for defiance of military conscription if troops were to be called up for deployment there.

– *The Economy.* As outlined in the previous section, the high costs of building, modernizing, maintaining and deploying a military and defence system have become concerns uppermost in the mind of the American public in the past year. The Reagan Administration's calls for a dramatically increased military budget while making substantial reductions in social spending, all in the midst of deep recession, have made the public acutely aware of the dollar costs of the defence establishment. Sensitivity to waste and cost-overruns is high, and the media's attention to a nearly item-by-item accounting of the cost of ships, missiles, planes and even fuel during the recent British-Argentine engagement in the South Atlantic has further sharpened the public's 'money response' to military affairs.

– *Nuclear War*. The American public is acquiring a new, or revived, level of consciousness about the threat of nuclear war. The orientation is not pacifist, nor is it unilateral in focus. It *is* a growing concern about 'omnicide' or the 'fate of the earth'. In rejecting the idea of a winnable nuclear war, or controlled exchanges, of effective civil defence, or normal postal service within the blast zone, the public has not eschewed the need for a strong military or an assertive national posture, but there are now doubts about leaders who speak of winning – rather than preventing – nuclear war. Their judgement in matters of war and peace is likely to be subjected to closer scrutiny.

The American Public
Public disposition towards the use of American military forces abroad is a special case, and is a function of several factors, none of which has become more important recently than the public's own *clear* perception of a threat to a *genuine* US national interest or moral obligation, and the public's belief in the truthfulness of US government representations of the situation in question.

Despite the sometimes turbulent economic and political relationship between US governments and those of Western Europe, Japan and other industrial democracies, the American public is not only disinclined to a 'divorce', but shows a rather strong loyalty to allies, particularly in cases of hypothetical attack.

Since the mid-1970s, pluralities and then the solid and growing majorities of the American public have sanctioned the use of American military force to assist friends under attack. The crucial element here is the word 'friends', for it is the existence of security commitments commingled with deeply-felt public affinities which account for a willingness to send troops overseas. In surveys by Gallup and Potomac Associates in 1975, 48% of the American people agreed that, if a major European ally were to be attacked by the Soviet Union, the US should use force in the defence of that ally. By 1980, Americans had become somewhat disillusioned with the theory that detente had reduced world tensions; instead they saw it providing a screen behind which the Soviet Union had become more expansionist. A 74% majority supported the view that US military action should be taken to repel a Soviet invasion of Western Europe. Similar dramatic growth occurred in public willingness to defend Japan in the event of an hypothetical attack on her by either the Soviet Union or China. Between 1975 and 1980, willingness to use US military force in such circumstances increased from 42% to 68% (see Table 5).

Yet the public clearly distinguishes between the use of force in defence of substantial allied commitments and the insertion of a US military presence merely on the orders of an administration in Washington. As the experience in Angola in 1975 demonstrated, the American public and the Congress had learned how to avoid the traumas of the Vietnam quagmire. Again in 1982, despite Government assertions to the contrary, Americans saw a Vietnam analogy in El Salvador.

El Salvador provided a litmus test of the public's ability to discriminate between those policies judged to be in the national interest and those which their Government put forward as necessary and proper. In late March 1982, 8 in 10 Americans interviewed in one survey said that they disapproved of the US sending any troops to fight in El Salvador. In the same survey, when asked whether they thought the Reagan Administration was telling the truth when it stated it had no intention of sending troops, 42% of the public said yes; 42% said no. Against this background, nearly two thirds (64%) said that they fully expected that the United States would send troops to El Salvador anyway, if the Government there does not win its own war against rebel insurgents (see Table 6). This public suspicion of the way in which the Reagan Administration determines the 'national interest' in world affairs has already begun to shadow public attitudes on another and more vital issue. The most fateful of questions, the future of arms control and of the war- and peace-making intentions of governments, is moving to centre stage in the arena of American public opinion.

Nuclear Awareness
The threat posed by international instability and even more deadly nuclear weapons and

20

Table 5: Should the US use Military Force to Defend X (if attacked by Y)?

			1980	1979	1978	1976	1975	1974	1972
1.	One of the US's major European Allies (if attacked by USSR)	*Agree*	74%	64%	62%	56%	48%	48%	52%
		Disagree	19	26	26	27	34	34	32
		Don't know	7	10	12	17	18	18	16
2.	Japan (by USSR or China)	*Agree*	68	54	50	45	42	37	43
		Disagree	28	35	35	37	39	42	40
		Don't know	4	11	15	18	19	21	17
3.	South Korea (by North Korea)	*Agree*	38	32	32				
		Disagree	51	56	52				
		Don't know	11	12	16				
4.	Taiwan (by China)	*Agree*	43	34	32				
		Disagree	42	51	48				
		Don't know	15	15	20				
5.	Thailand (by Vietnam)	*Agree*	30						
		Disagree	55						
		Don't know	15						
6.	Australia (by an enemy of US)	*Agree*	70						
		Disagree	21						
		Don't know	9						
7.	Philippines (by an enemy of US)	*Agree*	65						
		Disagree	25						
		Don't know	10						
8.	China (by USSR)	*Agree*	45						
		Disagree	42						
		Don't know	13						

Source: Gallup Organization; Potomac Associates in *Americans Look at Asia*, Watts, 1980

Table 6: US Role in El Salvador

1) The Reagan Administration has said it has no intention right now of sending American soldiers to fight in El Salvador. Do you think the Reagan Administration is telling the truth about that or not?

Yes, Administration is telling truth	42%
No, Administration is not telling truth	42
Don't know	16

2) Just your best guess, if the El Salvadorean Government cannot defeat the rebels, do you think the United States will eventually send American soldiers to fight in El Salvador or not?

Yes, US will send troops	64%
No, US will not send troops	27
Don't know	9

3) Would you approve or disapprove of the United States sending troops to fight in El Salvador?

Approve	18%
Disapprove	79
Don't know	4

Source: ABC/Washington Post Poll, March 1982.

delivery systems has become, at last, a public issue. While it is not likely that a large portion of the US public will become more knowledgeable about MIRV, MARV or throw-weights, it is virtually certain that the nuclear Pandora's box is now open and, as far as the American public is concerned, it is not likely to be closed until there are clear signs that progress is being made on arms limitations, reductions and safeguards.

For the American public at least, support for a nuclear freeze of any type, or support for any other formulation of nuclear arms control, should not be equated with a reversal or softening of an essentially assertive public posture on US foreign affairs. Rather, such support represents, as did public opinion with respect to proposed government policies towards El Salvador, a substantial erosion of consensus on what a valid national security stance actually is or ought to be. Survey questions couched in terms of a desire for 'toughness' or a desire to 'reduce tensions' show growing sentiment for co-operation on arms control. However a significant trend, dating from the middle of the 1970s, embodies a 'don't tread on me' outlook which continues to underlie American public opinion.

Support for specific arms-control proposals has not congealed in any way which would demonstrate that the public feels that it has (or should) pre-empt Presidential prerogatives at the negotiating table. But, unlike the early days of tentative protest against the war in Vietnam, the American public has rejected the idea that it does not 'know enough' to be concerned or to have a valid opinion, or that 'experts' should necessarily be left alone to decide the proper national posture in reducing the threat of nuclear weapons.

In fact it was the public pronouncements of a number of these 'experts' which gave rise to the re-born anti-nuclear movement in the US. Some of the early foreign policy and defence statements of President Reagan, as well as Secretaries Haig and Weinberger, led many Americans to see the present Government as bellicose, and too likely to push the world beyond confrontation and into a nuclear war. As public confidence in President Reagan's grasp and handling of foreign affairs began to slip, so rose the fortunes of the anti-nuclear movement.

As with El Salvador, the public was disinclined either to trust or believe statements made by the Government on what constituted the best policy. In an April 1982 survey by the *Washington Post* and ABC News, a 57% majority said that they did not feel that government officials could be trusted to make the 'right decision' about a nuclear freeze policy without being subjected to public pressure. By an even larger margin (64%) the polls showed that the public believed that it was pressure for a freeze that had given arms-control negotiations a higher priority within the Reagan Administration.

Underscoring what is clearly a gap between the Government and the governed is the public's sense that this Administration may not be seriously interested in reducing the threat of nuclear war. A 53% majority in an early Summer 1982 Harris poll rated the President negatively for his posture on arms-control negotiations with the Soviet Union, and 48% in the survey cited above (ABC/*Washington Post*) said that they felt that President Reagan had not done all he should to reduce the international build-up of nuclear weapons. Only 17% in a survey in May 1982 by the Associated Press and NBC accepted the proposition, often presented by the Administration that 'limited' nuclear war is both possible and winnable.

The arena in which the American debate – or struggle – over nuclear disarmament is taking place is generally described as containing two participants or sets of actors. The first can be thought of as the Department of Defense, adherents of the Defense Guidance Plan, etc. Without impugning the morals of this group, it is possible to conceive of them as the 'pro-nuclear' movement. On the other side, there is the anti-nuclear movement, advocating a freeze and disarmament measures. In some cases they, like their counterparts in the European movements, play down or discount Soviet intentions, both conventional and nuclear, and focus their attention on the reduction of US and NATO nuclear forces.

Each of these sets of actors, in presenting argument, testimony and public witness, speaks and acts as a surrogate of the public, taking it for granted that they speak in their best interests, and with the will of the people behind them.

Both sides are wrong. There is a third actor, and the third actor shares some of the perspectives of the first, and some of the second, but is accurately represented by neither. The third actor is the general public, and now that the public has begun thinking about the unthinkable, there is not likely to be a national consensus on nuclear arms policy until *three*, not *two* voices are listened to.

In sympathy with the anti-nuclear movement, the public wants to take steps towards reducing the threat of nuclear catastrophe. With these activists, the public feels that no conceivable dispute is worth destroying the world for, and that the realists on this issue are those who favour the control of nuclear weapons, not those who devise strategies for the use of the tools of omnicide.

Yet, along with the defence and foreign policy establishment, the public also firmly believes in the existence of a Soviet threat to world peace and thus to the American way of life. While seeking parity with, rather than clear superiority over the Soviet Union, the public nevertheless feels that the US some-how lost ground during the period of detente, and has become a less potent actor in world affairs than in decades past. With the defence establishment, the public feels in its heart that, despite the huge stockpiles of nuclear weapons at US disposal, it is not as well-protected in a dangerous world as it might be – and should be.

In response to a shifting rhetorical framework presented by political leaders, large segments of the American public have begun to question – and to challenge – the prerogatives of the strategic community on the issue of nuclear weapons and nuclear war. Under the pressure of a tight economy and government policies which reduce social services and increase military expenditures, the issues of strategic modernization and the cost of military procurement overall have begun to generate public resistance. Taken together, these two developments have begun to shake the public consensus which has supported the structure and direction of American – and Western defence efforts in the past. If there is a lesson to be learned, it is that the time for a new, constructive consensus-building dialogue among leaders, experts and the public has come. It has come, that is, unless it has already passed.

Public Opinion and the Defence Effort:
Trends and Lessons
Europe

RUDOLF WILDENMANN

For many years now public opinion in industrialized countries, as identified and measured in surveys, has followed a reasonably set pattern of clearly defined policy goals and, with only a few exceptions, it continues to do so even today. It is not surprising that between 50% and 70% of the population ask for an improvement in economic policies, with the emphasis at the moment on employment policies. Social security and related issues follow employment with concern over law and order also playing important roles. While different age cohorts and social groups may show varying degrees of emphasis on certain subjects, such variations do not significantly change the basic pattern.

What is remarkable about public opinion today is that defence does not figure at all as a policy goal. On the other hand the issue of 'peace' (as distinct from 'defence') has managed in the past few years to secure about 20% support from the general public and much more from the younger age groups. This is an extraordinary phenomenon. It is generally the educated section of the population which advances the issue of peace, not the blue-collar workers, and their definition of peace more or less completely rejects military defence.

Today's pattern also holds true if we divide mass public opinion into groups according to knowledge, political interest and political participation. We may identify five groups[1] within European countries and the US: 'activists', 'reformists', 'conformists', 'inactives', and 'fundamentalists' ('protesters' in the terminology of Barnes and Kaase). The degree of information they possess or the structure of their knowledge may be different but there is no decisive change in the pattern of their goals. It is also clear that the priorities of

peace provide a base from which the various peace movements work, with their strength varying according to whether they are Catholic or Protestant.

Topics which play an important role in the high level political discussions (such as energy, economic policies, the role of the law in society, etc.) are hardly of concern to publics. Moreover, the relation between democracy and defence, which is after all what fundamentally underpins NATO, does not now appear to constitute a basic consensus in Western societies.

Since there is no comparable data available besides the three positional elite studies carried out in West Germany[2], we have to take results from these studies as *pars pro toto*, in order to identify patterns in elites, acknowledging, of course, that there might be significant differences from nation to nation. In our studies we found the following rank-order of issues (scale from 0 to 10): *energy* 8.4; *fundamental rights* 8.4; *freedom of mass media* 7.8; *social market economy* 7.7; *full employment* 7.6; *detente* 7.5; *prices* 7.5; *foreign trade balance* 7.5; *law and order* 7.4; *good relations with USA* 7.4; *defence* 7.4; *European unification* 7.3; *social security* 7.2; *budgetary debts* 7.2; *terrorism* 7.0; *environmental conservation* 6.8; *economic growth* 6.6; *education* 6.5; *house construction* 6.5; *relations with USSR* 6.0 (and some others below that scale).

The greatest variation between political groups (clusters) can be found with respect to the social market economy and the assessment of detente. Each elite sector has its own, slightly different, rank-order of importance for policy issues but these patterns are very different from those of the mass public, and this situation has not changed dramatically since

1968, except that the issues of detente, European unification and education were then somewhat more strongly emphasized.

In a modern form, these differences in terms of interest, insight and emphasis between élites and the mass public reflect Alexis de Tocqueville's idea that democratic societies tend to be primarily concerned with their domestic well-being, whereas only elites ('aristocracies' at this time) concern themselves with the pursuit of long-term foreign or defence policies.

The following generalizations can be put forward on this basis of analysis:

- The mass public (almost by necessity) concentrates on its individual security in social life – on the family, occupation and employment, the well-being of its children, its idiosyncratic interests and hobbies.
- We should not complain about the lack of political interest on the part of the mass public or its poor judgment, but we should look rather into the socio-political structures and kind of 'political education' (in the sense of Walter Bagehot) which prevails.
- Opinions and attitudes (including non-attitudes) on the part of the mass public result largely from the influences of political leadership. If defence is presented in an unfavourable light or is not presented as an important policy goal to the public or if there is a lack of basis consensus, then this indicates a failure on the part of political leadership.
- The combined policy goals which seem to have been linked and fundamental in the late 1940s and 1950s – namely, stable economic conditions, social security, European integration and defence – seem today neither to be linked nor any longer to be fundamental. Without this combination of policies which appealed to the imagination of the younger generation 30 years ago, the policies of the 1950s would not have succeeded. If there is now a lack of consensus, we need to question the abilities of governmental machinery and party systems to resolve problems. Last but not least, we need to question the pattern used for the selection of party leaders.

Unfortunately there are many methodological errors in the surveys relating to the mass public and one of the most frequent is to put questions to them which only 'experts' are in a position to answer. Those carrying out such surveys then find themselves left with a mixture of reliable information, artefacts, and non-attitudes, simply because people feel compelled to answer questions even if they have no real insights or are simply not informed about the survey topic. It is therefore hardly useful to turn such answers into impressive tables and graphs.

Reliable information is most likely to be available when people are questioned as to their sentiments. For example, we could take as reliable the sampling of opinion as to the deterioration of trust in American governments, as distinct from trust in the United States herself. In many European countries this trend is obvious (as it is in the United States). We may conclude, too, that the fear of nuclear weapons and the risk of war is increasing everywhere in Western Europe, with the possible exception of France. Yet there still remains a strong feeling of necessity to be allied with the US through NATO (except again in the case of France) and, varying according to group, there is no trust of the USSR. The invasion of Afghanistan or the events in Poland have in fact increased distrust of the USSR, even if by and large they did not increase the fears of the risk of war in Europe, although in most countries the use of military force in the case of an attack still has the support of the majority. Negotiations with the East are regarded as being either useful or desirable or both. Trade with the USSR is seen as a means of maintaining a situation of non-war.

One theme comes through quite clearly. There is no desire whatsoever to engage in a war with the USSR. Peace should be maintained. War is not the way to solve differences within Europe, yet there are considerable differences of opinion as to how to avoid a war – which is not very different from the debates amongst policy-makers.

If we turn now to surveys of expert opinions and attitudes, only those carried out in West Germany[3] are available. Some of the important results are as follows:

- Very differentiated opinions are expressed *inter alia* on the usefulness of *détente* policies, on MBFR, on the implications of deterrence, on the production and location of new nuclear weapons, on the evaluation of political and military developments in the USSR and on the global versus European approaches to security. Major variations appear between governmental parties (then SPD and FDP) and the opposition (then CDU) including other sectors related to these parties (clusters). These variations are similar to variations found among elites with respect to defence or detente.
- The complicated nature of defence relations is mirrored in a diversification of policy assessments and possible goals. There is *no* general consensus as to what should be the underlying rationale for defence policies – as was once the case in the 1960s – except that there is a consensus in preventing war.

In 1950, the then Minister of Internal Affairs of the first Adenauer Cabinet, Gustav Heinemann, resigned when the question of German rearmament was favourably considered by Konrad Adenauer. In his letter of resignation, he pointed out that 'social rearmament' was necessary, not 'military rearmament', and that West Germany should aim at peaceful unification with East Germany and neutrality between the powers. Later, he founded his own party, the GVP, which was merged in 1956 with the SDP, and many of the GVP's leaders (for example Eppler, Rau, Posser, Heinemann) later became prominent figures in the SPD-dominated government. As President of the Republic, Heinemann was himself very active in the creation of the German Society for Conflict and Peace Research, even though he was no longer then directly involved in policy formulation. The former policies of the GVP have had a considerable influence on the contemporary SDP's positions, and on part of the FDP, as well as on other important political formations.

Military versus social spending is thus not a new problem in West Germany, and a number of politicians (and scientists), having now become members of German elites, are still very active in pursuing a different course in politics to that of the SPD/FDP when they were in power.

However, the question of 'butter' instead of 'guns' is not as simple as it may appear. All NATO countries are facing similar issues; the anti-nuclear movements reflect, in varying degrees, environmental, anti-nuclear and neutralist sentiments.

In the case of West Germany, the strength of the movement is also due to the fact that neither the governing parties nor the opposition took the movement seriously when it first appeared in the mid-1970s, even though empirical evidence was already available that about 15% of the population was sympathetic to such ideas.[4]

Several aspects of the phenomenon came together and there are several political dimensions of their possible consequences. Only those which are most central will be considered.

As Max Beloff remarks in his *New Dimensions in Foreign Policy* (London: George Allen and Unwin, 1961), it is hard for a democratic society not to escape the latent dangers of international relations. In the case of very protracted conflicts that are difficult to comprehend and require steady, reliable and rational policies, democratic societies in their perceptions tend to minimize these conflicts. Although the belief that democratic societies are bound always to say no at the wrong moment (as Walter Lippman in his 'Public Opinion' once contended – no at a time when armaments are needed and no at a time when the pursuit of peace is necessary) may not be correct today, it does seem true that the desire for European Unification (Hamilton Fish Armstrong) correlates with the perception of 'danger' from the USSR. It would also seem that democratic societies remain more concerned about the development of justice, liberty, freedom and welfare than about armaments.

It is becoming increasingly difficult to convince the younger generation that democracies need to be defended, that resources are scarce and that priority should be given to increasingly costly weapons when there seems already to be an abundance of them. In contrast, the post-war generation of the 1950s 'swallowed the frog' (D. Sternberger) of West German rearmament, simply because rearmament was linked to political concepts which foresaw an end to wars in Europe by the creation of new European perspectives and institutions. Such goals are no longer placed before today's younger generation. On the contrary, Europe seems to them to be on the point of stagnation wtih endless bureaucratic struggles about subsidies, market regulations and protective tariffs. One indicator for this disillusion was the very low electoral participation of the younger generation in the Direct European Elections.

This younger generation was raised in a period of prosperity and convincing democracy, when the capacity of democracies to resolve problems seemed to be immense. The 'restless generation', a term Max Kaase and I used in 1968, was very exposed to democratic socialization in schools and society. The more exposed, the more 'restless' it became (R. Wildenmann/M. Kaase, *Die unruhige Generation*, 1968). A rising percentage of each age group is receiving a higher education, and educational expectations are still on the increase. What M. Rainer Lepsius terms the *Versorgungsklasse* (the class of people provided for by the state) is to a very large extent independent of economic growth and takes it for granted that the reallocations of resources will be in its favour. Higher education resulted also in a greater interest and participation in politics. It widened the gaps between the various strata of society in terms of their respective influence over policy – it did not narrow them.[5]

In their writings M. R. Lipset and Stein Rokkan, analysing the rise of political structures in the second half of the 19th and early 20th centuries, stated that political and party systems were aligned along the lines of the political cleavages of these times. Transformed into a general approach this means that the following cleavages were covered:

- The reproduction of tangible and intangible capital in society, namely, productivity and natural science research and technology, mainly by the 'conservative' parties in Europe;
- Communication and social mobility as well as solidarity in society, in concrete terms, by the development of the Welfare State, mainly by social-democratic or liberal parties.

This leaves the problem of the relationship between man and his environment, as well as the problem of 'creativity', especially with regard to the capacity of developing new political structures – whether domestic or international. These new issues in democratic societies are now put on the agenda by the environmental and peace movements which are strongly in the interest of the *Versorgungsklasse*.

It is evident that, if democratic societies are to formulate a convincing foreign policy (especially with regard to defence), there must be reconciliation between these opposed forces. Unfortunately most political elites seem to identify problems after things have gone too far by which time it is difficult to resolve them by mutual agreement. Moreover there is still no attempt to establish a more systematic solution to the problem which Ferdinand A. Hermes defined as 'the people's peace and the tyrant's war' (1944, Notre Dame), in other words to create a variety of international institutions and procedures to control or resolve conflicts and (gradually) replace the uncertainties of a deterrent strategy and of the arms race.

The results of this brief investigation into public opinion both of the masses and positional elites strongly indicates that an extensive debate on defence should have taken place a long time ago. Given the enormous difficulties of formulating and carrying out a multidimensional defence policy under present conditions, and given that long-lasting emotional stability and solidarity are required in order for such policies to be successful, the failure of elite judgment as to these issues in the last 10 or 15 years becomes apparent. This applies both to the domestic and foreign policy dimensions of the problem. Western industrialized states managed to adapt their institutions and their political processes after the Second World War in order to meet the enormous problems of the day. They also attempt to create a European constitutional structure and were quite successful until the 1970s. Neither are adequate any longer. To regain the confidence of our public and political elites in defence policies, we must find a very different approach to today's fundamental challenges.

NOTES

[1] See Edward N. Muller, *Aggressive Political Participation* (Princeton: Princeton University Press, 1979); and Samuel Barnes and Max Kaase *Political Action: Mass Participation in Five Western Democracies* (London: Sage Publications, 1979).

[2] 1968: Wildenmann *et al*: 1972: Kaltefleiter/Wildenmann et al; 1981: Wildenmann/Kaase *et al.* In each case the sample consisted of top positional holders across society; in 1981 there were 1,750 respondents from a total of 3,150 top position holders.

[3] Schössler/Schmitt/Jung, Mannheim: SIPLA 1978-1981, three studies on 'Sicherheitspolitische Planung' carried out on about 600 'experts' participating in security policies.

[4] Regular yearly surveys 1976–1980, partially published.

[5] Muller and Barnes/Kaase *op. cit.* in note 1.

The Media and the Making of Defence Policy: The US Example

JOSEPH FROMM

Over the past decade the media in the United States have acquired a reputation as a major force in shaping national policy, credited with bringing down one President in the Watergate affair and forcing another to end American combat involvement in a war in Vietnam.

Nevertheless, the tangible influence of the American press and television on the decisions of government today is a subject of widespread and continuing controversy. There is no doubt that the spread of television into virtually every home has transformed the communication of news, information and ideas, with results that have yet to be accurately measured. It is a vehicle that has been utilized by the civil rights movement and the anti-Vietnam war movement successfully to proselytize a nation and ultimately to bring about a radical change of course. Conversely, it also has been exploited by Presidents, with varying degrees of success and most notably by Ronald Reagan, to win support for their policies.

In some areas of government affairs, it is possible to cite specific examples of the direct impact of the media on political decision-making or behaviour.

The 'supply-side economics' policy pursued by the Reagan Administration is a classic example. This controversial and unconventional theory of economic management was embraced by Reagan, as a candidate, largely as a result of the proselytzing endeavours of Robert Bartley, editorial page editor of the *Wall Street Journal*, and Jude Wanniski, his deputy.

On a different level, David Gergen, the President's Aide in charge of communications, told the *National Journal* that press was responsible for the Reagan Administration's quick retreat from a plan to grant tax-exempt status to racially-segregated schools. The White House, he said, had responded to 'the warning flags . . . first published in the columns, opinion pieces and editorials'.

In foreign policy, Presidential Counsellor Edwin Meese told a group of journalists earlier in 1982 that the impact of the media is especially noticeable. 'The press', he said, 'acts as intermediary between the public and the government as a national interpreter of events'. He pointed to El Salvador to illustrate the practical effects of this.

'The very fact', he said, 'that the press keeps asking if the President is going to send troops to El Salvador makes it an issue even though Mr Reagan has stated he is not planning such action'. The upshot, said Meese, was that Senate Minority Leader Robert Byrd sought to 'tie the President's hands'.

While one must resist the temptation to draw unwarranted general conclusions from these examples, they do illustrate the sensitivity of the government – particularly in the White House – to popular opinion as reflected by the press and television. One authority on the subject has concluded that the 'news media have become such pervasive forces that from a public affairs viewpoint, many events don't really take place unless they are covered by television, newspapers or news magazines'.

Nothing could illustrate the point more vividly than the emergence of the 'nuclear freeze movement' as a political force. It was only when television and the press 'discovered' the movement early in 1982, many months after it had established itself at grassroots level across the country, that the political leadership in Washington took note and reacted by displaying greater enthusiasm for renewed strategic arms negotiations with the Soviet Union.

29

Marginal Direct Impact

Against this background, it might seem logical to assume that defence policy is influenced as much if not more by the news media than policy in other areas – given the vast sums of money devoted to the armed forces and the implications not only for the nation's security but for the economy as well. In fact, defence appears to be something of a special case.

Systematic analysis of the subject is almost totally lacking. In attempting to calculate the influence of the media in the shaping of defence policy one must rely on personal experience, random interviews with representative journalists covering defence affairs and officials involved in the decision-making process and an examination of some of the more controversial national security issues.

A paradoxical conclusion emerges from such an inquiry. The direct impact of press and television on weapons decisions and strategy is marginal: yet the evidence indicates that the media may exercise a critical influence on the ultimate issue – the use of the armed forces to engage in war.

First then, it is necessary to examine the limited impact of the media on routine decisions – those involving the choice of weapons, manpower policies and strategic planning. One of the most respected television journalists assigned to the Pentagon offers this explanation: 'Strategic issues are too esoteric, weapons systems too complex and public understanding inadequate for the media to play a significant role. On high priced weapons systems, the press and television may force greater accountability but cannot force a change in the decision itself'.

James Reston, the distinguished *New York Times* columnist, provided another explanation for the limited impact of the media on specific policy decisions. 'When you talk about the media's impact', he said, 'you have to define what you mean. For example, the impact of ideas and criticism in the daily and periodical press is indirect. The criticism may bubble over policy on defence or policy on El Salvador and be argued in the press. But it is only when the other branch of government, in Congress, picks up that criticism that the press begins to have an influence since we do not have the power to subpoena'.

Among Pentagon correspondents and academic specialists in the defence field there is agreement only on a single weapons decision in recent years that may have been decisively influenced by the media – President Carter's April 1978 decision to defer production of the neutron warhead. Details of this episode bear recalling briefly.

On 6 June 1977, the *Washington Post* published a front page article by Walter Pincus under the headline 'Neutron Warhead Buried in ERDA Budget' with this opening paragraph: 'The United States is about to begin production of its first nuclear battlefield weapon specifically designed to kill people through the release of neutrons rather than to destroy military installations through heat and blast'.

Even though funds for neutron warhead development had been budgeted previously for some years without stirring controversy or even attracting notice, the Pincus article triggered an international furore that took the Carter Administration by surprise. Whether intended or not, the article set the tone of the controversy not only with the inference that there was something especially sinister about a weapon that killed people without destroying property but also with the hint that the Administration may have been guilty of deception by 'burying' the funding for the project in the budget for Energy Research and Development Administration (ERDA). The controversy was sustained by the American press as well as European media and, of course, Soviet propagandists.

The upshot was doubtless the most lamentable chapter in the four-year history of the Carter Administration's conduct of alliance diplomacy. After his top national security aides had negotiated what was considered an acceptable compromise with the European Allies on production and deployment of the neutron warhead, the President could not bring himself to make the final decision. On 7 April 1978, to the consternation of all concerned – and especially his closest advisers – he announced that manufacture of the weapon would be deferred.

What is noteworthy is not that a newspaper may have contributed significantly to the derailing of the neutron warhead but rather that

30

the incident is generally regarded as unusual if not unique. This is not to suggest that the press and television do not play a role – indeed, a most significant one – in the formulation of defence policy in the United States.

Shaping Popular Perceptions

Their influence can be defined in two ways. First the media, while not among the major players in the national security debate, serve as a conveyor-belt of information – and possibly misinformation – ideas and arguments calculated to influence the principal participants. Second the press and television contribute materially to popular perceptions that have a critical bearing on defence policy.

Taking the question of perceptions first, it is probably a safe generalization to assert that in determining the broad thrust of American defence policy – whether the budget should be greatly increased or curtailed, whether more super-carriers should be built or troops withdrawn from South Korea – nothing is more important than the popular perception of the Soviet threat and of the nation's preparedness to cope with it.

How radically and quickly American attitudes on these issues of national security can oscillate has been amply demonstrated in the past few years. In November 1976, the electorate, disillusioned by the failure of American military power in Vietnam, chose as President an obscure former Georgia Governor, Jimmy Carter, who pledged to reduce defence spending, withdraw American ground troops from Korea and – as he spelled it out later – to end 'the inordinate fear of communism'.

Four years later Ronald Reagan was elected, in a landslide, to replace Carter as President with a campaign that promised a massive increase in defence spending to finance modernization and expansion of the armed forces and held the Soviet Union responsible for all major international troubles.

Needless to say, the choice in both elections was influenced primarily by domestic affairs and, to some extent, personalities. But not to be discounted was the drastic change in the electorate's perception of the Soviet threat and American defence needs. Opinion polls show that, whereas in 1977 a large majority of

Americans perceived the US ahead of the Soviet Union in military power, in 1981 the ratio was reversed. And while 63 per cent in 1977 felt that military spending should be maintained at the current level or reduced, in 1981 89 per cent favoured the current level or an increase – with no fewer than 61 per cent supporting higher defence outlays.

What accounted for this extraordinary turn-around – and what part did the media play? While disenchantment with super-power detente was apparent early in the Carter Administration as the result of Soviet-Cuban adventures in Angola and Ethiopia, the radical transformation in attitudes toward military readiness is widely ascribed to four events which occurred in 1979:

– The Senate debate on the SALT II Treaty which focused national attention more on the shortcomings of America's defence posture than on the virtues of arms control.
– The fall of the Shah of Iran which brought home to Americans the vulnerability of Persian Gulf oil supplies and the failure of US policy designed to guarantee the security of the region with a surrogate power.
– The Iran hostage crisis seen by most Americans as humiliating evidence of the impotence of US military power – a perception that was powerfully reinforced by the rescue fiasco and the spectacle of a burnt-out helicopter in the Iranian desert.
– The Soviet invasion of Afghanistan viewed as the first conclusive demonstration of Soviet willingness to use her armed forces overtly outside the Soviet bloc.

These events – the overthrow of the Shah and the marathon hostage crisis above all – had a profound impact on the public consciousness in the United States, thanks in large part to the manner in which they were projected by the media. The torrent of news reports, commentaries, photographs and film concerning developments in Iran throughout 1979 and 1980 was overpowering.

The perception that became pervasive was that of the United States as 'a helpless giant' – powerless to save her most valued ally in the

Persian Gulf, to protect her diplomats imprisoned by Moslem revolutionaries in the American Embassy in Tehran or to rescue the hostages.

The cumulative impact of the events of 1979 as projected by the media produced a striking increase in popular support for additional defence spending and for action to overcome what was widely perceived as a position of military inferiority. The change was signalled most vividly in the Senate late in the Summer of 1979 by a revolt against the Carter Administration's defence budget and a vote allocating billions more for the military than requested by the Pentagon.

That this mood persists today is evidenced by continued Congressional support for high levels of defence spending and the Administration's success in resisting significant cuts in its Pentagon budget at a time when social welfare funding is being reduced sharply in an effort to narrow a $100-billion-plus federal government deficit.

Thus, while no methodical study has yet been undertaken to ascertain the impact of the media on the perceptions of the American public and Congress with respect to national security, it seems safe to conclude that it is critical. But a qualification is required: the influence of the press and television is exerted not as a result of deliberate positions they take on issues of defence but primarily through their normal activities in covering the news and through the pervasive role of television that brings news in its most graphic form into almost every home.

Transmission-Belt for Leaks
Similarly, in their role as transmission-belt of information, the media rarely exert influence in an overt or direct fashion but rather as a vehicle that is used by the actual players engaged in the game of formulating defence policy. To grasp what this means, it is important to understand the unique US system of decision-making in the national security field.

In contrast with most other countries – including most democracies – where defence policy is a virtual monopoly of the defence establishment and the Executive branch with little if any input by the Legislative branch, in the United States the role of Congress is important and has expanded greatly in recent years. The defence budget and programme are debated and approved by the Appropriations and Armed Services Committees in both Houses of Congress and certain specific aspects of national security – such as arms sales and aid – are scrutinized by other committees. This protracted and open process of examining defence issues obviously encourages efforts to influence the judgment of Members of Congress.

Another feature of the American policy-making process is the proclivity of the several branches of the armed forces and other competing forces in the defence community to utilize the media aggressively to advance their arguments and influence decisions. Finally, there is probably greater willingness by the media in the United States to publish 'secrets' than in any other country.

In this system, those who shape defence policy – in the Pentagon as well as in the Congress – look to the press to a remarkable extent to keep them informed about what is happening inside their own bureaucracies. The Air Force publishes twice daily a comprehensive reprint of virtually all articles related to defence and summaries of television comment. The first edition of this *Current News* is printed on yellow paper and is appropriately dubbed 'the yellow peril' because it often brings bad news to top officials at the Pentagon.

The system places a high premium on 'leaks' and the deliberate planting of information as a device for influencing policy. Representative Les Aspin of Wisconsin, among the most knowledgeable Congressmen in the ways of the Pentagon, says that Defense Department officials plant stories in an effort to influence, not the public, but decision-makers. He explains: 'Leaks come through bureaucratic wars – somebody who doesn't like a plan thinks that by leaking the existence of it, he will kill it; somebody who does like the existence of a plan thinks by leaking it, he will encourage it. . . . There are lots of games going on in this town and the press is the conduit for a whole lot of them'.

One of the most striking recent examples of leaking to influence the decision-makers involved an embarrassing disclosure concerning the defence budget. The story that appeared on the front page of the *Washington Post* on 8 January 1982, reported that a secret session of the Defense Resources Board had been warned that the Reagan defence programme as translated by the Joint Chiefs of Staff 'could cost $570 million more than his administration had budgeted over the next five years . . . dramatic evidence that defence spending threatens to run out of control'.

The leak, in the midst of a battle over major cuts in federal spending, was apparently intended to strengthen the hand of those who were critical of misleading projections of the cost of the military build-up and advocating tighter control of the programme. Although the Administration succeeded in warding off attacks on Pentagon military spending, a full-scale investigation was mounted that subjected all participants in the Defense Resources Board meeting to lie-detector tests.

The final stage of the neutron warhead controversy in the Spring of 1978 was marked by an aggressive campaign of leaking that was calculated – unsuccessfully – to induce President Carter to reverse or modify his decision to defer production of the weapon. A more successful campaign of leaks was waged in the Autumn of 1981 at a critical juncture in the Senate debate over the sale of AWAC (Airborne Warning and Control Aircraft) to Saudi Arabia. In this case, officials – presumably with the blessing of the Administration – provided reporters with information designed to demonstrate the limitations of America's most advanced air-borne early-warning system. The purpose was to allay fears that the Saudis could use the plane to attack Israel. The Senate approved the sale.

With rare exceptions, students of government in the United States say that the Administration is able to utilize the media more effectively than its critics in any controversy over a defence issue. Through his news conferences or speeches, the President can convert the press and television into a platform to present his point of view. The Secretary of Defense and other ranking officials also have easy access to the media to argue their case, an advantage not so readily available to their opponents.

Navy Secretary John Lehman provided a classic demonstration of what one authority on national security termed 'the pre-emptive strike' in the controversy over the sinking of the British destroyer HMS *Sheffield* in the Falkland Islands war. Within hours of the ship going down, Lehman, cutting short a trip to Europe, flew back to Washington to seize the initiative in the debate. At a meeting with a hand-picked group of Pentagon reporters, he advanced the argument that the sinking of the *Sheffield* demonstrated the indispensability of big-deck aircraft carriers to provide adequate defence against long-range missile attacks. In so doing, he went far to seize the high ground in advance against critics claiming that the episode proved the vulnerability of surface vessels and super-carriers in particular.

Leslie Gelb, the *New York Times* National Security Correspondent, who has held positions in the Defense and State Departments, maintains that 'any half-way competent and disciplined Administration can get its story published pretty much the way it wants'. The fact is that American Administrations have almost invariably won endorsement of their major defence decisions, however controversial they may have been and whatever treatment they have received by the media. That was true of the Nixon Administration's proposal for an anti-ballistic missile (ABM) system, the Carter Administration's decision to cancel the B–1 bomber, the Reagan Administration's decision four years later to revive the B–1, President Carter's 'race track' basing plan for the MX missile and the subsequent rejection by President Reagan of that scheme.

The Impact of Television
The role of television requires special attention. Upwards of 70 per cent of Americans rely on television as their principal source of news but the other 30 per cent include the best educated with the highest income in the population, and thus presumably the most effective in terms of influencing national policy.

Furthermore, of all forms of communications, television is probably the least suited for dealing with news and information on the complex questions of defence. Imagine the daunting challenge facing a reporter attempting to explain the 'dense pack' basing mode for MX in 90 seconds or two minutes. Dan

33

Rather, now anchorman on CBS Evening News, told an interviewer that television news 'tends to be a headline service, not an in-depth service'. He went on: 'Anybody who just watches TV news cannot be well informed. You have to read'.

The only systematic study available tends to underscore the inadequacy of television as a medium for informing the public about defence. On the basis of a survey of Walter Cronkite's CBS-TV Evening News programme in 1972 and 1973, Ernest W. Lefever concluded: 'An attentive American viewer relying wholly on the Cronkite show for 1972 and 1973 would have received a partial and highly distorted picture of the dangers confronting the country, the government's response, and the opposing views on national defence. The show carried almost no news on growing Soviet military might in missiles, aircraft, warships or manpower'. Lefever found also that the programme 'painted an overwhelmingly negative picture of US military developments' with 69 per cent of the stories casting the defence establishment in a negative light.

It should be noted that, if Cronkite struck an anti-military posture on his programme, he was doing little more than reflecting the mood of the day – with the nation still scarred by the Vietnam debacle and sentiment against the defence establishment running strong. How far the CBS programme stimulated or reinforced popular attitudes or influenced decision-making is another matter.

A better basis for judging the influence of television on defence policy is provided by a more recent series that CBS-TV screened in June 1981. The series of five, one-hour programmes at prime time – *The Defence of the United States* – was promoted as 'the most important documentary project of the decade'. The overall message questioned the seriousness of the Soviet military threat and raised doubts about the magnitude and direction of the massive defence build-up that the Reagan Administration was initiating. In short, it ran contrary to the mood of the nation in June 1981 – a mood characterized by profound concern about the Soviet military build-up and wide support for greatly increased Pentagon spending.

The avowed aim of the CBS series was to 'stimulate a debate' at the grassroots across the country on the Administration's rearmament programme. What is striking, given the extraordinary scale of the CBS-TV effort, was the apparently inconsequential impact. In fact, if this television blockbuster affected support for the Reagan defence programme among the public or in Congress it was not evident in opinion polls a year later and even less in the national security policy espoused by the Administration.

Negligible as the impact of television appears to be on the formulation of US defence policy generally, in one sense its influence may be crucial. The experience of Vietnam, the Iran hostage crisis and, more recently, the Lebanese War have raised serious questions as to whether, in the television age, the United States can use her armed forces in a foreign war – in particular, in undeclared wars – without tight censorship.

Although a subject of continuing controversy, there seems little doubt that the nation's attitude towards the Vietnam War and the decision to liquidate the US commitment to it was profoundly influenced by the fact that television brought it all into the American living room. To quote James Reston, the *New York Times* columnist: 'Maybe the historians will agree that the reporters and the cameras were decisive in the end. They brought the war to the people . . . and forced the withdrawal of American power from Vietnam'.

Similarly, live television coverage of the early months of the hostage crisis in Tehran – with the mobs chanting outside the beleagured American Embassy night after night – and Walter Cronkite's nightly reminding of viewers of the number of days the crisis had run – had a significant effect on the Carter Administration's policy, especially the decision to mount the doomed rescue operation. Hodding Carter, State Department spokesman at the time, said in an interview: 'That constant reminder of the failure to resolve the crisis had to have magnified the pressure. It had a definite effect on the process'.

More recently, television coverage of Israel's siege of West Beirut had a dramatic effect on public opinion in the United States –

and apparently on President Reagan personally – with the result that traditional support for Israel was sharply eroded and pressure developed for sanctions to force Israel to call a halt to her attacks.

The extreme sensitivity of decision-makers to the potential impact of television in conflict situations was illustrated by deliberations within the Reagan Administration over the commitments of US troops to a peace-keeping force in Lebanon. A participant at a National Security Council meeting weighing the decision reported that much of the time was devoted to debating how the public would react if the Marines were caught up in hostilities that were screened live by TV.

The implications for future American policy of the prospect of televised warfare are a matter of concern among those responsible for national security and especially among military officials. General William C. Westmoreland, who commanded American forces in Vietnam, said recently: 'Vietnam was the first war ever fought without any censorship. Without censorship things can get terribly confused in the public mind. Television is an instrument which can paralyze the country'.

It might be argued that Westmoreland is a biased witness, given his unhappy Vietnam experience. But his concern is felt, too, in media circles. Roger Mudd, a prominent television commentator, reflected the anxiety by raising the question whether a 'democracy which has uncensored TV in every home will ever be able to fight a war, however moral or just'.

Conclusions

There appears to be an exaggerated perception overseas of the direct influence of the media on American defence policy. The impact of the press and television on concrete decisions involving weapons, strategy and manpower is limited but they do make a major contribution to the 'national atmospherics' – popular impressions about the Soviet threat and American readiness – that, in the final analysis, determines the amount of resources the country is willing to devote to defence.

A controversy over the role of television in conflict is likely to develop in view of the concern that the US – or any democracy – may be hamstrung in the use of its military power, even in pursuit of interests deemed vital by the government. The stringent censorship imposed by the British in the Falkland Islands campaign will in all probability be studied – and debated – as a possible model for future US policy.

The Media and the Image of Defence Policy:
Europe

The Press has always sought to remark on the remarkable and to find fault with official explanations of the ordinary. The control that the Press (and in later days, the electronic media of mass communications) can exercise over the political process is that of an outsider and thus bound to be provocative. Without provocation, without the revelation of hidden facts and unorthodox or at least unconventional explanation of these facts the media cannot fulfill their purpose which is to satisfy curiosity, to arouse interest and to draw attention to issues that would otherwise go unremarked. Yet some ask more: they would wish the media at the same time to clarify issues and to respect their real proportions in order not to distort their meaning. This, however, is to ask too much for the Press has never been able to show things as they are without a measure of arbitrary distortion. Distortion is the price that has to be paid for bringing into focus complex and ambiguous issues.

Since war and peace, foreign and defence policy, international security, armaments and arms control are all highly complex and ambiguous matters, the media rarely manage to do justice to the issues involved. This difficulty is increased by the media's own business interests: they must try to win the public and that often means limiting the public's exposure to issues which are both unfamiliar and difficult to understand, otherwise the public will desert the media.

In former times, war and the military were taken for granted: every generation in most countries of Europe was expected to have to fight at least one war and preparation for war was part of national policy. If a generation was spared a war, they were considered lucky. War reporting in the eighteenth and nineteenth centuries, when the Press emerged as a permanent phenomenon in Western Europe, was no different from reporting a fire or an earthquake. Everyone expected such calamities. Moreover, war was widely seen as a means of policy. War reporting, therefore, was nothing more than observing and analysing the use of armed force. The legitimacy of that use was rarely questioned. War correspondents accompanied armies and navies in order simply to tell a story.

Three of the bloodiest wars of the last century and early in this were widely reported in the Press, albeit with a considerable measure of compassion for the ordeals of soldiers and victims: the Crimean War, the American Civil War and the Russo-Japanese War. War was identified with the noble image of 'Nations in Arms' and national feelings had generally accepted war as a national duty once national interest seemed to be at stake and the war 'just'.

This 'alliance' held more or less until the end of the First World War, despite the growth of Christian, liberal and socialist philosophy strongly condemning war and postulating general disarmament. However, the European Press reflected this unease and, when World War I broke out in 1914, there was articulate opposition to the general popular surge towards war. The traumatic experience of the war itself reinforced the moves towards disarmament and pacifism, and this was reflected in the European Press. Scepticism and criticism of the military establishments, defence and armaments blossomed in the liberal, democratic and socialist newspapers.

World War II again appealed to patriotism, and the 'just war'. Mass mobilization and mass suffering demanded that the war effort be identified with the highest national and humanitarian purpose. Fascism and Hitler made it easier to make that identification among the Allies. In the Soviet Union, Poland, Yugoslavia and Greece, it was not much different whereas in Germany war and national defence had been discredited.

In the post-war period a strong initial impetus for peace and disarmament was finally overcome by fear of a new aggression, this time from the East. For almost three decades, public discussion of security affairs was reduced to general expressions of reservation and the democratic left of Europe (and in the churches) and by technical descriptions of deterrence and defence on the centre and right. The European Press dealt with these matters in a strangely ambiguous and veiled manner. Latent scepticism combined with enthusiastic reporting on the new arms technologies, on the modern armed forces, on alliance politics, and on the strategy of deterrence by controlled escalation and flexible response – all highly abstract and complex subjects, difficult to deal with in the pages of the smaller newspapers in the 1960s and 1970s and almost impossible to present with any claim to reality and objectivity on television. There were some brave attempts to explain nuclear deterrence, escalation and conventional defence but more often the tone was one of breathless admiration for technical mastery.

In 1970, Helmut Schmidt, then Defence Minister, called the Bundeswehr an industrial organization that 'produces security' and the media accepted, by and large, the official explanations of deterrence. There was not much controversy until the late 1970s and criticism was confined to compulsory military service, where it existed, to the high cost of armaments and to the absurdity of armed East-West confrontation. The era of negotiations tended to deflect criticism of the military but such debate as took place was a privileged communication between a few specialists in the media and within the bureaucracies and legislatures. The central issues were not debated. They were insulated and widely misunderstood by the general public – like modern works of art: complex, ambiguous, awesome, and, at times, awful. The media employed few specialists and had little interest in defence, armaments and arms-control policies, strategy and security. Editorial staffs

were therefore ill-prepared when the old controversies of the 1950s over the rearmament of West Germany, nuclear arms in Europe and deterrence exploded again in the late 1970s and swiftly engulfed significant parts of the educated public – in churches, at universities and in high schools with many teachers leading the opposition against nuclear arms and NATO policies.

This lack of preparation was due mainly to the latent opposition within the media against military security and nuclear weapons. Since the late 1960s, many former participants in the student revolt against the Vietnam War and American policies had joined the editorial offices of television and radio stations, newspapers and the wire services. In West Germany many of them had invoked the constitutional privilege of declaring themselves conscientious objectors to conscription and had carried on a propaganda campaign against military service. The ground was prepared for the setting up of organized resistance to the State's laws on military service and to the politics of military security in Europe.

The Impact of Detente

The years of detente after 1966–67 had changed the perceptions of the 'potential enemy' or 'potential aggressor' in the East. The Harmel Report on the Future Tasks of the Alliance had declared that the relaxation of tensions with the East was compatible with and even complimentary to defence and deterrence. But this combination, while entirely rational as a policy, was ambiguous as to precisely how the Soviet Union and the other Communist-governed countries of Eastern Europe were to be approached for limited co-operation and a security partnership. The central proposition of the Harmel Report was neither understood nor accepted by large segments of West European Society. Detente had been looked upon by many politicians, academics and journalists as an alternative to East-West confrontation in Europe – much as arms control had been understood as a substitute for armaments and defence. If the Soviet Union and her allies in Eastern Europe were to be considered as prospective partners, why should they then be looked upon as 'potential aggressors' to be countered by NATO with new arms and defence measures? The basic concept remained that of qualitative superiority of the West over the East in military forces and arms technology. The West European Governments relied on this assumed qualitative superiority in order to limit defence efforts and, in particular, military expenditures beyond an agreed and rather modest level. NATO relied on stabilizing security by mutual and balanced force reductions (MBFR) and the Vienna Negotiations encouraged expectations for arms control in Europe as the Conference on Security and Co-operation in Europe (CSCE) had done since 1973. Detente policies were invoked to justify opposition to conscription, to armed security and to defence expenditures. The democratic left in Europe was particularly impatient with the East-West confrontation and NATO programmes and its many supporters within the media transmitted this impatience to the public, as did many teachers in schools and the proponents of peace research at academic institutions. Social-democratic Governments in Western Europe came under relentless criticism from within their own parties, from trade unions, from their youth organizations and from the churches for their alleged lack of awareness of the risks of confrontation and the dangers of war resulting from armaments programmes and the high levels of military forces. The traditional pacifism of the European left, embedded in all the Socialist and Social-Democratic Parties of Western Europe (and in large segments of the Liberal Parties as well) was revived by the hopes of the detente period and the aim of detente was anticipated as reality long before the process had time to develop and arms control to be established. The 'Spirit of Helsinki' was often taken for a fact, whereas in reality it still remained simply a promise of better times to come.

The media, never well-equipped for dealing with complex matters of international relations and by tradition emotional rather than capable of detached examination of unpleasant facts, had left reporting and commenting on military and security affairs to a very few specialists. These were considered by the editors with a mixture of awe, condescension, suspicion and mild neglect yet they held a near monopoly. Privileged they may have been but their impact was sharply limited by the space and time the editors made available for them. Thus a strange situation had emerged: a small number of professional journalists of varying quality virtually controlled all information and commentary on defence and security affairs but they did little to shape editorial policies. This became evident when the first epic controversy arose over 'the neutron bomb'.

As far as personnel were concerned, many of the correspondents who had covered World War II survived into the post-war period. These professional journalists specialized in war and military affairs but the interest shown by their editors has varied sharply. For example, the last war the French press really covered in depth was the Algerian War of Independence 1954–62.

The Vietnam Legacy

The war in Vietnam changed things. It became a permanent subject of newspaper and television interest in most of Western Europe with ideological and political factors tending to dominate both the reporting and the evaluation. This led observers generally to wrong conclusions about the nature and the eventual outcome of this war. By 1965 it was generally proclaimed that this Second Indo-chinese War could not be ended by a military victory and that therefore only a political solution could end the struggle. Reporting and comment tended to reflect this dominant conviction in Western Europe, in particular in the French media but also in Germany, Scandinavia, Italy and the Netherlands. The effect of this general conviction was to under-estimate the significance of the strategic equation, the balance of military forces after the withdrawal of US forces in 1973, the impact of the arms support given to North Vietnam by the USSR and China, and the strain of combat on the forces of South Vietnam and the population. Last not least, reporting underestimated the political significance of armed combat in the strategy and psychology of the Vietnamese Communists. When South Vietnam collapsed this belied the forecasts of ten years of reporting in the Western press. The interdependence of political and military factors had been wrongly interpreted in favour of an assumed permanent military stalemate that left only a negotiated settlement as an outcome. European public opinion, however, shaped by the media and by the elite in universities, churches, humanitarian institutions and political parties, did not correctly perceive the lessons of the event, namely that it was the physical and moral exhaustion of the forces of resistance in the South that had finally led to collapse under military pressure.

The image of the Vietnam War on television has shaped the ideas relating to military security, the use of armed force, national defence and the role of violence in politics of an entire generation. Although the reporting of European television and the higher quality press was by and large correct, preconceived notions were not shattered by the evidence on the ground. Even the advance of the columns of North Vietnamese tanks into the city of Saigon did not dissipate the false impression that South Vietnam had been smashed by its own people in revolt, helped, but not led by the North. The subsequent annexation of the South by the North and the later military invasion of Cambodia by the Vietnamese have been treated only with cursory interest. The War was over and that was what counted in European perceptions.

Since the Vietnam War, the problems of peace and military security in the East-West context and in Europe itself have been overshadowed by the reporting of more distant wars. Nevertheless the constant reference to war has affected public attitudes to nuclear deterrence and military defence in Europe. The continuous reporting of human suffering and damage impresses the horror of war on peoples' minds and tends to identify defence and military security with war in Europe. The emotional reaction of the media to armed conflict elsewhere, irrespective of the causes and the course of events, has reduced the determination to defend even one's own country and Western Europe against a possible threat from the East. The reporting on all wars since Vietnam has followed the same pattern: war is senseless; it can serve no rational purpose; it must end in catastrophe; and there is no legitimacy in using the military instrument for any political end including the defence of freedom

and independence. One can observe this 'anti-war' reporting in the case of the Gulf War between Iran and Iraq, in the Lebanese War and in the conflict between Britain and Argentina over the Falklands. Reporting has tended to concentrate on the cruelty and senselessness of war, which can be expressed visually or written about descriptively. While this is to be commended from a humanitarian and philosophical point of view, it does not help to distinguish the causes of war and hence between defence and aggression and between deterrence and war-fighting. The European media seem to have the most serious difficulties in this respect. There is an exception: the British media coverage of the conflict in the South Atlantic. The reporting here reminded one of traditional war reporting: confidence that the cause of their country was right and pride in performance. While interesting in itself, that may not be an attitude that is helpful in explaining the need to defend Western Europe against a superior military force.

Erratic Coverage

Coverage, then, tends towards the spectacular and the spectacular dominates not only the television screen and the headline but also the understanding of defence and security, often equating them with war and insecurity. Second, only very few media organizations employ professional journalists specializing in military and security affairs. For many years in West Germany only two nationally-distributed daily newspapers – the *Frankfurter Allgemeine Zeitung* and *Die Welt* – published articles and reports on defence and security issues. Even today regular, systematic reporting and comments on these subjects can be found only in these two newspapers, while others, such as the *Süddeutsche Zeitung* of Munich and the *Frankfurter Rundschau*, tend to keep up their reader's interest by a certain amount of copy dealing with security, arms control and defence. The weekly press is represented especially by *Die Zeit* of Hamburg and, with some qualifications, by *Der Spiegel*.

Third is the question of regularity. Only the *Frankfurter Allgemeine Zeitung* offers substantial continuous coverage of security and defence matters. The bulk of the press and the radio programmes address defence and security if and when there is a public debate, usually a controversial one, and when the issue can be easily defined. This was the case with the 'neutron bomb'. It is also the case with such issues as chemical weapons, nuclear arms, NATO strategy or when there is discussion of the possibility of a limited war in Europe or limited use of nuclear arms in Europe. Television on the other hand has screened a number of informative and explanatory films on nuclear arms and strategy, on the balance of forces, on arms control and on the military threat to Western security.

West Germany may not be typical of all Western European countries. Others probably do less since national defence is unlikely to have the same degree of urgency and the same controversial character as in a frontier country, where destruction would first occur in the case of conventional or limited nuclear war. Moreover in Germany the traumatic experience of a lost war dominates whenever the use of military force is discussed. Responsibility for war and for preparations for war weigh heavily on the consciences of many politicians, churchmen, journalists, and academics. It is the main theme of any discussion of the ethics and morality of national defence and deterrence, since the nuclear fact, as Professor Kurt Biedenkopf has pointed out, imposes on people a state of extreme psychological tension bordering on the unbearable.

For this reason alone arms-control proposals are followed closely in public once the issues have been clearly shaped and recognized by the media. However, the public attention span is short and this is why the media have not consistently featured long drawn out negotiations like MBFR or SALT very prominently; the subjects are too complex and detailed knowledge indispensable if one is to understand what these discussions are all about. Occupation with such themes is even less in evidence in such countries as Britain, France, Italy and Spain. The Nordic countries, the Netherlands and Switzerland, on the other hand, seem to resemble the situation in West Germany. Great occasions in international politics, such as summit meetings, can confer some sudden interest on the

subjects under discussion but the treatment given usually consists of a resumé of the record prior to the event and of the problems encountered. The British and West German media generally do quite well on such occasions. The MBFR and SALT negotiations, for example, have been rather well reported since they began and CSCE has been adequately reported. On the other hand, French, Italian and Dutch reporting has been less frequent and continuous during the last ten years' or so, although the NATO 'dual track' decision of 1979 and the problems of its implementation related to the INF (Intermediate Nuclear Force) negotiation have received considerable attention in the media of nearly all West European countries.

Influence in Concrete Cases
One can single out four particularly critical and significant cases of media influence on the political decision-making process during the last few years:

- the 'neutron bomb' decision;
- the storage of chemical warheads;
- the storage of nuclear warheads;
- the *Pershing* II and GLCM deployment decision of 1979.

These and other related issues (such as 'no first use') have much to do with the perception of the East-West theatre balance in Europe, the perception of threat from the East, the concept of extended deterrence and the Alliance strategy of flexible response by controlled escalation. In other words, the issues are complex and highly technical. They are not easy to understand and to discuss.

Public debate lives on simplification and hence the media have simplified and often oversimplified the issues as have many politicians taking part in the debates. The peace movement in Europe has generally adopted a clearcut and summary formulation of the issues and has largely falsified the original propositions as they did in the case of the 'dual track' decision. Soviet propaganda has seized the opportunity offered and its disinformation campaign has been and is being manipulated by internal communist agitation within the peace movement in several West

European countries. The media, of course, have acted as media tend to do: they support or at least record the opposition to Government policies and strategy. In this respect the affiliation of a certain number of journalists with parties of the Democratic Left, with the labour movement, with churches and with student groups tends to reinforce the position taken by those organizations or groups. In such cases the media no longer act independently but rather under external influence.

One can argue, of course, that this is how most information or at least most elements of opinion are reported. However, there have been examples of rather biased programmes produced with the help of those in opposition to government policies and dominated by the 'counter-experts' of the peace movement without government or independent contributions arguing a genuine case in objective terms. Spokesmen for the Soviet Government have been granted easy and generous access to programmes for interviews and lengthy statements where spokesmen for the Government have been excluded or not been offered the same conditions. In fairness such manipulation has by and large remained the exception. On the whole the media have represented both sides in the debate even if they have tended to lean towards emotional explanations and to be critical of official policy and they have mostly featured the danger and the horrors of nuclear war where the issue was, and remains, one of deterrence and arms control.

The most spectacular case is that of the Reduced Blast/Enhanced Radiation (RB/ER) weapon or 'neutron bomb'. The coining of the label 'neutron bomb' decided the shape of the issue and the explanation offered first in the *Washington Post*, according to which this weapon would kill humans but would spare property, decided the terms of the debate. Europe rejected the 'neutron bomb' almost out of hand with public statements by politicians, churchmen, academics and journalists, few of whom had more than the vaguest idea of what this weapon was intended to do. The debate has since been clarified and broadened but not entirely in favour of NATO policies. In 1977–78 public opinion in Western Europe, in particular in West Germany and the

Netherlands, had suffered a shock when first confronted with the neutron weapon. Discussion of its characteristics and significance for deterrence and defence brought out a clearer picture of its purpose but did not lead to the desired quietening of public opinion. The neutron weapon remains a highly sensitive and divisive political issue, invariably spoken of in press reports and on television in the context of its use by NATO in the early stages of a war in Europe.

During that first phase of public discussion, the 'neutron bomb' overshadowed all other nuclear weapons and the entire issue of Theatre Nuclear Force (TNF) modernization. However, no sooner was the neutron issue taken off the political agenda as a result of President Carter's decision in the Spring of 1978 to defer production when public attention turned to TNF. From 1979 that issue was fuelled by the 'dual track' decision on the modernization of long-range TNF (or INF – Intermediate Nuclear Forces). Soviet propaganda paired the neutron weapon with the ground-launched cruise missile (GLCM) and later also with the *Pershing* II. The press and television generally questioned the usefulness or desirability of new TNF systems. Press and other media commentary together with the arguments of the opponents to these NATO options in public debate created an unfavourable environment for the implementation of NATO plans. In 1981 – 82 the neutron weapon issue was revived by US procurement decisions. On this occasion it became clear that no West European government or parliament would accept deployment in their countries. In retrospect, it can be seen that the neutron weapon issue changed the entire psychological climate for TNF modernization.

The debate on the 'dual track' decision and hence on LRTNF modernization has also changed since the end of 1979. While there has been no general rejection of GLCM and *Pershing* II deployment in some parts of Western Europe, the issue has become dominant in domestic politics in West Germany and in the Netherlands and is a latent problem for any Belgian Government. The situation in Italy and in Britain seems less critical. In West Germany it is expected that the public debate in 1983, the year in which first deployment of both missile systems is envisaged, will be conducted in an emotionally charged atmosphere. The arguments have already been formulated, political parties have taken positions (some of them only provisional) conditional on the expected results of the Geneva INF negotiations. The press is in possession of more facts and figures than ever before and the Government has given more information and more political guidance for the understanding of the problem than in any other matter on public debate concerning security. In the press at least this is still an open issue -- while the case of the 'neutron bomb' is politically closed.

Attention has turned also to nuclear and chemical weapons stockpiled in Europe. Some magazines, like *Der Stern* in Germany, have featured articles on these stockpiles prominently for some time and thus created an issue, seized upon by the peace movement. The stockpile issue has come up again and again in political debate at regional and local levels. The peace movement and, in particular, action groups of the extreme left (such as the Communist Party and other persuasions of the radical ecologist factions) have prepared 'peaceful sieges' of US and German nuclear weapons sites and have placed obstacles on the roads. *Der Stern* published a map of such sites in West Germany in 1981, although the sites marked were partly wrong and markedly in excess of the real number. *Der Stern* had pictured West German territory as a nuclear weapons launching pad and this bellicose picture of West Germany has been taken up both by the Communist and left-wing radicals and by official propaganda and information media in East Germany.

In this way all the issues mentioned above have been linked in order to present a kind of deadly network covering West Germany likely to attract pre-emptive strikes on a territory already overburdened with nuclear arms and delivery systems even without additional deployments. The fact that 1,000 nuclear warheads have been withdrawn since 1979 as part of the 'dual track' decision and that the replacement of *Honest John* by *Lance* has resulted in a reduction of systems and operational warheads has hardly been mentioned in media reports.

While Soviet propaganda did strongly influence part of the press and the electronic media it appears on the strength of current evidence, that this influence is reducing.

One must conclude that the media in Western Europe and particularly in West Germany have played a considerable role in determining public opinion on the issues in question. The interplay between the media, the peace movement, certain politicians and academics as well as 'counter-experts' opposing official policies and NATO programmes has been remarkable and certainly not without impact on the public, as the mass demonstrations of October 1981 and June 1982 showed.

Conclusions

Defence and security, foreign policy and military policy have become the object of closer if not always serious scrutiny by the media. The nature of the media offers easy access to dissenting opinion, all the more so since it can present itself as non-conformist and can call official policy into question. The opposition groups can raise artificial or irrelevant issues through the media and make unrealistic arguments without proper correction since those working in the media have only general knowledge and experience. Unless debates are arranged with competent representatives of Governments or advocates for the official policy, 'counter-experts' go unanswered. Since radical minorities are committed to agitation and organized to carry it through, entire audiences can – and on occasions have been – seen or heard to support the most extravagant arguments and alternative policies, such as the replacement of military defence by 'social defence', by which is meant passive resistance to a foreign occupier instead of fighting a defensive war. Deterrence is being systematically attacked as counter-productive and as leading to a general war without any evidence offered other than historical 'lessons' that 'armies will always wage war in the end'. The Press is less exposed to organized manipulation by dedicated groups than the television and radio networks but the press remains particularly wary of official explanations and statements of fact. Both have to be scrupulously correct and at the same time plausible to be accepted. Since to divulge military secrets no longer deters indiscretion among officials or investigative reporting by journalists, the debate can be dominated by selective reporting and by artificial constructs of strategy, arms programmes and defence.

The general lesson for official information policy is clear: Governments and NATO must cope with the new realities of the political process. Neither the media nor the general public can handle or absorb the information on which decisions must be based. The result is confusion and polarization on artificial, irrelevant or falsified issues whether these are nuclear policies, NATO's strategy of deterrence or the military requirements for effective defence. Governments must recognize that the media suffer great difficulties in explaining the background to political decisions to the people. The necessary clarity is often submerged by abundant or even overabundant flows of news, the relevance of which cannot always be recognized and the quantity of which can no longer be absorbed.

This makes selection paramount and confers on the media the privilege of choosing between items and arguments, entirely at their own discretion. The selection of news has always been the major editorial task but guidance when needed could be obtained by reference to established opinion, to the accepted authorities and by reference to debate between differing opinions in appropriate fora. Today the concept of national interest is no longer accepted as a matter of fact, nor can Alliance decisions be translated into national policy simply after a debate in Parliament and government decision. Nor do the media have the space or time necessary for explanation since the subjects of defence, security, arms control, and strategy do not appeal to the larger public. Hence proper selection and formulation, presentation and research become all the more important for correct reporting and balanced argumentation.

Modern journalism in Europe is not exactly conducive to such an approach, since it tends to focus on the expression of personal opinion and to side with minorities. The minorities in question claim the role of a legitimate opposition. They stake their claim in the name of non-conformism and as representatives of the citizens, who do not feel properly represented in parliaments. This claim alone makes them interesting and attractive to the media. They also make good journalism by promising spectacular scenes and lively debates which make for good political entertainment. In this way the reasons behind official decisions can be overburdened with controversy. The public begins by being confused and is then exposed to their distinct propaganda message: opposition to official policy in the guise of 'struggle for peace' and 'peace festivals' are arranged by popular 'artists for peace'. Political propaganda programmes are shown on television or broadcast on the radio carrying a message against NATO's 'dual track' decision or the 'neutron bomb' or nuclear stockpiles and usually against all of them at the same time. The Press reports favourably on such happenings, unable to see through false appearances. Part of their public, in particular the younger generation, feel in any case sympathy for the cause propagated. The media in turn follow what they perceive to be a general feeling or preference. In this way the media tend to neutralize themselves and to lose influence. In short, they are being manipulated in their desire to follow what they take to be the fashion. Governments and defence establishments that have long dominated the news and impressed the public with their authority must now make greater efforts to get across their part of the news and the truth. Education of journalists is both necessary and difficult because of concern in the media that journalists might be manipulated by Governments. The establishment of independent fora for the education of media representatives which would help to draw them into discussions on security, defence, arms control, strategy and military policy generally would seem to be the most promising approach. Media representatives must be trusted to perform the role of watchdogs. To do that effectively they should not be left alone with the committed agitators. Yet it is not easy for the media fully to explain matters, for the need to restrict classified information often results in counter-productive denial of news or lack of explanation. This has been the case with the Soviet SS–20 deployment. Not only are there differences of opinion within the community about the number but even simple counting difficulties contribute to the confusion. They cannot, therefore, be held entirely responsible for the programmes or articles they produce. It has to be recognized that the media can neither be used to justify nor to explain Government decisions. Governments must explain and defend their policies themselves and compete with those who would oppose these policies. It is not possible or desirable in a democracy to attempt to exercise control over the media even in the cause of national security. On the other hand, media sympathy for the cause of disarmament can be easily obtained since this is a natural sentiment and a sensible attitude towards war and peace. Governments must see to it that this inclination is not exploited by those who think only of disarmament without due regard for security and who are in no position to influence the policies of those powers on the other side of the East-West divide with whom they seek security through adaptation.

The Media and the Image of Defence Policy:
Japan

MASASHI NISHIHARA

In every mass society, the press and television have become major actors in the political arena and Japan is no exception. The media exerts an important political influence, first by disseminating facts or selecting from facts those that it chooses to disseminate and, second, by encouraging the public to adopt certain political values through editorials, commentaries, and even through the tone given to the headlines of news articles. Much of the credit for the successful anti-nuclear campaigns in Japan during the first half of 1982, aimed at influencing the UN Special Conference on Disarmament, should go to the mass media.

Political leaders, while utilizing the media to disseminate their views, often run the risk of being exaggerated or distorted by the media. Opponents and critics readily use the views reported to attack them and, on occasion, even to force their resignation. Because of newspaper *exposés*, many Japanese Government leaders, including several Heads of the Defence Agency (equivalent to a Defence Minister) and of the Joint Staff Council, have experienced political difficulty. Press coverage may relate to views on the Constitution, on the Japan–US Security Treaty, on nuclear issues, on the Self-Defence Forces and other defence issues, not to mention occasional political scandals. Successive Cabinets have made their defence policies deliberately ambiguous, hoping thereby to minimize the effects of media criticism.

While the mass media's political role is thus unquestionably important, there are very few cases, at least in postwar Japanese politics, in which the mass media have clearly influenced the public views on defence issues and led the public to demand that the Government shift its policy. For the past thirty years, some major newspapers have persistently criticized the Liberal Democratic (Conservative) Government for its conventional rearmament programmes, begun in 1954, and pressed their pacifist or 'dovish' views. But that has not prevented the Liberal Democrats from forming the Government for the entire postwar period, except for the sixteen months after June 1947. The Government survived in 1951 over the issue of the Peace Treaty with the Allied Powers, in 1960 over the problem of a revised Japan–US Security Treaty, and in 1972 over the matter of regaining control of Okinawa from the US. Despite the bitter attacks by the press of a government policy that has steadily increased defence spending in spite of an economic recession, Prime Minister Suzuki's Government retained much popular support for its policy during its lifetime.

There are therefore clear limits to the political influence of the Japanese media and this raises questions of how the media, particularly the press and television, function, why they have tended to be 'dovish', and how they have presented certain specific issues.

The Big Five
More than half of some 120 daily commercial newspapers, national and local, have morning and evening editions. This may be an additional factor contributing to their influence although, since they have to compete with television news programmes in the evening, the evening editions have substantially smaller circulations. Nevertheless the total circulation, counting morning and evening editions as two, amounted to some 66.3 million copies a day in 1980.[1] If morning and evening editions are counted as one set, the total circulation was still 46.4 million copies and, if this latter figure is adopted, there were some 400 copies for every 1,000 people in Japan. This compares well with other countries such as the Soviet Union (397 copies per 1,000 population), Great Britain (388), West Germany (312), the United States (287), France (214) and Italy (113).[2]

45

Five daily newspapers with nationwide circulation enjoy uniquely dominant positions in the world of Japanese news media. None of them support any particular political party nor are they supported by any party. The 'big five' are *Asahi* (7.5 million copies for morning editions in 1980), *Mainichi* (4.6 million), *Yomiuri* (8.4 million), *Nihon Keizai* (1.8 million), and *Sankei* (1.9 million). Between them they have 53 per cent of the total newspaper circulation, national and local. Although *Yomiuri* has now become more centrist, it used to carry, together with *Asahi* and *Mainichi*, almost uniform layouts and similar 'dovish' editorial views and reporting preferences but the fact that *Yomiuri*'s circulation now outnumbers those of *Asahi* and *Mainichi* has much less to do with its editorial policy shift than with its aggressive sales and promotion policy. *Nihon Keizai*, equivalent to *The Wall Street Journal* or *The Financial Times*, emphasizes the reporting and analysis of economic affairs, but still treats major political events at great length. It is considered to be a well-balanced, high-quality paper. *Sankei* is the most 'hawkish', stressing the importance of a stronger defence posture and closer ties with the United States. It also tends to be alarmist about Soviet military power and Communist ideology.

In the Tokyo area there are seven television stations (two public and five commercial) running programmes continuously from six in the morning until midnight or later. Although 98.2 per cent of Japanese households own colour television sets, the television news programmes appear to have a very limited impact on the public. Television networks in the Tokyo area, for instance, allocated in 1980 only 10 per cent of their time for news reporting and commentaries, in contrast to 60 per cent allowed for entertainment.[3] Only 7 to 10 per cent of those polled watched news and commentary programmes. In contrast, over 70 per cent of the adult population read a newspaper every day, and about 92 per cent read newspapers with varying degrees of frequency.[4] Also relatively high are the percentages of those who always read the 'serious' pages: editorials (25.6 per cent); politics (46.0 per cent); and foreign news (22.3 per cent).[5] A survey conducted in Tokyo in 1975 produced some interesting statistics: asked why they made use of different types of media, about 60 per cent of those surveyed said that they read newspapers 'to learn of trends in public opinion and acquire their own basis for judgements and opinions', while only 30 per cent relied upon television for such purposes.[6] This is because television, while providing news analysis, rarely gives strong opinions. The exceptions are a few popular commentators such as Ken'ichi Takemura and Ryūgen Hosokawa. Both happen to put over conservative views. One media survey showed that there was 'substantial public support to make Takemura Prime Minister'.[7]

Why is the Press 'Dovish'?

The 'dovish' editorial policies of *Asahi*, *Mainichi* and *Yomiuri* can to a considerable extent be explained by their history. Founded at the time of the Meiji Restoration of 1868, they established the role of government critic and believed that they should enlighten the public on how Japan should be modernized. They did not see their role to be that of reporting events and analyzing them in a balanced manner.[8] Papers which supported particular governments tended to be damaged when that government fell. On the other hand, the government often attempted to control a critical press by using the security police to harass editors and writers and by controlling the amounts of paper available. Clashes between the government and the press continued until the 1930s when the government adopted strict censorship and intervened directly by interfering with press personnel management.

The journalists' failure to fight the government's control of the press in the pre-war years left them with a sense of guilt. They felt that if only they had fought harder, they might have prevented Japan from getting involved in an unwinnable war. This feeling persists today.

A constant point of reference in post-war Japanese debates on defence policy is Article 9 of the Constitution, originally drafted by the Occupation Authorities in February 1946 and put into effect in May 1947. This Article renounces Japan's right to belligerence 'as a means of settling international disputes'. When, in 1947, General Douglas MacArthur, then Head of the US-dominated Allied Occupation Forces, talked about Japan becoming a neutral, peaceful country like 'a Switzerland of the Orient', the majority of Japanese endorsed his views. The Government, the press and the public all agreed. However, when the Cold War developed, Prime Minister Shigeru Yoshida, often referred to as the 'Adenauer of Japan', took a more realistic view of Japan's security by approving US foreign policies. The press immediately suspected that this was the beginning of the road to Japan's rearmament and began to warn the public of the danger. For the Socialists and Communists, as well as for most journalists, pacifism became an ideology, and they failed to give pragmatic consideration to Japan's national interests. All security issues, including Article 9 itself, have been debated between the idealists (or, as Masamichi Inoki has called them, the 'utopian pacifists') and the realists.

The occupation authorities naturally encouraged a free press, although they did censor press coverage of the occupation policies. They also encouraged the formation of labour unions in the newspaper companies' work force. Workers, now led by the Socialists or Communists, began to criticize their newspapers' editorial policies and to demand the removal of all those in positions of authority who were suspected of having supported the Government during World War II. The *Yomiuri* Company in particular had a series of serious labour disputes starting late in 1945. The disputes ended in victory for the Company in the following year, but only with the help of the occupation authorities. Many other newspapers also encountered the same difficulty, and their editorial policies have tended ever since to be affected by the ideological leanings of their workers. *Asahi*, for example, is often labelled 'red' partly at least because of its strong leftist unions.

The Pacifist Argument
Issues related to defence are naturally wideranging, and they are often compounded with problems of international security, foreign policies, and budgetary priorities. What is unique to the Japanese press is that their analyses of major East-West tensions treat American policies much more critically than Soviet policies. Moreover almost all defence issues are debated on legal grounds, the basis of which is Article 9 of the Constitution, rather than on pragmatic assessments of security needs. At the risk of oversimplification, typical press arguments on current issues may be summed up as follows:

1. The Reagan Administration's military programme intensifies East-West tensions and demonstrates a lack of seriousness about arms talks with Moscow. The road to peace lies through positive reductions of forces, including unilateral reductions. Japanese defence build-up is against the wishes of peace-loving peoples.
2. The USSR 'military threat' in the Western Pacific has been exaggerated by the US, which plays down Soviet internal weaknesses such as low economic productivity and ethnic tensions. The Japanese defence build-up provokes the USSR.
3. The Polish crisis has been aggravated by the Administration's policies of sanctions against General Jaruzelski's Poland and the Soviet Union. Japan should not support President Reagan's policies.
4. The Suzuki Government's policy of increasing defence was a step to military power. It was against the Constitution. Spending over one per cent of GNP for defence will lead Japan down a dangerous road.
5. Japan's economic power should be used for peace, not for war. Japan's security can be maintained externally by friendly relations with all major powers and internally by solid welfare and education programmes.
6. The Self-Defence Forces (SDF) should be placed under strong civilian control, to avoid any resurgence of their political power. Japan has to be set an example of anti-militarism. The Falkland War showed how silly the military of both Great Britain and Argentina were in fighting over such a useless, unpopulated island.
7. For Japan's SDF to participate in UN international peace-keeping forces

would be a dangerous step towards involvement in international conflicts. It too is against the Constitution. Japan has to show the world its strong, sincere desire for peace.

8. Japan should not possess any 'offensive' weapons. It also is against the Constitution. The Government should not give in to American pressure for greater defence efforts. Siding with the US is a dangerous course.

9. The American military presence in Okinawa can easily involve Japan in regional and global conflicts. It should thus be reduced to a minimum. Japan should have tighter control over the movement of US troops and arms in and out of the island.

10. Japan is the only victim of an atomic explosion. This should be the basis of Japanese peace diplomacy. The introduction of US nuclear weapons, including transit through Japanese waters of US ships carrying nuclear arms, should never be allowed.

In short, the leading daily newspapers attempt to present two views: that the Japanese should wish to see a militarily weak Japan contributing to world peace by not siding with major powers and by using its economic power constructively; and that successive Conservative Governments, being reactionary, are driving the nation along a wrong and dangerous road. These arguments are not just made over editorial pages but also in columns (Op-Ed pages) to which selected writers are invited to contribute and through the somewhat sensational wording used in news article headlines. *Asahi*, for instance, often carries a series of special reports, such as 'Japan Turning to the Right', 'Is the "Soviet Threat" Real?' and 'The Tilt to Military Expansion'. Every Summer, most newspapers run a series of anti-nuclear articles to commemorate the Hiroshima and Nagasaki disasters in August 1945. Every Autumn (and particularly in the last two years) the news media have paid special attention to how new budget allocations are decided for defence items.

The press also seems to have been 'outraged' by President Reagan's military pro-

grammes and alarmed by the neo-conservative political trends in Britain, Canada and Japan (and, should one also add, in Mitterrand's France?). In 1982, journalists of pacifist inclination have been encouraged by the success of the peace movements in Europe. Disproportionate coverage has been given to anti-nuclear campaigns. During the Spring of 1982, *Asahi*, for instance, had almost daily news articles, columns and editorials about the 'grassroots' anti-nuclear movements in Japan. They reported how many local communities had declared themselves to be 'nuclear-free' communities and that groups such as writers, theatrical performers, academicians, religious believers and housewives had taken part in joint petitions against nuclear weapons. As a climax to these campaigns, some 27 million signatures were collected on a petition to be presented to the UN Secretary General in early June 1982.[9] Yet *Asahi*'s headline read: 'One Hundred Million People's Petitions Submitted to UN'.[10]

Limits of Influence

Despite this activity, an examination of Japan's post-war political history clearly demonstrates the limits to the actual impact of such pacifist editorial policies upon the defence policy of the country. While raising the controversial issues (such as 'Will the Japan-US Security Treaty Endanger Japan?') and enlightening the public about such issues, most national newspapers have failed to weaken Conservative Governments or to force them to adopt more pacifist foreign and security policies. Several examples may be cited.

The constitutionality of a proposed Self-Defence Force (SDF) began to be debated soon after the Korean War broke out in 1950. The media and the opposition parties criticized the Government and maintained that the Constitution prohibited the Japanese from exercising the right to self-defence. The Government interpretation was that the Constitution did not prohibit self-defence, and they went on to establish the SDF in 1954. Despite press editorials critical of the SDF, a *Mainichi* poll taken in September 1953 showed that 48 per cent supported rearmament, while only 33 per cent opposed it.[11] This issue of constitutionality subsequently came up on countless occasions, notably in a number of well-known court cases. Major newspapers have pointed to the ambiguous constitutional basis of the SDF but popular support for it has gradually increased over the years and, by 1978, as many as 86 per cent of those polled recognized the SDF as necessary for the country.[12]

The Japanese-US security relations have also caused anxiety with the major newspapers. The issues involve nuclear deployment, US military bases, defence co-operation, joint exercises, and military technology co-operation. They often pertain to legalistic arguments as to what is or what is not possible under the existing legal framework. There have been several occasions for tension. For instance, US sources, whether intentionally or unintentionally, have claimed that US warships have visited Japanese ports with nuclear weapons on board, despite the Japanese Government's persistent denials and its policy of not allowing such visits. The latest such incident was a casual claim to that effect made in May 1981 by Edwin Reischauer, who was US Ambassador to Tokyo during the 1960s. As it was printed in *Mainichi*, it became a political bombshell.[13] The major daily newspapers implied that the successive Japanese Governments had been intentionally hiding the facts from the people who, they claimed, totally opposed the visits of nuclear-armed US warships to Japan. However, a subsequent poll by *Asahi* revealed that 33 per cent of those polled supported such transit visits and 10 per cent even favoured US-sponsored nuclear deployments on Japanese soil.[14]

Perhaps the greatest impact that the Japanese press has had on the public has been its constant opposition to the revised Security Treaty between the two countries, signed in January 1960 and ratified in June of that year. Opposition groups, primarily Socialist and Communist Parties, left-wing labour unions and student organizations, were able to make their presence felt to the point that President Eisenhower had to cancel his visit to Tokyo at the last minute, causing him considerable embarrassment. This climate of opposition to the Treaty was certainly fostered by the mass media, which maintained that, if the new Treaty were ratified, Japan would be drawn into dangerous Cold War conflicts. In a pre-ratification *Mainichi* opinion survey of March 1960, 22 per cent favoured the Treaty; in a post-ratification *Mainichi* survey (August 1960), only 15 per cent favoured it, although 34 per cent thought they could not avoid accepting it.[15] Despite the opposition, despite such luke-warm support and despite the resignation of Prime Minister Nobusuke Kishi, he was in fact replaced by Hayato Ikeda, from the same ruling party, who carried on basically the same defence policy. This demonstrates the limits to the impact of the media.

Defence expenditure is currently one of the most contentious security issues in Japanese politics. The ratio of the defence expenditure to GNP is treated by the opposition parties and in the pacifist newspapers as a symbolic criterion for the Government's defence posture. Until 1965 the ratio was over 1 per cent and in 1955 it was as high as 1.8 per cent. As GNP increased sharply, the ratio went below 1 per cent, although the defence expenditure itself still increased in real terms. Late in December 1981, the Suzuki Cabinet increased its defence budget from 0.91 per cent of GNP for FY 1981 to 0.93 per cent for FY 1982. *Asahi*'s headlines included, 'Another Step Toward a Military Power', 'A New Era of Military Expansion', and 'Suzuki Selling Out to US'. It also criticized the fact that the planned rate of increase for the welfare budget over the previous year was lower than for the defence budget. The same newspaper invited liberal sceptics and opposition party leaders to give their comments, which were naturally critical.[16] Yet the public has basically accepted the government's policy for gradual defence improvement. All polls taken during the recent years of defence increases have revealed that the majority of respondents accept 'the present level' of SDF strength. The people appear generally to recognize that Japan cannot forever depend upon another power for her survival.

Conclusion

The news media certainly play a vital role in drawing the public attention to the issues, but, at least in Japan, they have failed to persuade

49

the public to adopt their editorial views. For some 20 years after 1945, the majority of Japanese were attracted to 'utopian pacifism', but, since about 1965, they have outgrown pacificism much faster than the press and appear to accept the world as it is with a mixture of cynicism and sophistication. Perhaps the Japanese people have been impressed that, despite the newspapers' constant warnings about the dangerous consequences of having a Security Treaty with the United States, Japan did manage to stay clear of the Vietnam debacle. Japan has not been involved in conflict since 1945. What is more, Japan has successfully overcome economic difficulties including the the two oil shocks of 1973 and 1979. The public seems to have been convinced that much of the credit for this should go to the distinctly conservative leadership of the Liberal Democratic party. *Yomiuri*'s gradual shift to editorial moderation is considered to be an attempt to conform to this change in popular climate. The fact that Takemura, the popular television commentator mentioned earlier, publicly criticizes *Asahi*'s views and expresses his own pro-Government views, emphasizes this conservative political climate. The people are opposed to nuclear weapons, but they seem to sense that demonstrations alone do not bring peace.

Japanese politicians and officials are extremely cautious in their remarks and in their conduct for they know that they will be extensively reported in the press and that any press criticism may be used by the opposition parties to attack them. Consensual decision-making, characteristic of Japanese political practice, requires a minimum level of co-operation from the opposition parties. The Government and the governing party, while enjoying a clear majority in the Diet, have still to move slowly on defence issues. It is in this sense that the role of the press in forcing a slow change in defence policy implementation is likely to remain important in the future.

NOTES

[1] *The Japanese Press 1981* (Tokyo: Japanese Newspaper Publishers and Editors Association, 1981), p.62.

[2] *Ibid.*, p.15. This publication actually cites '570 copies per 1,000 Japanese people', based on the figure of 66.3 million copies rather than 46.4 million copies. The writer feels that the figure of 46.4 million should be used because morning and evening issues should be counted as one newspaper copy rather than two. That would be more comparable internationally.

[3] *Japan 1981: An International Comparison:* (Tokyo: Keizai Koho Centre), p.68; and *Asahi nenkan 1979, bessatsu*, p.437.

[4] Young Kim, *Japanese Journalists and Their World* (Charlottesville, Va: University Press of Virginia, 1981), p.18. This is based on the 1969 survey, conducted by the Japan Broadcasting Association (NZK).

[5] *Ibid.*, p.19. This is based on the 1974 survey.

[6] *Ibid.*, p.21.

[7] John Marcom, Jr., 'Japan's Leading Pundit Gains Fame with Tidal Wave of Gab on the Airwaves', *The Wall Street Journal*, 11 May, 1982.

[8] *Asahi* started in 1879, *Mainichi* in 1872, *Yomiuri* in 1874, *Nihon Keizai* in 1876 and *Sankei* in 1933.

[9] *Asahi*, 1 May, 1982, morning edition. Buddhist groups claimed that they would collect 70 million petitions. *Asahi*, 1 June 1982, morning edition.

[10] *Asahi*, 11 June 1982, evening edition.

[11] *Mainichi nenkan 1979, bessatsu*, p.114.

[12] *Bōei Handobukku 1981*, p.391.

[13] The circumstances under which this incident occurred are well described by a *Mainichi* journalist, Yoshihisa Komori, who interviewed Reischauer. See his *Kaku wa mochikomareta ka* (Have nuclear arms ever been brought into Japan?) (Tokyo: Bungei Shunjū Sha, 1982).

[14] *Asahi*, 14 June, 1981, morning edition.

[15] *Mainichi nenkan 1979, bessatsu*, p.114. For the 1960 incident see, for example, George Packard, III, *Protest in Tokyo; The Security Treaty Crisis of 1960* (Princeton, N.J.: Princeton University Press, 1966).

[16] E.g. *Asahi*, 27 December, 1981, morning edition.

The Management of Defence Expenditure

SIR FRANK COOPER

This Paper is intended as a basis for international discussion – no more, no less – not least because of the variations from country to country of government institutions, procedures and attitudes. Inevitably the Paper reflects to a significant degree experience within the British system but it deliberately covers a wide area of ground.

Defence is – amongst other things – a major enterprise. In many countries defence ranks high on the list of public spending agencies; it is frequently the largest single management authority, particularly if account is taken of both military and civilian personnel; it often stands at the forefront of purchasing organizations both nationally and even more so within Government where it accounts for a very high proportion of central Government purchases of supplies and services; and it frequently operates large industrial undertakings of its own and has a significant impact on the fortunes of defence-related industries and on employment prospects in them.

The management of defence expenditure is superficially akin to that of a large, international conglomerate. Many of the same kind of characteristics exist – for example, international issues, major investment questions, and the deployment of a wide variety of personal professional skills. It is also true that the difference between 'policy' and 'management' is frequently incapable of disentanglement except in the most arid sense. Yet there is one overriding difference – there is no profit and loss account. The defence tests are either success through the preservation of peace coupled with the maintenance of a successful foreign policy or failure through the outbreak of war due either to inadequate force structure, which represents a failure in the management of defence expenditure, or to a political failure to convince a potential adversary that what may be an adequate structure will be brought to action. Beyond these lie the ultimate test of the success or failure of arms in battle.

There are many constraints on defence and its management. It is worth identifying some of them.

Constraints on Management

It would be as well to say a brief word first about the old question of whether the allocation of resources to defence should be determined by the threat and commitments or by what nations believe they can afford. Historically it is difficult to dispute the proposition that the threat only dominates when national interests – almost national survival – are perceived to be at serious risk. This is not to approve or applaud such a stance but to recognize that, particularly in Western democracies (not least in time of economic recession), there is a strong tendency for the electorate and Government to go down the road of what can apparently be afforded without disturbing too much the general tenor of national life. This path is arrived at by some alchemic process of subjective judgement rather than by logical argument. There is no objective way of deciding the size of a defence budget. Total resource allocation is neither a science nor an art.

The essence of democracy is choice. There is a constant interplay between external and domestic factors and within the domestic economy. Two of the most important choices that democracies have to make are the size of the public sector in relation to the private sector and the distribution of resources and expenditure between the various programmes that make up the public sector. Most public programmes have a definite and clearly desirable output – for example, schools, hospitals and roads. Defence expenditure is seen as more akin in the public eye to expenditure on insurance. It differs, however, very significantly from the payment of an insurance premium in that it actually reduces the probability of the disaster against which it seeks to insure. Nevertheless, like many private citizens, Governments are sometimes tempted to under-insure – all the more so when economic growth is low or non-existent.

It is this background which tends to encourage medium and small democratic countries to look at each other and gives rise to suggestions that the level of a country's defence expenditure should be determined by the proportion of GDP that its allies devote to defence. This approach is a fallacy, one that is manifestly illogical and ignores the fact that what matters is the quantum of defence that is required.

There are many factors which bear directly upon the management of defence expenditure. It may be helpful to list briefly some of the major ones:

- The national system of government
- International commitments and obligations
- Good or bad intelligence
- The clarity with which defence strategy and objectives are defined
- National political priorities and public attitudes to defence
- The current politics and problems of governments (almost invariably dominated by the short-term)
- The long-term nature of defence exemplified by the emphasis on long lead times and heavy forward commitments
- Government procedures – notably, in the budgetary area:
  decision-making procedures
  availability of funds – single or multi-year basis
  annuality or flexibility of funding
  public accountability
  public purchasing policy
- The scope of the defence industrial base and scientific base and availability or otherwise of industrial competition
- The impact of factors partially or wholly outside national control such as the world economy, oil prices, foreign exchange, availability of manpower, inflation
- Rising costs of technology and the nature of modern weapon systems

- Manpower – availability, cost, skill
- The military life-style and tradition
- The nature of a country's history, its experience of warfare and military affairs
- The irresistible urge to replace existing defence systems
- The competence of the military/civilian bureaucracy
- Vested interests

This list is not remotely exhaustive and the weight of the various factors varies from time to time and from nation to nation. It is not intended to examine each item in turn. It is simply intended to illustrate some of the problems – some real, some artificial – that inevitably play a significant part in the management of defence expenditure. The central practical problems in defence management rest in relatively few areas – particularly rising real costs and the measures to deal with them; major investment decisions; and the reconciliation of the long-term nature of defence with short-term political and economic pressures. Yet ever present are other dimensions, not least the politics of national priorities, the state of the domestic economy, international obligations and public support. There are too the practical problems connected with resource allocation.

How are the resources to be devoted to defence determined? Most countries seek to plan a national programme over a period of years within the framework of a system which combines analysis with dialogue and debate founded upon a central assessment of how the economy is likely to perform over the period of the plan. In recent years many countries have been faced with difficult defence management problems because of high rates of inflation (which has made full inflation-proofing nigh on impossible), lower rates of growth than expected, and rises in public expenditure either relative to the private sector or in absolute real terms, or both. Cash flow has become increasingly important and more difficult to control. For the defence manager this has resulted in the need to make continuous short-term revisions, often of an undesirable nature. These revisions of necessity fall upon capital investment items, stocks, and military activity levels.

These difficulties can be made even more severe by the rules of public accounting which do not always harmonize with the demands of a long-term capital programme. Any business would be extremely difficult to run if it had no cash reserves or overdraft facilities. There is a strong case in the modern world for all defence managers to have a degree of flexibility, approved by the legislature, in managing the cash resources allocated to them.

How is the allocation of resources within the defence budget to be managed? There is no serious alternative to the production of a long-term plan and updating and costing it at regular intervals. Such a plan has to take account of internal and external factors. It depends crucially on the assumptions fed into it, and, with an alliance, on the successful reflection or reconciliation of national and international aspirations and priorities.

There is no one currency in which the output of a defence programme can be measured. In consequence there is no way of proceeding from data to decision through scientific and quantifiable processes. These can and will illuminate some of the choices; but the ultimate decisions are a matter of judgement, often as much political as military. There has to be a continuing dialogue and full debate, and this is provided for through detailed procedures – frequently time-consuming – within and between governments.

Rising Real Costs

The continuing rise in the real cost of defence equipment is well known. It is more than doubtful whether the consequences in terms of policies or management have been adequately studied, let alone turned into constructive attitudes for the future.

The principal reason for these cost rises can readily be identified. At their head stands the demand to exploit the outburst of advanced technology which poses new threats and demands new responses. In particular much entirely new technology has been introduced into warfare (for example, guided weapons in ever-increasing variety, computerized fire control systems, thermal imaging, satellites and nuclear propulsion). There have been major new twists in technology (switching to short-take-off/vertical-landing flight capability (V/STOL); turning torpedoes into true guided weapons; and towed array sonar). And there is real cost growth as each mark or generation of equipment becomes more complex and improved.

From studies done in the British Defence Ministry it seems that something like 60% of the equipment budget is likely to experience growth in real terms of 6–10% per annum in terms of capital and production costs. It is dubiously profitable to seek more accurate figures for the subject is detailed and complicated. The problems of comparing like with like, of weighting for multi-role or changed role, the effect (not necessarily positive) of changes in reliability and maintainability and the measuring of effectiveness obviously present formidable difficulties. Nevertheless, the increases are real. Some typical consequences are shown in Table 1.

Table 1: Relative Production Costs of Successive Generations of Equipment

Example	Nth Generation	N+1th Generation	Years Between In-Service Dates	Multiplication (Real Cost)	Average Real Annual Rate of Increase
Frigate	*Leander*	Type 22	14	3.0	14.0%
FGA Aircraft	*Hunter* F6	*Harrier* GR1	16	4.0	19.0%
Trainer Aircraft	*Gnat* Mk1	*Hawk* Mk1	19	1.5	2.6%
Helicopter	*Wasp* Mk1	*Lynx* Mk2	12	2.5	12.5%
Infantry Vehicle	FV 432	MCV 80	20	3.5	12.5%
Guided Missile	*Sea Cat*	*Sea Wolf*	13	3.5	19.0%
Artillery Shell	5.5 in.	155 mm L15	11	2.0	9.0%

Source: Statement on the Defence Estimates 1981: Cmnd 8121–1, HMSO, April 1981

This type of problem further manifests itself in terms of the investment costs of research and development (R&D) compared with money spent on production. In general the overall ratio of production to development is low – typically three or four to one. The ratio tends to become even less favourable as the planning stage is replaced by real time development.

It must be broadly true that a higher production to development ratio represents good investment. But this generalization needs to be treated with some caution. The overall ratio says nothing about total procurement costs of particular equipments or the availability of alternatives. High development costs aimed at reducing subsequent production costs could be advantageous; likewise a high production ratio could reflect unsatisfactory increases in production costs. Above all, the ratio says nothing about relevance and effectiveness.

Another phenomenon which affects the defence manager is the impact of the defence Relative Price Effect (RPE). RPE is imperfectly understood. Public sector costs tend to rise faster than prices in the economy generally and the rate varies from programme to programme. Defence prices are no exception. The main reasons appear to be: a). changes in labour productivity in manufacturing industry generally compared with defence industries; and b). movements in import prices relative to domestic costs per unit of output.

The defence RPE tends to rise when manufacturing labour productivity has improved and when relative import prices rise – and vice versa.

Historical data from a number of Western countries who reported sophisticated defence deflators covering the 1970s suggests that defence prices increased at a faster rate than general inflation, the difference being an average of 1.3% per year over the period as a whole. Substantial sums are involved and present a significant problem for the managers of defence expenditure which can only be dealt wwith either by increasing the resources allocated to defence or by adjusting the defence programme.

Manpower costs have also risen in real terms. Again quoting from British experience over the last 20 years, there was a definite upward and real trend at an average annual rate greater than 3%. However, in the latter part of the period increases have moderated to between 1% and 2%.

The major consequence of these factors taken together has been substantial reductions in the number of equipments it is possible to maintain in service. This is most noticeable in terms of ships and aircraft. If one takes 1960/61 as the base year (= 100), by 1980/81 aircraft were 50 and destroyers and frigates 45.

Meeting the Challenge of Rising Costs

Real cost escalation has been with us for many years. It seems unlikely that any Government will be able to fund over a long period of years real cost escalation on the scale indicated. Hitherto, defence managers have reacted by cutting commitments, reducing the quantities of equipment, abandoning some equipments, keeping equipment in service longer, and improving the efficiency of defence management. Inevitably, with the passage of time the room for manoeuvre diminishes.

Britain has at least been successful in a sustained drive to invest a larger percentage of the defence budget in equipment. In particular, the number of United Kingdom based civilian staff has over the last six years been reduced by more than 50,000 (up to 20% of the total) and much has been done to reduce overheads in many areas. In consequence the percentage of the defence budget devoted to equipment has risen spectacularly and so too has the real amount spent as shown in Table 2.

What more can be done? There are a number of relatively conventional initiatives which are being pursued: avoiding over elaborate operational requirements; using commercial equipment; collaboration with allies; more emphasis on sales potential; reducing through-life costs; sensitivity analysis; improved contracts procedures; exploiting stretch potential; and continuing the drive to cut overheads of all kinds.

Yet it seems unlikely that these initiatives will result in solutions which will halt the trend. Are real solutions in sight? Are they possible? External and internal pressures on defence managers almost invariably tend to aim at the replacement of an existing weapons

Table 2: British Defence Expenditure

	74/5	75/6	76/7	77/8	78/9	79/80	80/81	81/2*.	82/3*
Percentage of defence budget devoted to equipment	31	34	35	38	40	40	44	44	46
Spending on equipment at constant 1982 prices (£m)	4025	4489	4411	4511	4683	4899	5542	5604	6005

* Estimated

system. What kind of new ship, tank, or aircraft? But is this the right question to ask? Is this the way to solve the problems of the next century? An alternative formulation might, for example, be what kind of equipment will be required in the next century to execute that part of the land battle which is currently undertaken by tanks? But even this formulation may not be fundamental enough since it needs to be related to opportunity costs in other parts of the defence programme and the overall balance of capabilities required to fulfil defence objectives and ensure defence effectiveness. What is to be feared is that conventional and conservative questions will produce conventional and conservative answers and that these, coupled with rising real costs, will inevitably diminish the quantity of defence to a point where, however high the quality, it cannot provide an effective defence posture.

Where does the answer lie? There is almost certainly no single solution. One major factor could, of course, come from measures of multilateral disarmament but the possibilities of progress are at best uncertain. Is it perhaps inevitable that the range of capabilities provided by a single nation will diminish and that increasing measures of specialization will be enforced either by *force majeure* or by deliberate intent? Military specialization in terms of capabilities and tasks has been canvassed over the years. Progress so far is not encouraging. Countries have been more prepared to give up capabilities than to exchange them with others. There is no sign of early results on a significant scale. Indeed many will argue strongly that diversity is a source of strength.

In recent years greater effort has been devoted to equipment collaboration. There are a number of good examples of both joint development and joint production in a variety of forms. Another approach is the so-called 'family of weapons', where two or more countries agree to undertake the separate research, development and production of associated weapons. This has much to commend it but it does require a degree of international reliance and trust which are not always easily found.

Will economic pressures and costs bring about further measures of industrial specialization? For example, some countries have given up manufacturing various types of aircraft and other equipment. Is there scope for specific specialization arrangements, where two or more Governments agree to depend on one another for the supply of certain types of equipment with the goal of eliminating duplication in Government-funded technological and industrial capability? Such an approach might produce considerable dividends, though it would be difficult to achieve in practice. It may be that pressures on the industrial market can achieve more than Governments. For example, firms engaged in similar fields could merge their activities to form a single international company. Governments would contract with a single company leaving the international division of work to the company. Again firms might join together to establish temporary or permanent international consortia to supply particular equipments. Such consortia would arrange for different parts of the work to be undertaken in different countries. No doubt arrangements of this kind would need to overcome a number of difficulties not least in the legal, contractual and procedural fields.

Another form of specialization is for two or more countries to make reciprocal purchases

55

without commitment to permanent and long-term specialization. Thus country A might meet its needs for certain types of armoured vehicles by placing an order with country B, while country B might make a reciprocal purchase of helicopters from country A. Are these possibilities not worth pursuing? One particular difficulty is that most countries seek to define their operational requirements in obsessively detailed and elaborate terms. There could be an advantage in countries specifying their requirements in shorter and simpler terms, stating the problems and objectives but leaving the solutions unspecified. They could also on occasion set a target cost for the project.

Solutions such as these could share out R&D, achieve longer production runs, and lower unit costs through larger volume production, but it is difficult to believe that they will resolve the dilemma of rising costs or, as James Farrow put it, the *Quality/Quantity* quandary.

Is there a real way forward? The only safe statement is that sticking to one's last is the way to disaster. Change is difficult but change is necessary and possible. It demands hard questions and receives harder answers.

There is, however, a further area which is as yet inadequately explored, namely that it does seem very possible to make much better use of assets not exclusively devoted to defence. Virtually all countries have ships, aircraft and vehicles in use for commercial and other purposes. Given the development of modern technology, there does seem a real prospect of enhancing military capability at a marginal rather than full cost. Adaptation for alternative use seems not merely practicable but highly desirable. Many examples spring to mind – the use of container ships for the operation of helicopters or vertical take-off aircraft; the ability to adapt commercial shipping rapidly for helicopter operations and refuelling at sea; the conversion of civil aircraft to the in-flight refuelling role; and the widespread opportunities for the use of civil aircraft, helicopters and vehicles for defensive purposes and the relative ease with which a variety of military equipment – particularly missiles – could be fixed to them. Special training and special legislative powers might

well be required but proposals of this kind do seem to offer a real prospect for the future. Put simply, if it is not possible to afford all the defence-dedicated systems that the planners require, is it not possible to turn modern defence technology to advantage by making use of non-dedicated assets?

Setting Priorities
This leads on to the endemic difficulty of changing defence priorities in short order despite the natural predilection of most democratic governments for short-term measures. Defence equipment programmes are long-term and involve substantial forward commitment of resources. The British position with respect to major equipment projects (some 60 per cent of all equipment expenditure) shows a more or less linear decline in planned allocations remaining from about 92 per cent at the end of year one to 40 per cent in year ten, assuming that the programme is already in full development or has entered the production phase at the start of year one.

This is not to say that commitments cannot be changed but the cash cost will be high with considerable disruption to R&D and production programmes. Moreover, major projects require massive capital investment and the further they get down the road, the more they acquire a certain momentum of their own which is difficult to stop – even if it were right on policy grounds to do so.

Increasingly manpower, both military and civilian, inhibits changes in priorities. The need to recruit and train skilled personnel also involves considerable lead times and high investment costs both in people and in the facilities to train them.

Treaty obligations and other commitments tend to militate against change and to 'institutionalize' relationships. This situation is not necessarily undesirable in itself for, where defence relationships between countries and between *blocs* are institutionalized, change can be destabilizing. Changes in weapons technology are inevitable and can in themselves, on occasion, be destabilizing.

Nevertheless, it is the task of a defence manager to see that expenditure is used to produce an effective defence posture and pro-

56

gramme. Budgetary and administrative controls – which are increasingly the norm – have a negative rather than positive effect. Alliances provide a forum for debate, dialogue and consensus and they can offer a monitoring system over members' programmes albeit through somewhat laborious processes. The real problem of the next twenty years remains, namely how to sustain an effective defence against the background of real cost rises and exploding technology. How is the problem to be tackled?

Two suggestions are put forward with some diffidence. It can be said with reasonable safety that those who take major investment decisions now are unlikely to be in positions of authority when the investment matures. They rarely have to account for them. It might be a salutary discipline if, when these decisions were taken, it became mandatory to ask and answer two questions. What alternative would be adopted if this decision were not taken? What could be done to improve existing systems? In both cases the answers should be made part of the public decision-making process.

Secondly, there is a need for both international and national policy reviews. Virtually all planning is conservative and incremental. As a general rule it is a war which stimulates imagination and innovation – and results in change. Reviews should not be frequent – this would be totally against the long-term nature of defence – perhaps once a decade. They need to concentrate initially on strategy and major defence objectives before looking at defence equipment, manpower and infrastructure. Aims and standards should be formulated. There is much to be said for such reviews being undertaken by groups specially assembled for the task and therefore able to take a rather more dispassionate look than those immersed on a day-to-day basis of defence management.

Public Confidence
Defence to be effective requires public support and needs to command public confidence. It is doubtful whether any democracy with a disunited people could sustain a war. Public confidence is crucial to the question of allocating resources to defence. The traditional pattern in most Western democracies is for the executive to submit proposals for the defence programme and the consequential expenditure to the legislature. The form of the debate and approval varies from country to country but no legislature regards defence expenditure as anything other than a major area of interest.

Arrangements for overseeing the efficient disbursement of money are also important. The legislature, frequently with strong and independent professional support, exhibits a deep concern for ensuring that money has been spent on the purposes for which it has been provided and increasingly exhibits also an interest in probing wider questions of efficiency and economy.

The level of public understanding and debate of defence issues is frequently low. Too often issues are distorted by being presented as quarrels between interested parties: between the fighting Services; between Ministries; between the United States and Europe; between East and West; and between government and defence industry. Except in contexts of this kind, it is often the case that little attention is paid to management and resource allocation issues, perhaps because they are not of particular interest to most of those not engaged in the process.

There are, of course, constraints to any debate. Military secrets should not be passed to potential adversaries. Nor should advanced technology. There is also the much ignored fact that discussion tends to be inhibited by the closed nature of society in many non-democratic countries. Open discussion is denied to the closed societies of the East, whose legislatures and citizens do not have the same opportunities to consider the form and scale of their government's defence policies. This is a vital difference between the West and East. In the long term, a knowledgeable and informed public opinion throughout the world is one of the best guarantors of peace.

There are those who argue that public debate demonstrates weakness, lack of direction, uncertainty, lack of will, and simply provides information to potential adversaries. The true counter to this argument is that in a democratic nation its defence policy, its defence programme and its effectiveness in war depend on public understanding and support from those who foot the bill. It is also relevant that governments have a monopoly in defence – though doubtfully in wisdom. That monopoly needs to be probed, prodded and questioned – otherwise it will not command public support nor will it be efficient or effective.

Among the worst features of the management of defence expenditure are its frightening complexity, its inability to simplify, its continuing search for consensus, and the fact that it apparently only becomes really creative as a result of war. It finds difficulty in explaining itself to itself let alone to the ordinary citizen.

Further changes are inevitable and great skill will be required to identify the objectives to be sought and the policies to be pursued. Hard and innovative thought is needed. The demand on national resources has to be fully justified and accounted for in an open and proper way. The crucial points need to be identified and action taken.

Nevertheless, an attempt must be made to simplify issues in such a way that they are comprehensible in broad terms to the individual citizen and stand a reasonable chance of commanding his support. The

almost inexhaustible store of weapons technology, rising real costs, the vicious effects of inflation, and the element of genuine incredibility which lurks about many defence issues argue strongly for seeking simplicity. The support of the nation is an essential part of defence management.

Conclusion
This Paper raises more questions than it answers. The reason is straightforward – there are no quick or easy answers. The practitioner in defence management knows full well the complexity of the defence environment in which he works. He knows the sensitivities of national and international politics, the influential weight of national history and military experience, the impact of economic growth (or lack of it), the clash between competing national priorities, the pressure of industrial policy, and the efforts that countries within an Alliance must make in order to be sure of adequately understanding each other. It is factors such as these which produce a lively debate, force out facts and encourage analysis. Controversy and argument about defence in a democracy are a source of strength not weakness and are an essential part of earning public support.

The Critique of Nuclear Deterrence

ADAM ROBERTS

The purpose of this Paper is to enumerate some of the main grounds for concern about nuclear deterrence and also to try to suggest where the critique of nuclear deterrence leads.

The ambitious title suggested for this Paper is, of course, simplistic. There is not a single critique of nuclear deterrence: there are several. Arguments about nuclear weapons are always, like other arguments, shaped by their intellectual roots and their national environment.

The most 'successful' anti-nuclear arguments so far – in the sense of leading to decisions by particular states not to manufacture or deploy nuclear weapons when they could have done so – have for the most part not been critiques of absolutely *all* nuclear deterrence: often they have had a less fundamentalist character, stressing particular aspects of a state's situation which might indicate a preference for a non-nuclear or at least a less nuclear approach. Such limited prudent arguments, important as they are, are not the main focus of this Paper.

It is the somewhat more general arguments against nuclear weapons and deterrence that form my subject here. At various times since the Second World War there has been, particularly in the NATO countries and also in Japan, a great deal of public criticism of reliance on nuclear weapons. There have also been many detailed written critiques, both of nuclear weapons generally, and of the paraphernalia which has surrounded them: strategic doctrines, delivery systems, alliances and so on. In this Paper I cannot do full justice to all these critiques, but they do have enough in common to make some crude attempt at synthesis and analysis possible.

In looking critically at nuclear deterrence, this Paper focuses mainly (but not exclusively) on Western Europe. This is not just due to the parochialism of the writer: in the past few years several issues relating to nuclear weapons have arisen particularly in, or in relation to, the Western European member-states of NATO; and it has been there that public expressions of concern about nuclear weapons have been most evident.

As far as the NATO member countries in Western Europe are concerned, generalizing wildly one can say that their governments have relied on two principal types of nuclear deterrence: the extended (and probably over-extended) deterrence involving the US nuclear forces in the defence of Western Europe; and the less extended deterrence provided by the national nuclear forces of Britain and France. Both types of nuclear deterrence have for a long time involved an element of threat to use nuclear weapons first in the event of massive attack – an approach which is increasingly criticized. But many critiques of a rather more limited character have been made of one or other of these types of deterrence. Such critiques, often focused on the one issue of credibility, were used largely to justify a different but still definitely nuclear approach. Thus critiques of extended deterrence contributed significantly to the development and maintenance of the British and French national nuclear forces, while McNamara's 1962 critique of national nuclear forces was connected with his advocacy of a particular type of extended deterrence. While *both* critiques may have been correct, the example confirms the obvious: that not all critiques of nuclear deterrence are necessarily compatible with each other; and that it is desirable to be reasonably clear as to whether a critique applies to nuclear deterrence in general, or just to a particular form or application of it.

My focus in the Paper on the more sweeping anti-nuclear position – the one to which I am closest – does not imply any easy assumption that the total abolition of all such weapons is a realistic possibility. The argument that nuclear weapons have been invented, and that man, having eaten of the fruit of this particular tree of knowledge, cannot now disinvent them, is reluctantly taken as read in this Paper. Indeed, it seems clear that the existence of nuclear weapons (being large in their effects, but relatively easy to conceal) makes general and complete disarmament an even more unattainable goal than it was before. But it is not obvious what corollary follows from the assessment that, for the fore-seeable future, we will live in a world of nuclear weapons. We also live in a world where concentration camps, napalm, torture, chemical and biological weapons, and heroin have all been invented: yet most states and individuals manage to avoid relying on most of these things most of the time, and they have been brought under various kinds of national and international control. Nuclear weapons are already subject to several types of restraint and control, but perhaps, if we are going to go on living with them, further limitations will have to be accepted.

Deterrence vs. Nuclear Deterrence

The subject of this Paper is *nuclear* deter-rence, not all deterrence. The distinction is especially emphasized here because, in con-temporary parlance, including even some professional usage, the concept of deterrence (like that oft-misused adjective 'strategic') is still sometimes equated in a facile way solely with nuclear weapons. This is especially so in the US, which happened to assume a wide range of international responsibilities in the very years, after 1945, when she happened to have a temporary monopoly of nuclear weapons.

However, deterrence can be found at many levels of animal and human life, and in many conceptually quite distinct forms. If deter-rence is defined as being no more than the clear threat of sanctions in the event of viola-tions of territory or of basic norms, then it can assume forms that are very specific (making punishment fit the crime); and its forms may not necessarily in every case be physically vio-lent. However, the concept of deterrence does more normally contain an element of violence and even terror.

A very strong case can be made for many forms and uses of deterrence, and it would be

intellectually absurd to criticize them all col-lectively. Many forms of deterrence have proved very enduring over time, and are to be found in countries with very different ideolo-gies and political cultures. In many cases, such forms of deterrence have a clear and even positive social function.

However, as bases for regulating the be-haviour of individuals and groups, at least some forms of deterrence have long, and per-haps increasingly, been recognized as having severe limitations. In many countries, the pro-gressive reduction of the types of crime subject to the death penalty may be a case in point. In many spheres of activity the most extreme threats are not necessarily the most effective: hence the curious necessity, recognized in many countries, to make people wear car seat belts under pain of summary legal action rather than under pain of death. The observa-tion of some criminologists, that deterring crime successfully depends more on the cer-tainty of being caught than on the extreme character of the threatened punishment, may have wider application.

In international relations, deterrence is usually, and quite reasonably, associated with the threat of using violence, and it is very deeply rooted in the system of states. For bet-ter or for worse, the world of sovereign states which we inhabit is a world in which the survival of states, or at least of their govern-ments, depends to a significant degree on their ability to discourage or to defeat foreign mili-tary attack if they fail to discourage it. True, there are many lightly-armed states (Iceland and Ireland are just two examples), but they may in some cases owe their security either to geographical accident or to deliberate accom-modation with a greater power: just as the fact that most citizens are unarmed does not mean that force has no role in society, so the exis-tence of some relatively lightly-armed states does not itself prove that factors of power balance and of deterrence are not important in international relations.

But a state's efforts to discourage attack do not have to assume the form of threatening to retaliate on a massive scale with indis-criminately destructive weapons against the adversary's society. Historically, deterrence has often been the product of a threat to inflict losses on an attack locally: to deny an attacker victory on the ground; to ensure that any victory gained by an attacker will have few, brief or bitter fruits; to retaliate against hostages specifically taken for the purpose; or to retaliate against an attacker's homeland, but with conventional rather than nuclear means. Deterrence before Hiroshima did not consist only of that airpower element about which George Quester has written eloquently[1], but also of many more ancient military forms and methods.

Today, when considering deterrence, it is well to remember that the great majority of states in the world are neither nuclear powers themselves, nor members of nuclear alliances. While many of these states have themselves been involved in war (as too have all the nuclear powers), and many are hardly cases for emulation, there may be something to learn from at least some of them about how non-nuclear deterrence can still operate in the nuclear age; how nuclear blackmail seems in practice to be less of a threat than the theoreticians would have us believe; and how a state, even today, can manage its security policy effectively and with public support.

Non-nuclear deterrence has by no means always worked in international relations. Its failures may be a matter of considerable historical dispute, but the fact that there have been some is hardly in doubt. There was a good deal by way of deterrent threats before the First World War, but war broke out nonetheless. Moreover, conventional military balances are often very unstable. The point here is not to eulogise non-nuclear deterrence, but simply to register that it is a pervasive phenomenon, that it existed before 1945, and that it continues to exist today.

Just as a serious (but by no means flawless) case can be made for deterrence in general, so such a case can be made for nuclear deterrence in particular. The record of the nuclear powers and alliances is itself a powerful if not unimpeachable argument: World War III has been frequently forecast, and its history has been written many times, but it has not actually happened. Even if every nuclear doctrine so far developed can be shown to be flawed – containing such embarrassing impurities as patent bluff, gross political sim-

plification, moral dereliction, and unwitting invitations to the adversary to take countermeasures – nuclear deterrence itself may still have, as intended, a certain frightening and impressive quality. It is no part of the argument of this Paper that nuclear deterrence can be easily abandoned by all the states which at present rely on it. The strengths as well as the weaknesses of nuclear deterrence have to be recognized.

Limitations of Critiques

At least where matters of defence and security are concerned, intellectual critiques of existing policies can represent no more than the beginning of a long journey. It is quite easy to criticize almost any defence policy as having crippling defects but the exercise will be condemned to futility unless there is something else to offer in place of the policy being criticized.

There is ample evidence from other fields of human activity that simply telling people about the perils of their situation, or advising them what *not* to do, is of distinctly limited value. If criticism of an existing policy is to be effective, there has to be a reasonably clear alternative, or at least a plausible vision of one. If there is no alternative policy in sight, then through a process of psychological denial people may well reject all evidence of the danger of their situation.[2]

The evidence of the public opinion polls tends to confirm the inadequacy of simply opposing an existing policy. Despite the obvious dangers of nuclear weapons, one poll after another, both in Britain and other countries, suggests that although particular weapons systems may be opposed by a higher percentage, a simple unilateral rejection of nuclear weapons and alliances never gets much above 30 per cent support – about the same as pacifist movements got in the 1930s. This would seem to point to the need to move the framework of debate away from the somewhat sterile single issue of multilateral v. unilateral disarmament.

Some may argue otherwise, and may say that there is political or intellectual merit in criticizing nuclear deterrence irrespective of the question of alternatives. Thus Philip Green, in his book *Deadly Logic*, made a spirited attack on nuclear deterrence, and on its theoreticians, particularly in the US:

> The false attribution of expertness to an intellectual elite, which has in effect passed a test of political acceptability, narrows rather than enlarges the channels of influence. Pseudo-science such as that of deterrence theorists thus constitutes a dis-service not only to the scholarly com-munity, but ultimately to the democratic political process as well.[3]

However, he specifically stated that it was not the job of the academic to propose what should be put in the place of the nuclear deterrence which he castigated. While one can well understand the anxiety of the American academic in the 1960s not to get caught up in the Washington policy advice shuttle, the consequent reluctance to propose any policy direction at all does look like intellectual escapism.

There is a second limitation of many criti-ques of nuclear deterrence, namely that they sometimes contain quite serious elements of inconsistency. Take for example the question of minimum deterrence. In Britain, some anti-nuclear writers have criticized US nuclear forces for being far larger than a minimum deterrence policy would require; and have then dismissed the British nuclear force on the grounds that it is a pathetic symbol of her fading imperial grandeur, quite lacking in any practical strategic value. While these two statements may not be logically compatible, there is a tension between them which is sel-dom, if ever, explored.

Anti-nuclear critiques often appear to be inconsistent on a more fundamental point. Absolute arguments may be presented against nuclear weapons, but the inevitable and depressingly hypothetical follow-up question, 'Should the US (or USSR) give up these weapons unilaterally?' often produces a cautious, even equivocal answer. Such inconsistencies appear not just in political exchanges, but also in state-to-state relations. Thus Japan, an almost allergically anti-nuclear country which has repeatedly stressed her three anti-nuclear principles, has been involved in a close security relationship with the US ever since the post-Second World War occupation.

Advocates of nuclear deterrence are no less guilty of inconsistency. For example, many of them are poor at explaining why it is good for their country to have nuclear weapons, but bad for other countries to do so; and at explaining whether, or in what circumstances, they would 'press the button'.

Such inconsistencies, on both sides of the nuclear debate, are a tribute to the complexity of the problem, and amount to an unintended confession of the partial and inadequate character of our various prescriptions for tackling it. One might end up accepting inconsistencies, in the spirit of Walt Whit-man: 'Do I contradict myself? Very well then I contradict myself.' At all events, the reader is warned that some degree of inconsistency may be inevitable in a critical exercise of this kind.

Headings of Criticism

Below are listed (not in any order of priority) some of the main headings of criticism of nuclear deterrence. They seem to me to be the most serious lines of criticism; and some lines which I take less seriously (e.g. that there is no possible threat to any of the nuclear states, and therefore nothing that needs to be deterred) I have simply omitted. There is considerable overlap between the different headings.

1. Where Does It All Lead?

However impressive the achievements of deterrence in general, or those of nuclear deterrence in particular, may have been so far, this nagging question remains. To critics of nuclear weapons, it is saying that what nuclear deterrence has worked up to now is the equivalent of the man who has fallen from the top of a skyscraper saying 'So far so good' as he passes the tenth floor. Even if some past gloomy prognostications have been proved wrong, and even if one does not foresee im-minent major war, the question remains: How long states can rely on nuclear deterrence without there being a conflict involving the use of these weapons? As Lawrence Freedman has written:

> An international order that rests upon a stability created by nuclear weapons will be

the most terrible legacy with which each succeeding generation will endow the next. To believe that this can go on indefinitely without major disaster requires an optimism unjustified by any historical or political perspective.[4]

The sense of unease about the ultimate direction of nuclear weapons policies is apparent in many statements and actions of governments of nuclear weapons states. For example, the three nuclear powers which were the original parties to the 1963 Partial Test Ban Treaty (PTBT) stated in the preamble;

Proclaiming as their principal aim the speediest possible achievement of an agreement on general and complete disarmament under strict international control in accordance with the objectives of the United Nations which would put an end to the armaments race and eliminate the incentive to the production and testing of all kinds of weapons, including nuclear weapons . . .

Five years later, the 1968 Non-Proliferation Treaty (NPT) not only reiterated this language in the preamble, but also stated in Article VI of the body of the Treaty:

Each of the Parties to the Treaty undertakes to pursue negotiations in good faith on effective measures relating to the cessation of the nuclear arms race at an early date and to nuclear disarmament, and on a treaty on general and complete disarmament under strict and effective international control.

Such statements, which go far beyond the modest references to disarmament in the UN Charter itself, are perhaps one type of indication that the nuclear powers at least feel the obligation to pay lip-service to the possibility of a better world. It is all reminiscent of George Orwell's discovery, when writing *Down and Out in Paris and London*, that none of the tramps he met actually called himself a tramp: they were always gentlemen 'temporarily in difficulties'.

Even if one rejects the theory that arms races inevitably lead to war, the lack of any persuasive vision, especially perhaps in Western countries, of a better future for international relations is as disturbing as it is striking. For as soon as even the possibility of nuclear disaster begins to loom in people's minds, the whole armaments process can easily seem like a series of small decisions, each in its own terms perfectly rational, which leads only to the utter irrationality of genocidal war.

2. The Catastrophic Character of a Nuclear War

It is absurd that it should have become necessary, over a generation into the nuclear age, to reassert the obvious: that a nuclear war between the super-powers would be a catastrophe, not just for this or that country, but for human civilization. But it needs to be said. Even if attempts were made to limit such a war, it would still be an unparalleled disaster, and perhaps most of all in Europe – both East and West. Alexander Pope's lines might become horribly applicable:

Now Europe's balanced. Neither side prevails
For nothing's left in either of the scales.

The widespread and justified feeling that nuclear war represents a vast and looming threat, greater than any issue which might be in dispute between the Eastern and Western Alliances, and that it is reliance on nuclear deterrence which has made nuclear holocaust possible, leads on to the conclusion that it would be better to accept the possibility of foreign attack and occupation than to risk the destruction of civilization. The slogan 'better red than dead' is a somewhat simplistic encapsulation of this position: since socialist states tend to be fairly heavily militarized and have even got into armed conflicts with each other, it is more doubtful than ever whether 'red' and 'dead' are real alternatives. Overall, one cannot be happy about the narrow and simplistic depiction of choices which leads to such conclusions and slogans. Simply to make a state vulnerable to occupation by a nuclear superpower is not a very attractive proposition in itself, and might not in the end contribute greatly to international stability. All this points to the need for (though it does not establish the possibilities of) non-nuclear means of defence, to which reference is made at the end of this Paper.

But as long as defence is presented as an essentially nuclear matter, based on the threat to unleash total war, it is inevitable that at times of international tension or crisis, or at times when new weapons decisions are under discussion, many citizens will conclude that such a defence is worse than the evil against which it is supposed to protect them.

3. How Much Stability Has Been Achieved?

Public scepticism about nuclear deterrence may owe something to doubts as to how much stability has in fact been achieved by these weapons, whether such stability as exists may be due to other causes as well, and whether stability really is supremely desirable as a goal.

The evidence that international relations today are unstable, while it should not be exaggerated, is indeed plentiful. The Soviet intervention in Afghanistan in December 1979, the continuous stream of wars in the Middle East, and the Argentine invasion of the Falkland Islands in April 1982 (the most flagrant attack there has yet been against a territory held and administered by a nuclear power) have all been reminders that we still live in a world in which norms against resort to force are far from strong. Of course deterrence theorists can reply, in each of the cases cited, that if only deterrence had been stronger, if only commitments had been clearer, if only the politicians had had more sense than to negotiate with the adversary, if only a few warships had been sent in time . . . These arguments have considerable merit: but so, too, does the perception that some degree of muddle, confusion, and misunderstanding may be inevitable in politics and international relations, and that the causes of some conflicts are very deep-seated.

True, it was never claimed for nuclear deterrence that the possession of nuclear weapons by a few states could bring about general stability. But in the US some claims very close to this were made, and apparently believed, at the height of East–West detente. Now, almost a decade later, talk of a 'generation of peace' and of a five-cornered structure

of power all sounds hopelessly dated. The considerable confusion in US foreign policy-making in the past few years – in part the consequence of the rival foci of power in the State Department, the Pentagon and the White House – has contributed greatly to the sense that, in tackling nuclear problems, man has more power than wisdom at his disposal.

For all the concern about international stability, and about the means by which governments reach decisions, Europe seems remarkably stable; and the argument that nuclear weapons have contributed to this stability is serious. The continent which was the cockpit of two world wars in thirty years has now experienced no major war for over thirty-five years. Part of the explanation for this may be that Europe is where the two great nuclear Alliances meet. But there is something absurdly simplistic in the oft-repeated contention that it is nuclear weapons which have kept the peace in Europe. In the past, for example in the nineteenth century, Europe has had long periods of peace, which was hardly due to nuclear weapons. Today, other factors may be involved. It is possible that Europe has been kept at peace not so much by nuclear weapons in particular, as by the general presence in Europe of two major outside powers; that the memory of two past World Wars, both sparked off in Europe and largely fought there, is itself a deterrent to war; and that the remarkable internal political stability of most European countries has contributed to international stability. Certainly the wide range of factors contributing to European stability needs to be borne in mind: where such factors are not present, nuclear deterrence may be inapplicable, as witness the distinctly lacklustre results of (and disappearance of) NATO's Asian clones, CENTO and SEATO.

European critics of nuclear weapons sometimes make a rather different argument: not that these weapons have contributed relatively little to stability, but that they have contributed too much, that the Cold War, now descending on us again, has frozen Europe into an absurd and brittle condition of ideological division. Undoubtedly, part of the attraction of the European Nuclear Disarmament (END) movement has been its appeal to a vision of Europe which, however vague, represents a sharp move away from what is perceived as the thraldom to the two major blocs. Edward Thompson expressed the matter with characteristic pithiness when he said:

I am not quite sure how the third, European, perception so suddenly emerged, although we did something about it ourselves. It is this. We are pig-in-the-middle while an interminable and threatening argument between born-again Christians and still-born Marxists goes on above our heads.[5]

The case of Poland is sometimes cited as proof of the deleterious consequences of the division of Europe into two nuclear blocs. The political developments of 1980–81, sparked by the growth of Solidarity, symbolized to many people a reassertion of a European political culture against super-power control; and the introduction of martial law in December 1981, after very heavy pressure from the Soviet Union for a restoration of order, seemed as clear a triumph of the bloc principle as had the military *coup d'état* in Chile eight years earlier, in 1973. A few people in the West, including some theoreticians of nuclear deterrence, had before December 1981 expressed rather frankly their concern that a greater degree of Polish independence could be bad all round for international stability, especially if it served to encourage neutralism and unilateralism in the West. Thus in his 1981 Reith Lectures Laurence Martin said that 'the Polish crisis is dangerous for NATO as well as the Warsaw Pact'.[6] No statesman in the West reacted to the imposition of martial law in December 1981 quite as cynically as Louis Philippe in 1831, who said of the suppression of the Polish revolt in that year: *'L'ordre règne à Varsovie.'* But the thought may still have been there in some form.

The very mention of Louis Philippe is a reminder that international solidarity among conservatives pre-dated the invention of nuclear weapons and the emergence of NATO and the Warsaw Treaty Organization. One cannot lay the blame for the order, such as it is, now reigning in Warsaw entirely at the door of nuclear weapons: almost any imaginable security system, whether autonomous or within an alliance, is bound to place some premium on order. But a conception of order which sees a threat in a non-violent workers' movement with limited goals is vulnerable to the charge that it reduces the possibilities of peaceful change, and thwarts assertions of national independence and political freedom.

4. *Instability in Weapons*

Alongside the general instability of international relations, there is a more particular instability of a technical character, Neither weapons nor the cost thereof has stood still. In the NATO countries in the past few years there has been a succession of bitter controversies surrounding new nuclear weapons and delivery systems: the neutron bomb; cruise missiles and *Pershing* II; the British *Trident* programme; and the MX missile. Whatever the technical explanations for them, these weapons give rise to quite genuine concerns: the 'neutron bomb', that it is a nuclear 'solution' to a conventional problem (massed tank attack) and is thus a first-use weapon; cruise and *Pershing* II, that they are nuclear weapon systems whose deployment was decided upon in haste before they had been tested, that they are of a type and range bound to be regarded as a direct threat by the USSR and to be targeted accordingly, and are to be located on land in densely-inhabited parts of Western Europe; the British *Trident* programme, that its expense involves some de-emphasis on conventional forces, and that it was bought 'off the shelf' with an offensive power vastly greater than the Ministry of Defence wanted; and that the MX missile, originally intended for an elaborate new basing system, is perhaps the first major weapons development in history which has nowhere to go.

It may be regrettable that so much of the public debate has centred on these new weapons, rather than on underlying issues of overall defence policy, or on existing weapons which may be even more dangerous, such as the so-called 'battlefield' nuclear weapons in Europe. But there are reasons for the attention given to the new weapons systems, not least that their accuracy seems to fit in with certain ominous statements about nuclear 'war-fighting'. Moreover, the argument made for some of these new systems, that they are absolutely essential to the maintenance of deterrence or to the credibility of the Alliance, serve as unintended reminders of the weaknesses of nuclear deterrence. If the whole nuclear house of cards is as fragile as some of the experts would have us believe, small wonder that some want to demolish the house rather than replace or add to the cards.

The number and scale of recent weapons developments, both in the East and the West, do seem to demonstrate a dangerous dynamism in the technology of nuclear weapons and delivery systems. As in the Cuban Missile Crisis of 1962, so also with the Soviet Union's SS–20 missile programme today, new weapons deployments seem themselves to contribute to an increase of tension between states. To the extent that this is so, and it is of course far from being a complete explanation of international tension, the arms competition between East and West may have the character of a self-perpetuating process, not only continuously producing new weapons, but also the condition of tension which is needed in order to justify the defence efforts of states.

The deployment of multiple independently-targetable re-entry vehicles (MIRV) has been a sad example of the destabilizing effects of new weapons systems. In the mid-1960s, when they were being developed, many warned that they might create a situation where each side had more means of nuclear attack than the other side had nuclear targets, a situation in which ideas of pre-emptive blows are bound to flourish. Such warnings have been more than amply fulfilled in the intervening years.

5. *Disturbing Trends in Strategic Thinking*
It is not just in the hardware itself, but also in the purposes and strategies attached to it, that there is evidence of inner dynamism and restlessness. Deterrence and war-fighting can never be totally distinct modes of thought, and perhaps one should not be surprised at the re-emergence of a war-fighting approach. What is particularly odd and alarming about this re-emergence is that it includes an element of faith that one side might prevail in a nuclear war, or that such a war once started might be geographically limited.

Before pointing to particular disturbing trends, one general observation about contemporary nuclear strategic thought should be made: much of it, for understandable reasons, has a highly mathematical and technical character. Strategists working out how many MIRV can be got into an ICBM may be the modern equivalent of mediaeval theologians working out how many angels can be got on the head of a pin. To the layman much of this exercise seems academic in the worst sense, not least because the actual conflicts in the world never involve such neat numerical balances, and always involve a large political element. While academic strategists, who have largely taken over from bishops the role of blessing the bomber, discuss multiple warheads which they hope will never be used, in Afghanistan tribesmen fight a nuclear super-power with weapons which might be from the Imperial War Museum.

The current disturbing trends in strategic thought have their origins in an earlier failure. The attempt to reach a stable state of nuclear deterrence, based on the concept of Mutual Assured Destruction (MAD), suffered successive blows not just because the Soviet Union developed other ideas, but also because MAD itself seemed to have several built-in flaws. For military men it is a somewhat bleak and depressing approach, and for civilians it is hardly better. MAD seemed to a few Western Europeans to foreshadow an era in which the nuclear forces of the two super-powers cancelled each other out, leaving the Soviet Union with a preponderance of conventional military power in Europe; and some Americans had even stronger objections to it. The return by the United States to a declaratory policy of counter-force has been due to many factors, but also produces its own problems. If counter-force is better than MAD in that it is more discriminate, it is worse in that it seems to put a premium on acting pre-emptively, and to require continuous quantitative and qualitative improvement of nuclear arsenals. This argument, though hardly new, is still persuasive.

In the past few years, there has been particular instability in matters of strategic doctrine. The various US statements on the possibility of a limited nuclear war in Europe, or

66

indicating that a nuclear war might be less than a catastrophe for the United States, may have been intended to strike fear into the hearts of the Soviet leaders (and may indeed have done so), but their principal visible effect has been to cause alarm and despondency in Western Europe and in the United States herself.

A related but even more ominous sign of the instability of weapons and strategy has been evident in the 'window of opportunity' theory. It is true that the idea of a 'window of opportunity' can help to explain at least the timing of the outbreak of some past conventional wars. As far as nuclear weapons are concerned, the 'window of opportunity' theory presumes that one side might exploit a temporary preponderance in nuclear weapons to attack the nuclear forces of the other side – or at least to use the threat of such an attack as a lever for exerting very heavy pressure on the adversary. This theory has always been questionable, because it implies a decision to launch an enormously risky adventure for reasons which seem more technical than political, which are difficult to square with almost any ideology or ethical system, and which in any case seem to take little account of the degree of confusion, malfunction and muddle (to say nothing of mass murder) likely to attend such an exercise.

However wrong-headed they may be, the various American (and Soviet) statements indicating some degree of willingness to fight a nuclear war, and some expectation that one side might prevail in such a war and recover within a few years, may be an outcome not only of the warped minds of their authors, but also of a more general belief that in order to maintain nuclear deterrence it is necessary to talk tough and even to accept openly the possibility of a nuclear war. One could conclude, therefore, that the heightened fear of nuclear war in the past few years is an inevitable consequence of nuclear deterrence itself. Many would challenge this, including the late Bernard Brodie, who argued eloquently that 'the balance of terror is decidedly *not* delicate'.[7] But military doctrine as well as deployments seem to have been informed, especially in recent years, by a more restless and Manichaean spirit than Brodie's.

6. *Risks of War by Accident or Miscalculation*

The possibility of war occurring as a result of some technical accident – the mis-reading of radar information, computer malfunction, the freak detonation of a nuclear weapon in a plane crash – has been the subject of much attention since at least the early 1960s.[8] Numerous precautions have been taken by the nuclear powers to guard against such dangers, and the evidence would appear to be that these precautions have been effective. However, the continuing stream of reports of accidents involving nuclear weapons, and of control computers malfunctioning, suggests that an accidental or unauthorized detonation of a nuclear weapon is by no means impossible. Moreover, any regression to situations or strategies placing a high premium on pre-emption or quick reaction could heighten the risk of an accident degenerating into an accidental war.

War arising from miscalculation, rather than from a technical accident pure and simple, seems more plausible. Indeed, there has been a strong element of miscalculation in the outbreak of many past wars: for example, miscalculation about the capacity of one's own forces or those of an adversary, about the likely reactions of third parties, or about the degree of commitment of an adversary to a particular cause or piece of territory. Rival involvements of the super-powers in Third-world countries, especially those with political systems or frontiers whose legitimacy is contested, may offer particular risks of a war arising at least in part through miscalculation. Kissinger's fears that the Middle East of the 1970s might be like the Balkans in the decade before 1914 was one expression of the concern about the wisdom of super-powers hitching their wagons to unstable stars in troubled areas.

7. *Possibly Indecisive Character of Nuclear Weapons*

Although immensely destructive, nuclear weapons may not be quite so decisive. True, the evidence is persuasive that they did help to end the War in the Pacific in 1945, though in circumstances where it was clear that Japan's defeat was inevitable anyway, due both to the military victories of US forces, and to the entry of the USSR into the war.[9] Like strategic bombing, of which they are the logical and terrible culmination, nuclear weapons may perhaps sometimes be more effective in hurting an adversary's society than actually stopping his forces from fighting.

In peacetime, the threat of use of nuclear weapons seems to be a blunt and largely unusable instrument. In the period since the Second World War there have been relatively few cases in which their use has been threatened in any way as a means of securing a particular change of policy, and these threats do not seem to have been outstandingly successful. The success of US policy in the Cuban Missile Crisis is perhaps the most striking exception, but it owed much to local naval preponderance. The idea that non-nuclear countries must necessarily be vulnerable to nuclear blackmail finds relatively little validation in the actual events of the past thirty-seven years.

8. Nuclear Deterrence and Obstinacy

It is frequently asserted that nuclear weapons have made states cautious, and there is some evidence for this. But it is by no means the whole truth. Nuclear weapons may also have a particular tendency to lead to obstinacy in the foreign policy-making of the powers which possess them. The US persistence in remaining in the quagmire of Vietnam appears to have owed much to a belief that a superpower has to demonstrate its steadfastness, commitment and resolve, otherwise its willingness to use its forces (including nuclear forces) on behalf of other allies around the world might be doubted. The whole problem of great powers being concerned with face, and with demonstrating *urbi et orbi* their determination or willingness to use force, is scarcely new, but it may have been made more difficult by the development of nuclear weapons.

9. The Particular Problems of Extended Deterrence

One of the reasons for the current concern about nuclear weapons is that many US commitments to distant territories – commitments which have traditionally been of great concern to western strategic writers – pose especially sharp problems now that the Soviet nuclear forces are so large. The scope of these problems of extended deterrence is peculiar to the US: no other nuclear power has them in so clear or extensive a form. The issue is not simply the distance of commitments from America herself, but also that they involve the issue of first use. The arguments over extended deterrence are numerous and complex, and one may dismiss some of the more extreme attacks on the idea. The French view, that because it would not be logical for the US to risk nuclear war for the sake of Europe, she will therefore not do so, betrays a curious faith that what is illogical must therefore be impossible. But if extended deterrence cannot be written off by logic alone, the attempts to resolve the obvious problems of extended deterrence by new strategic doctrines or new weapons have something of the air of the attempts to make the Ptolemaic system credible by the frenetic adding of epicycles. It is possible that one partial resolution of the problem might come from a recognition that nuclear weapons are not the centre of the strategic universe, and cannot do very much more than cancel each other out. This raises the difficult question of 'no-first-use' policies, discussed below under a separate heading.

The problem of extended deterrence today, at least in the European context, is simply an extreme version of the classic problem of nuclear deterrence itself. Either it seems all too credible, to the extent that it frightens allies and leads to counter-action by adversaries; or it does not seem credible enough. The fears being expressed simultaneously in Europe, though for the most part by different people, that the US would be all too willing to fight a so-called theatre nuclear war in Europe, and also that the US nuclear guarantee is hardly credible, confirm this. Although the idea of extended deterrence is not yet by any means dead, its evident weaknesses so far as Europe is concerned may suggest the need to find solutions going beyond the inevitable Alliance fudge-words of 'flexible response'.

10. Nuclear Weapons and the Laws of War

The relationship between nuclear weapons and the Laws of War is an area of vast complexity and deep moral ambiguity in which the layman fears to tread.

The use of nuclear weapons against most targets, and especially of course their use against cities, would obviously risk running counter to the most basic principles of the Laws of War: discrimination, protection of non-combatants, and general prohibitions of the use of weapons which are particularly inhumane. The immediate carnage resulting from such use of nuclear weapons would on its own be enough to justify such a statement. The long-term after-effects – psychological and physical – have been well documented in Hiroshima and Nagasaki. Weapons which have severe after-effects, even when the conflict in which they were used is long over, have traditionally been restricted under the Laws of War.

Yet there are in fact relatively few formal international legal prohibitions which explicitly govern the use of nuclear weapons in war (as distinct from their testing and deployment in peacetime, which comes under the rubric of arms control). As a class, nuclear weapons have escaped the kind of formal international prohibition on use which has been applied (mainly through the 1925 Geneva Protocol) to gas and bacteriological weapons. The failure of states to conclude any binding multilateral agreements explicitly restricting the use of nuclear weapons in war is remarkable, especially in view of the fact that in the nuclear age some eleven major multilateral agreements on various aspects of the Laws of War have been concluded. In relation to 1977 Geneva Protocol I, additional to the 1949 Geneva Conventions, Britain and America have gone so far as to state explicitly in reservations that the terms of this Protocol do not apply to nuclear weapons. However, in a number of statements the US has recognized that the principles of law relative to the use of weapons in war 'apply as well to the use of nuclear and similar weapons'.[10]

The reason for the dearth of laws-of-war type controls over the use of nuclear weapons is that there is a degree of tension between the underlying ideas of the Laws of War on the one hand, and of nuclear deterrence on the other. The Laws of War seek to limit war: in particular, to reduce its cruelty, and to ameliorate its effect on non-combatants, on persons who are *hors de combat*, and on neutral states. Most forms of nuclear deterrence, by contrast, seek to prevent war by making it so utterly frightful that states will fear to resort to it. Thus these two major approaches to the control of war appear to clash irreconcilably.

One may doubt whether in fact the clash between ideas of deterrence and the Laws of War has to be so absolute. The two approaches can be compatible in some respects. To accept certain principles of limitation of the use of force does not necessarily make the outbreak of war more likely, and indeed it may make it less so. If war does break out, the Laws of War may combine with deterrence to keep the war limited: for example, in Europe in the Second World War, explicit deterrent threats, clearly articulated on several occasions, underpinned the 1925 Geneva Protocol's prohibition on the use of gas and bacteriological weapons. Indeed, that agreement, including the reservations appended to it by many states, has the character of a 'no-first-use' agreement, although it also goes beyond this.

There are respects in which a laws-of-war approach may not be altogether incompatible with nuclear deterrence, but this is not necessarily in every case an occasion for rejoicing. Because assured destruction of an adversary's society is plainly in conflict with the Laws of War, a laws-of-war approach could easily be used as a subtle argument for counter-force strategies, the disadvantages of which hardly need further elaboration here.

So far, however, nuclear deterrence has not been effectively integrated into the laws-of-war stream of thought, and it appears indeed to largely reject this major traditional approach to the control of armed conflict. For all the limitations of the Laws of War, so sharp a rejection of an approach which is still deeply imbued in much of our thinking about the problem of war is itself a reasonable basis for criticism of nuclear deterrence.

11. Continued NATO Reliance on First Use

Under the rubric of 'flexible response', NATO has continued to rely on a policy of possible first use of nuclear weapons – a policy which

69

is increasingly questioned, not least by soldiers and ex-soldiers.[11]

If nuclear weapons have to be developed and deployed, the most obvious restriction on their employment would appear to be a policy of no first use. This could be a matter of unilateral deployments and declarations, or of multilateral agreement of the laws-of-war type. The most recent expression of a no-first-use commitment was contained in the message from President Brezhnev which was read out by Soviet Foreign Minister Gromyko in his speech at the United Nations on 15 June 1982. Since China has also made some no-first-use declarations, of the five recognized nuclear powers it is only the three NATO members which do not have such a declaratory policy.

The reasons why NATO has not felt able to accept a declaratory policy of no first use need to be recognized. Partly they are the outcome of history and inertia. In an era of US nuclear dominance, and European exhaustion following the Second World War, the idea of reliance on possible first use was more understandable than it is today, at least in the sense that it posed far fewer practical problems. Today, granted that the aim of NATO is to deter all war (not just nuclear war) between East and West in Europe, the adoption of a no-first-use policy would not be at all easy – especially as the Warsaw Pact states have numerical advantages in some categories of conventional weapons, and geography, as in Berlin, does not favour a purely local defence. The idea underlying NATO's approach to deterrence – namely that *any* aggression must be seen to risk incalculable consequences – seems to go against the grain of the no-first-use idea. Moreover, it is often doubted whether 'no first use' statements amount to very much more than paper promises.

While these objections are serious, they are far from being conclusive. Even if the idea of a formal no-first-use declaration is rejected, there is still a powerful case for moving away from a strategy of actual dependence on first use.

However, many reasons can be advanced for supporting not merely an avoidance of dependence on first use, but an open policy of no first use. NATO threats to use nuclear weapons first are increasingly incredible, because of the extreme vulnerability of Western European societies to retaliation and the uncertainty as to whether any nuclear war could remain limited. Moreover, in any European conflict, any NATO decision to use nuclear weapons would be far more likely to divide the Alliance than unite it, and might thus achieve the opposite effect from the intended one. To get away from reliance on first use might also reduce the need for at least some of the land-based nuclear weapons systems in Western Europe, the presence of which has caused great public concern. Furthermore, no-first use policies might, by clarifying the limited nature of the role of nuclear weapons, assist public acceptance of the need to maintain or increase a non-nuclear defence capacity. There have been some proposals, which might or might not involve negotiated agreements, to try to link a NATO no-first-use approach to certain reductions in Warsaw Pact forces, and such proposals might offer a means of tackling the admittedly difficult problem of a perceived imbalance in conventional forces. Words are important, and statesmen go to great lengths to explain the purposes and intentions behind the enormous power they possess. Clearly enunciated policies limiting first use, accompanied by necessary changes in military deployments, might contribute both to a sense that nuclear weapons are subject to some reasonably clear governing idea, and also to East–West stability. The failure to move in this direction confirms the general impression that the nuclear arms race has a dynamic of its own, unrestrained by human intellect or purpose.[12]

12. The Limits of Arms Control

For over twenty years, arms control has been widely regarded as the best available means for keeping weapons development, especially in the nuclear area, under some kind of limitation while at the same time maintaining a balance of power. This approach has a serious and well-articulated rationale.[13] Moreover, many important arms-control measures have been agreed, including the 1963 Partial Test Ban Treaty, the 1968 Non-Proliferation Treaty, and the 1972 SALT I Accords. However, these and similar agreements can be criticized on many grounds, and they have plainly been an inadequate brake on the momentum of the arms race. By the beginning of 1982, with the SALT II Treaty still in difficulties, and with other negotiations on nuclear and conventional arms control apparently becalmed, some of the hopes held out for arms control a decade or two earlier seemed to have been disappointed. Whether anything can be salvaged in the various negotiations now proceeding – including the talks on intermediate-range nuclear weapons in Europe, and also START – remains to be seen. But the limited nature of the achievements of arms control so far, and its failure to improve East–West relations in a lasting way, add to the sense that arms control has delivered rather less than was once hoped of it.

The accusation made against arms control is not merely that it has failed to tame the tiger of the nuclear arms race, but also that in some respects it has whetted the tiger's appetite. It does seem to have contributed to the current preoccupation with numbers and equivalences; and it has also contributed to the idea of bargaining chips – weapons projects developed so as to form a kind of currency to be used in arms-control talks. Because of these factors, arms control may even have contributed to the arms race it was intended to curb.

This is not to suggest that arms-control talks should be abandoned. For one thing, the criticisms summarized above do not apply equally to all arms-control negotiations and agreements. Moreover, the first eighteen months of the Reagan Presidency have been an object lesson in the folly and political costliness of soft-pedalling arms control. What the criticisms above do particularly suggest is that arms control, although it may help at the margins, is not likely on its own to improve political relations, to stop the arms race, or to offer a way out of the dilemmas of nuclear deterrence.

13. Moral Criticisms of Nuclear Deterrence
The application of moral principles to international relations is notoriously strewn with pitfalls, and the old saying, that the road to hell is paved with good intentions, might yet be proved more literally true than its anony-

mous author can ever have intended. The question of the morality of nuclear deterrence is by no means simple, and no course proposed is free of moral difficulty.[14] But the moral problems involved in reliance on nuclear weapons are serious and need to be faced. Although morality is sometimes perceived or presented (particularly in discussions about the problem of war) as a series of absolute and abstract rules imposed from outside, it is perhaps better seen as a necessary condition of human existence in a world which has always been dangerous; and as a means of asserting general interests as distinct from purely individual ones, or long-term interests against short-term ones. Hence moral considerations are not, and certainly should not be seen as, separate from practical ones.

The recent increase in public concern about nuclear weapons does have a moral element, a sense that to base a defence policy on the threat of genocide is wrong. Even though plenty of criticisms can be made of the adequacy of this position, it does have a strong basis and it does exist as a powerful political fact. One could put it even more strongly: a policy which could involve us in the roles of Nazi and Jew at the same time has unique moral defects. Moreover, a policy which explicitly relies on the possible first use of nuclear weapons is particularly questionable on moral grounds, especially where (as in the case of NATO) such a policy is the result of a reluctance to make necessary efforts in the field of non-nuclear defence.[15]

Although the idea that nuclear weapons are uniquely evil is vulnerable to criticism (other means of warfare also being indiscriminate, and some imaginable uses of some nuclear weapons being quite discriminate), there is a moral and practical case for trying to prohibit or in other ways restrict the use of nuclear weapons as a class. As many have remarked, there is simply no firebreak in war anything like as clear as that between non-nuclear and nuclear weapons.

14. The Economic Costs of Nuclear Weapons Systems
The question of the costs of nuclear weapons has featured prominently in recent public debates, especially in Britain where the cost of

the *Trident* D–5 programme is a particularly sensitive matter. It is certain to take a larger slice of the defence budget than did the *Polaris* system it is due to replace. The old idea that nuclear weapons offer a cheap form of defence – 'a bigger bang for a buck' – is not easily sustainable today. The evidence on this is not just that the nuclear weapons states (China perhaps excepted) also happen to have defence budgets which, whether expressed in dollar equivalents or as a percentage of Gross National Product, are somewhat above the international average. It is also that nuclear weapons systems, being basically unusable for almost any rational purpose, have not proved a substitute for more conventional air, naval and ground forces. Nuclear weapons and their associated delivery systems are simply one more claim on already stretched defence budgets and, because of budgetary constraints, the pursuit of nuclear deterrence may, for some states at least, involve some inevitable degree of reduction of conventional defence and deterrence.

15. *The Failure to Protect Populations*
It is an odd fact that the western states which are either nuclear powers themselves, or are closely allied to nuclear powers and are likely to have nuclear targets on their territory, have done relatively little to protect their populations from the effects of nuclear attack. This is particularly clear in the cases of the US, Britain and France. One might also note in passing that there are no anti-nuclear civil defence preparations whatsoever today in the city of Hiroshima. All this does not prove that democracies are incapable of planning for the worst. The highly developed civil defence preparations of Sweden and Switzerland suggest that something can be achieved.

What is the explanation for this paradox, that some non-nuclear and neutral states have made a serious effort to protect populations whereas the Western nuclear powers have not? In nuclear powers there seems to be some official reluctance to admit that the seamless web of nuclear deterrence might fail. When the governments of these powers have tried to introduce civil defence programmes (as in Britain and the US in the early 1960s, and again in the last few years) they have done so

in an amateurish way, and have run into a deadly combination of apathy and opposition, based in part on a concern that precautions against war looked like preparations for it. The considerable professional disagreements about how much, if anything, civil defence measures could salvage from the catastrophe of a nuclear war have added to the reluctance of many governments to go in for more than half-hearted half-measures where civil defence is concerned.

All these considerations apply less strongly in some of the non-nuclear states, including Switzerland and Sweden. It is less difficult for them to concede the obvious, that nuclear deterrence might fail. Since they are non-nuclear, their civil defence policies can hardly look provocative. To the extent that they might not be nuclear targets in a war, there are greater possibilities of protecting the population, for example from hazards such as fall-out. A further significant factor is that the countries which now take anti-nuclear protection seriously have long traditions of interest in civil defence, pre-dating the invention of nuclear weapons; and their defence policies, overall, are of a kind which is comprehensible to the population.

Within nuclear states, by contrast, the position regarding civil defence is peculiar and ugly. The populations lack even those elementary forms of protection which might at least help in the event of a major nuclear weapons accident. By contrast, the governments are reasonably well protected. A system of nuclear deterrence which leads to such a bizarre outcome is not easy to defend.

Where Does the Critique Lead?
The preceding headings – which are certainly incomplete – involve several distinct strands of criticism. There is the danger of nuclear weapons accident and of nuclear war, concern about which must be at the heart of any critique of nuclear deterrence. There is the lack of confidence that any war, and especially any nuclear war, between East and West could remain limited. There is the sense that the calculations of strategic planners, both East and West, have acquired a logic and momentum of their own. There is the doubtful morality of relying on essentially indiscriminate weapons,

and the doubtful practicality of relying on what amounts to a threat to commit mass suicide. There is the uncomfortable fact that nuclear deterrence has not led towards stable super-power relations, or to extensive measures of arms control. Because of the criticisms enumerated, nuclear deterrence does not seem to be a system which should inspire much confidence even in the relatively short term, let alone *sub specie aeternitatis*.

But any attempt to proceed beyond this point must start by acknowledging the inadequacies of what one might call the politician's fallacy: the assumption that because one can denounce the faults of an existing system, therefore one's own preferred nostrum must work. To a large extent we have got into the present situation precisely because the possible alternatives were widely deemed to have failed, or to be inadequate. The mere reiteration of shop-soiled ideas is not likely to achieve very much.

Thus the well-known deficiencies of the idea of general and complete disarmament are not reduced – indeed they may in some respects have been increased – by the development of nuclear weapons. As for the idea of world government, some of the very problems that have made the nuclear situation worse – the extreme distrust between the super-powers, and their commitment to unilateral arms build-ups as a means of achieving security – also have had the effect of ruling an international security authority even more firmly off the agenda than it was in the first place.

Because of the difficulties and defects of such multilateral approaches, a thorough-going critique of nuclear deterrence cannot avoid pointing in a unilateral direction. But this does not mean that the debate has to be framed around the one idea of unilateral disarmament as conventionally conceived: i.e. a single act of renunciation, in which it is perfectly evident what kind of defence which is rejected (nuclear deterrence), while that which is to take its place is not so clearly defined. Moreover, the conventional argument for unilateral disarmament, that the moral gesture by one country would be likely to affect other potentially nuclear countries, may reasonably be doubted.

To formulate defence policy on the basis of a single anti-nuclear moral imperative is questionable, both because there are bound to be accusations of continuing to rely, consciously or unconsciously, on another state's nuclear umbrella; and because the usual unilateralist emphasis on a single country acting alone seems to down-play the value of a collective attempt, which could be within the framework of existing alliances, to get away from the present and questionable state of affairs where defence is largely equated with nuclear weapons.

As distinct from unilateralism as traditionally presented, a different approach, justified as much on prudential as on moral grounds, needs to be considered: namely the attempt to develop non-nuclear policies for defence and deterrence, relying to the greatest extent possible on conventional military forces, or on militia-territorial type forces, or on organized civil (i.e. non-violent) resistance as a means of discouraging attack or resisting occupation. Thus the choice presented here is not just between nuclear deterrence on the one hand, and conventional deterrence on the other, but may involve an element of unconventional defence and deterrence. This could involve the use of resistance in depth, at least in populated areas, against possible foreign attack and occupation. Such resistance might assume either guerrilla or non-violent forms.

However, I have written on such approaches elsewhere,[16] and must observe my own warning against shop-soiled ideas. There is no use putting a greater burden of weight on such approaches than they are capable of carrying. To take civil resistance, it has occurred (and continues to occur) in a quite wide variety of circumstances, not least in occupied areas. Its successes, though few, have not been entirely negligible. However, there are many fundamental difficulties in trying to make this technique the sole basis of a state's defence policy, and it rather has the character of being a special option for special circumstances.[17] As for a territorial-militia type of defence, this does have considerable strengths, as Yugoslavia's maintenance of her dependence since 1948 has demonstrated: yet this case also shows that such an approach is not necessarily a total escape from involvement with nuclear powers: Yugoslavia has at times sought a modest degree of reinsurance with the US. Moreover, the Yugoslav approach would not easily be transplanted to the very different geographical and social terrain of Western Europe. But other ideas for a non-nuclear defence might have greater validity there, including some which have been put forward for a re-vamped conventional defence with greater reliance on the much-vaunted precision-guided munitions and on territorial forces.

Whatever the difficulties of such approaches, and they are undeniable, it is well to remember that the overwhelming majority of states muddle through in one way or another without nuclear weapons, and the problems of non-nuclear defence, though serious, should not be exaggerated.

The fact that many states have remained non-nuclear does not mean, however, that a completely non-nuclear world is a realistic possibility. For the foreseeable future it is not. Even a complete renunciation of all nuclear weapons by the western states alone is not only exceedingly unlikely but also – if one is to be frank – not necessarily to be desired. The fact that nuclear deterrence has crippling weaknesses does not mean that it has no validity whatsoever.

At this late stage one important observation, both methodological and substantial, should be made. Even though the emphasis throughout this Paper has been on general criticisms of nuclear deterrence as such, inevitably, by the mere act of searching for evidence and thinking about issues, one focuses not on the general, but on the particular. To a large extent, it is particular ideas about the role of nuclear weapons which one questions, particular strategies which one criticizes, particular nuclear weapons or deployments about which one is most concerned. It is not only inevitable, but also right, that concern with the general issue of nuclear deterrence should not be at the expense of attention to more particular and limited issues.

So far as NATO member states are concerned, many of the criticisms of nuclear deterrence enumerated in this Paper might point to particular and limited conclusions which can be briefly encapsulated as follows:

- It may well be that, just as civil nuclear power generation has not lived up to all the early hopes for it, so also nuclear weapons have introduced considerably less of a revolution in warfare than has often been thought, especially in the NATO member states. To a large extent, though perhaps never completely, nuclear weapons simply cancel each other out, and other forms of military preparation and deterrence have not lost their importance.
- The idea that only the most extreme threats deter, or that they are particularly effective in doing so, is fallacious. The most extreme threats, and the weapons which go with them, may not only inspire the adversary to take counter-measures, but may also deter us as much as potential adversaries. This is a particularly serious consequence because the primary mechanism by which NATO deters is simply by hanging together, and it cannot do so on the basis of making threats which are, and will remain, internally divisive.
- Naïve doctrines of prevailing in a nuclear war, and misleading justifications of civil defence conveying the idea that nuclear war might be less than a catastrophe for civilization, are evidence of the bankruptcy of much nuclear deterrence theory, and should be abandoned.
- The issue of a 'no-first-use' policy regarding nuclear weapons, and the changes in deployments to go with it, needs to be reconsidered. While the difficulties of this approach, and its inherently meliorist character, are evident, it could make possible the introduction of a defence system which had a higher degree of credibility, which was understandable to the public, which reduced the pressure for new and controversial nuclear weapons deployments, and which reinforced the crucial firebreak between nuclear and other weapons.
- In order to deter attack effectively without resorting to the threat of first use of nuclear weapons, the conventional military forces of some NATO countries need to be restructured or even increased; and preparations for unconventional forms of defence, which also have some deterrent power,

74

deserve to be more fully considered within NATO than they ever have been in the past.

– Despite all the difficulties of so doing, the continuing validity of the underlying principles of the Laws of War (especially the avoidance of the use of particularly inhumane weapons, and the protection of non-combatants) needs to be vigorously asserted. The issues raised by this approach are not simple, but cannot be ignored in view of the obvious necessity of maintaining clear limits on the use of arms in a century which has already seen far more deaths in war than any other, and in a world which is grossly over-armed and seems likely, for better or for worse, and to a greater or lesser degree, to remain so.

NOTES

[1] George H. Quester, *Deterrence Before Hiroshima: The Airpower Background of Modern Strategy* (London: John Wiley, 1966). For an interesting discussion of pre-nuclear deterrence more generally, focusing mainly on events before the First World War, see particularly Richard Rosecrance, 'Deterrence and Vulnerability in the Pre-Nuclear Era', in Christoph Bertram (ed.), *The Future of Strategic Deterrence* (London: Macmillan Press, 1981), pp. 24–30.

[2] For an interesting essay arguing this point, see Lester Grinspoon, 'The Truth is Not Enough', in Roger Fisher (ed.), *International Conflict and Behavioural Science*, (New York: Basic Books, 1964), p. 238*ff*.

[3] Philip Green, *Deadly Logic: The Theory of Nuclear Deterrence* (Ohio: Ohio State University Press, 1966), p. 276.

[4] Lawrence Freedman, *The Evolution of Nuclear Strategy* (London: Macmillan Press, 1981), p. 399.

[5] E. P. Thompson, *Zero Option*, (London: Merlin Press, 1982), p. 37.

[6] Laurence Martin, *The Two-Edged Sword: The Reith Lectures 1981* (London: Weidenfeld and Nicolson, 1982), p. 33.

[7] Bernard Brodie, *War and Politics* (London: Cassell, 1974), p. 380.

[8] See for example the report, *Accidental War: Some Dangers in the 1960's*, prepared under the auspices of the Mershon Center at Ohio State University in 1960, and published in Britain by Housmans, London 1962.

[9] See for example the account of the Japanese decision to surrender in L. Giovanetti and F. Freed, *The Decision to Drop the Bomb*, (London: Methuen, 1967), pp. 275–95.

[10] US Delegation to UN General Assembly, Press Release, 10 December, 1968.

[11] See for example, Field Marshal Lord Carver *A Policy for Peace* (London: Faber and Faber, 1982), pp. 11, 58–60, 101–6.

[12] For recent advocacy of a no-first-use policy for NATO, see McGeorge Bundy, George F. Kennan, Robert S. McNamara and Gerard Smith, 'Nuclear Weapons and the Atlantic Alliance', *Foreign Affairs*, Spring 1982. See also the reply by Karl Kaiser and colleagues in the Summer issue, and Michael Howard's letter in the Fall issue.

[13] See for example Hedley Bull, *The Control of the Arms Race* (London: Weidenfeld and Nicolson, 1961).

[14] For some excellent discussions of these issues, see Geoffrey Goodwin (ed.), *Ethics and Nuclear Deterrence* (London: Croom Helm, 1982).

[15] For a discussion of nuclear weapons in relation to the 'just war' tradition, and proposing a no-first-use approach, see James Turner Johnson, *Just War Tradition and the Restraint of War: A Moral and Historical Inquiry*, (Princeton: Princeton University Press, 1981), pp. 357–65.

[16] In the volume I edited, *The Strategy of Civilian Defence: Non-violent Resistance to Aggression* (London: Faber, 1967); and in my *Nations in Arms: The Theory and Practice of Territorial Defence*, (London: Chatto and Windus, 1976).

[17] This was my conclusion in *Total Defence and Civil Resistance: Problems of Sweden's Security Policy*, a report prepared for and issued by the Research Institute of Swedish National Defence, Stockholm, 1972, pp. 151–81.

Domestic Consensus and Nuclear Deterrence

HAROLD BROWN

The Breakdown of Domestic Consensus on Nuclear Policies

Over the past eighteen months, a substantial breakdown has taken place in the domestic consensus on nuclear policies in Europe and the United States. In Europe, mass demonstrations have occurred against the deployment of new US cruise and *Pershing* II ballistic missiles. These include not only young protesters, ecologists, and other cause-adopters. Many middle-aged, middle-class, conservative Europeans have also joined. Especially among the Protestant churches, leaders have condemned in ethical and religious terms the development and possession of nuclear weapons, nuclear deployments, nuclear strategy and nuclear deterrence.

Somewhat later, parallel phenomena have appeared in the United States. One movement to educate the public about nuclear war is led by physicians, galvanized by the realization that destruction of civilization includes destruction of physicians. Another is the Ground Zero movement. That makes no prescriptions, but tries to awaken the public to what the effects of a nuclear war would be and to the importance of taking steps to prevent nuclear war. Respected public figures, many of them well experienced in defence, foreign policy and arms-control matters, urge a nuclear freeze or a 'no-first-use' doctrine or both. The Conference of Catholic Bishops in the United States is considering a pastoral letter on nuclear issues. In its early draft, it asserts a 'no-first-use policy' as a matter of pastoral doctrine. It denies the morality of retaliation in kind to nuclear attack if that retaliation is aimed at or collaterally inflicts massive civilian casualties. And it questions the morality of retaining a nuclear capability at all.

The present protest movement exceeds in size anything yet seen in the United States, and equals that of the nuclear disarmament campaigns in Europe in the late 1950s and early 1960s. Moreover, it may well have more influence in electoral politics, Non-Communist parties in Europe either sharing power or with a chance of coming to power (the British and Dutch Labour Parties, the 'Greens' in West Germany, and segments of the Dutch Christian Democratic Appeal Party (CDA) and German Sozialdemokratischepartei deutschlands (SPD) not only oppose the 1979 NATO decisions but also favour unilateral disarmament, at least in terms of a denuclearization of their own territories. Some of these positions are rather imprecise. Others might not be implemented by their present proponents if they come to power. Nevertheless the public protests and party positions indicate severe disquiet about situations and about policies. These include the nature and direction of the nuclear arms competition, the nuclear doctrine of the Western Alliance, the policy of nuclear deterrence, and the delegation of decisions on these matters to the experts, professionals and political leaders who now have that responsibility. Domestic consensus has clearly eroded in most Western countries with respect to national and alliance nuclear policies. Why?

First, US-Soviet relations have markedly deteriorated. Indeed, they are now worse than at any time since the Cuban missile crisis, perhaps since the death of Stalin. Some observers and publics see Soviet assertiveness and expansionism (in Poland and in Afghanistan, and previously in various parts of Africa) as increasing the chance of a nuclear war. Others perceive an increase in the willingness of the United States to take risky military action as having the same effect. The former view is based on Soviet actions; it continues to dominate US opinion. The latter is held by many in Europe. They point to the Reagan Administration's own policies and to its rhetoric about Soviet intentions and behaviour.

Second, the prospects for arms control appear bleak. A major element in public unease is the failure of the United States to ratify the SALT II Treaty, even though that can be attributed largely to the Soviet invasion of Afghanistan. Another is the absence in US security policy under the Reagan Administration, until recently, of an arms-control and reduction component. In the past a serious commitment on the part of the United States and other Western governments to negotiations on nuclear arms has offered hope to publics in the countries of the Alliance. (Some opponents of arms-control negotiations would claim it has been a false hope.)

The Reagan Administration has now made a commitment, still rather ambiguous, to continue to observe SALT II. It has resumed strategic arms talks in the form of START, and continued negotiations on intermediate-range nuclear forces (INF). These actions have helped to limit suspicions that arms control no longer plays any part in US policy. To the extent that US proposals have been seen as reasonable, they have operated to lever the US position among informed European publics back up the precipice over which it was falling. But there is still uncertainty on both sides of the Atlantic as to how serious this commitment to negotiations is. Moreover, the setting forth of negotiating positions in the form of public speeches, however necessary under the circumstances, is unlikely to be helpful to the negotiating process.

The problem of perceptions of fairness of US positions is not eased by the inadequacies in Soviet proposals. The USSR is not expected by many among Western publics to make fair proposals – or rather, many Western commentators see fairness in Soviet proposals whose reciprocal equivalents they would find unfair if made by the United States. While it is not realistic to see arms control as a road to peace separate from the resolution or habituation of major political differences, arms control can and should stabilize military balances. The new barriers in that road are, therefore, a significant concern.

Third, governments have in their nuclear strategies appeared to give more emphasis to fighting rather than to preventing nuclear wars. Numerous declarations by various officials in the Reagan Administration, which the President himself has lately been careful to avoid, have been a significant factor in public disquiet both in Europe and in the United States. These include statements, or implications, that nuclear wars can be won, or that they could well be limited in geography or intensity, or that even all-out nuclear wars can be survived given enough shovels. Some Europeans have expressed particular concern that geographical limitation could mean limitation to Western and Eastern Europe with the United States and the USSR as sanctuaries. Failures and malfunctions of warning systems have heightened public fears that nuclear war could occur, if not by plan then by accident.

In short, a reversal has taken place since 1979 of what had been an easing of concerns in the United States and Europe about nuclear weapons through most of the 1970s. That relaxation had developed from an expectation, realized to a significant extent during that period, that budget limitations, arms-control efforts and nuclear strategies would all act to limit the Soviet–American competition and reduce the risk of nuclear war. During the 1980s, publics have with good reason come to be less confident about the effectiveness of each of these limits. When further reminded about the real existence, and presence in their midst, of nuclear weapons by the proposals for new missile deployments, their concerns have been transformed into a major political force.

At the same time, another public in the United States and in some cases also in Europe has become increasingly worried since the early 1970s by the build-up of Soviet forces and what they consider the failure of the United States and the Allies to meet the challenge. They are concerned about the possibility that the USSR might undertake what it may see as limited nuclear wars or a winnable all-out nuclear war. While the claims by these groups and their opinion leaders about US strategic nuclear inferiority are at best misleading, the concerns polarize the publics and further undermine domestic consensus on nuclear policy. These groups press to have nuclear capabilities that exceed and doctrines that match what they consider to be those of the USSR. They and the officials who share their positions widen the spread of views and make it less likely that any particular doctrine or programme will be generally accepted. Moreover, the unlimited force requirements and costs that could be derived from such an approach deepen the divisions in the electorate.

In the US, in Europe, and in Japan as well, there is a widespread perception that the Soviet Union is ahead of the Alliance in strategic nuclear, medium-range nuclear and conventional forces. On both the left and on the right, proponents respectively of social welfare programmes and of greater military strength push for a choice of one at the expense of the other. The more extreme among them exaggerate the real need for choice between the two as much to reduce the activity they oppose as to increase the activity they support. Although this conflict is, in my judgment, more a political one than the consequence of a genuine and sharp economic limit, it further polarizes public opinion and makes agreement on all defence programmes more difficult. The cost of nuclear forces is about one-quarter that of conventional forces. But the concern in the countries of the West is greater about nuclear than conventional war. Moreover, the question of 'how much is enough?' can be more sharply posed to publics with respect to nuclear forces. For both reasons, real or overstated competition for funds with non-military needs can hit sharply at nuclear force programmes. Continuing economic distress – 'stagflation', unemployment – intensifies these effects. That has significantly eroded support for nuclear programmes in conservative business circles in the US, and I would judge in Europe as well.

PD-59: The Role of Public Views

In the past, public attitudes have not been given much attention in the definition of US and NATO nuclear policies. A recent example is the formal US adoption in PD-59 of the countervailing strategy. This refinement in US nuclear strategy was prompted by several concerns. The first was the major build-up in Soviet offensive nuclear capabilities. But the emphasis in Soviet writings on nuclear warfighting and war-winning strategies also

played a part. So also did the planning and programmes for protection of Soviet political and military leadership in case of nuclear war, and perceptions, however questionable, of a massive Soviet civil defence programme.

In the countervailing strategy, the United States would put at very high risk the elements of Soviet power and society believed to be held as valuable by Soviet leadership. Thus either in limited or all-out nuclear war the Soviet leadership would stand to lose more than it could possibly gain. By these steps, including the ability to respond to the unlikely contingency of a limited attack in a (believably) limited way, the US aim has been to continue to deter both limited and all-out attack by the USSR. The method of this deterrence is to be through persuading Soviet planners that they could not win a nuclear war at any level because both sides would lose.

Thus the policies embodied in PD-59 were directed primarily toward planning for US strategic nuclear forces, and the deterrence of Soviet attack on the United States. They were, however, consistent with NATO's plans for the use of nuclear weapons in either selective attacks or all-out nuclear war. The studies and analyses which formed the basis of PD-59 were completed in 1979. An outline of the proposed doctrinal refinements was presented in the unclassified January 1980 Annual Report of the Secretary of Defense. It had been foreshadowed in earlier public statements, and was subsequently discussed both in closed Congressional testimony and in NATO Ministerial Meetings. Those presentations had been accepted as rather routine.

The public announcement of PD-59 was delayed until the Summer of 1980 primarily because other events in Iran and Afghanistan took priority. The August 1980 public statements made all the doctrinal points described above. At the same time, the Carter Administration attempted to use this modest refinement in US nuclear strategy as a response to charges that the USSR had achieved strategic nuclear superiority. It hoped thus to gain support from (primarily US) publics who were swayed by those changes. To a degree, this backfired. It encouraged widespread though mistaken interpretations by the public and by some experts in the United States and Europe that PD-59 signified a major step toward a strategy and plan for fighting a limited nuclear war. Moreover, few hardliners were impressed. Thus the handling of PD-59, by trying to gain the support of conflicting constituencies, lost more than it gained. The ground should have been more carefully prepared among journalists and non-governmental experts.

Overstatements by some officials, in describing PD-59, of belief in the feasibility of fighting nuclear war helped to increase public fears that governments take the prospect of nuclear war lightly. Perhaps the saddest aspect of all was the failure of the following Administration to learn from the effects of the inadequate emphasis, in its predecessors' public handling of the matter, on PD-59's overwhelming concentration on deterrence rather than warfighting. Instead, Reagan Administration officials appeared to clasp nuclear warfighting to their bosoms. The public reaction, in the US as well as Europe, was predictable.

Steps to Rebuild the Consensus

In the future, political leaders and governments will have to pay more attention in defining and articulating their nuclear policies, to re-establishing and sustaining public support and confidence.

First, they will need to be sensitive to understandable concerns, and be prepared to respond directly to rational arguments about the possibility and potential consequences of nuclear war. Moderate and reasonable publics in the United States, Europe and Japan have such concerns and express such arguments.

That the nuclear arsenals of the superpowers could end civilization not only for them but for the countries of Europe and Japan as well is a legitimate reason for public alarm, even though it is not a new reason. The damage to society that would result from use of the nuclear arsenals is no greater than it was ten years ago; indeed it may be marginally less. The increase in popular concern derives more from a public perception that such a war has increased in likelihood.

The deterioration of US–USSR relations that drives that perception is also real, and serious. Yet the enormous destructive potential of the nuclear capabilities of both sides, in a continued approximation to parity, continues to introduce caution into the policies of both super-powers. Just as before, their nuclear arsenals act as a strong deterrent to Soviet–American military conflict. Moreover, in Europe and the Far East, the existence of US conventional and theatre nuclear forces, and the mutual Alliance commitments, make any Soviet adventure too dangerous to be undertaken at all lightly. In South-west Asia, where US forces remain offshore, nuclear force is – properly – more remote, and a political-military security structure is lacking, the potential danger of war is probably greater. But in the light of the enormous complexity of the regional political situation in South-west Asia and the great variety of its rivalries and hatreds, both the USSR and the West will have a number of non-military options to promote their interests. As a result, they may not feel driven to undertake military actions. In any case, neither super-power could have great confidence that such actions would succeed in the light of the military and political uncertainties.

Yet, even if these concerns of publics are addressed, the fundamental problem of the threat of nuclear war will still exist. In order to retain or regain public support for national and Alliance nuclear policies, political leaders must convince their publics that they are doing what can be done *to minimize the chances that a nuclear war will occur.*

All Western nuclear policies should continue to have deterrence as their central objective. Essential strategic nuclear equality is also a requirement, politically even more than militarily. Other objectives, such as escalation dominance, warfighting, or successful defence against a nuclear attack, are very unlikely to be at all feasible. Actions or doctrines seen as pursuing them as major goals could not only undermine deterrence but would probably further erode public support for nuclear policies. However, Western nuclear policies should seek to maintain and improve deterrence of Soviet aggression by creating and declaring the existence of various nuclear responses appropriate to the nature of a nuclear attack. Thus the US would not be limited to an all-out response, against all classes of targets and with the entire forces, independent of the nature of attack that prompts the response. These options should pose likely costs to the USSR that outweigh reasonably foreseeable gains to her. The nuclear forces must therefore provide capabilities for attacks of various magnitudes against a variety of classes of potential targets. It is also of critical importance that the nuclear forces should have a high degree of survivability and should not require either quick decisions on their use or plans for launch under attack.

Arms-control initiatives can also serve to reduce the possibility and risks of nuclear war. The actual achievements of arms control have been modest, but they have not been a trap. The United States and the Allies need to pursue control, limitation, and reduction efforts seriously and forcefully. This will test whether the Soviet leadership is prepared to accept equitable and verifiable agreements. A more explicit acceptance by the current US Administration of the SALT II provisions as upper limits on forces would give some reassurance to publics on numbers of launchers, warheads, fractionation, and numbers of new missile systems permitted to be developed. Freezes of particular categories of weapons should not be excluded from consideration, though, because deterrence has complex ramifications, my own view is that a general freeze has serious pitfalls. For example, to freeze nuclear-armed bombers and cruise missiles but non-nuclear air defences undermines the stability of deterrence. Even major reductions in present forces on both sides would reduce public concerns more than they would reduce the damage potential of nuclear war but, if carefully crafted, such reductions could improve the stability of deterrence, which should continue to be a major goal of strategic weapons programmes and arms control alike. Thus efforts towards nuclear arms limitation and reduction remain urgent, but publics must not be deceived into thinking that arms-control efforts – even the most successful that have been achieved, such as the ABM Treaty and the SALT Agreements, or conceivably achievable by the START negotiations – will remove the threat of nuclear destruction.

The West needs also to define a set of technical, political and military security policies more effectively aimed at reducing the incentives for nuclear proliferation. These will not be easy to devise, still less to implement. A world with more nuclear states would not necessarily (though I think it likely to) increase the risk of nuclear war between the super-powers but surely the interactions of all states would become more precarious and complex. The super-powers share a common interest in postponing the spread of nuclear weapons.

To reduce the risk of nuclear escalation from a conventional war, Western governments need to design a strategy and programme for improving conventional military forces.

Many difficulties stand in the way of programmes to improve the conventional balance. The industrialized democracies can surely afford the economic costs of such a posture but they will confront major political inhibitions, at a time of slow economic growth, to even marginal changes in the allocation of resources. Moreover, the governments differ in their attitudes toward the threat posed by the Soviet Union. They vary in their views of the appropriate division of military responsibilities in Europe, the Pacific and elsewhere. Major splits mark their perceptions of the nature of the problems in South-west Asia, and of the proper balance between political and military responses to those problems.

The patchy progress in meeting the force structure, equipment, and development objectives agreed to in the NATO Long-Term Defence Programme (LTDP) by heads of government at the 1978 Summit is hardly encouraging. Moreover those improvements in the NATO-Warsaw Pact balance continue to be needed, along with further concentration on concepts that might radically improve tactics, training and force utilization.

Despite its difficulties of achievement, a more reassuring conventional balance is, paradoxically or not, one of the major ways to reduce dependence on nuclear deterrence and in turn to reduce the chance of a nuclear war. It would raise the nuclear threshold and provide an incentive for reductions in nuclear weapons both unilaterally and in arms-control agreements. It would also create some basis for a believable no-first-use commitment. Whatever its dangers (which could well still predominate in that case) such a commitment would have advantages in gaining support for security policy in general. An improved conventional balance could at the same time even produce a greater acceptance of present nuclear doctrines and programmes by publics in Europe, in Japan and in the United States.

To reduce the pressures for the early use of nuclear weapons in case of a war, NATO needs to readdress the requirements for battlefield nuclear weapons. Consideration should be given to reducing their number as the new artillery rounds are produced, and to their eventual replacement by systems of at least one or two hundred kilometres range. These replacements would need to be assigned to the same categories of targets. Their accuracy, yield and target acquisition systems would have to be the same, in order to pose the same threat to massed attackers. All of those features are technically feasible. Organizational and command arrangements may be more difficult but the greater range and the higher level of control would, advantageously, reduce the risk of being overrun and the pressure for devolution of release authority. Automaticity of use would be reduced. Some may argue that would reduce the effectiveness of deterrence. I believe the reduced risk of escalation to nuclear war substantially outweighs that fear and such a shift would surely increase public confidence that nuclear war had been made less likely.

To reduce the chance of nuclear war through misperception or a misunderstanding of intentions or actions, the US and the Soviet Union need to improve their procedures for crisis management. A hotline exists but it needs to be upgraded in reliability and function. It is not clear that procedures exist at both ends to ensure prompt delivery of messages to a level where decisions can be made.

One possibility is the establishment of a joint US–USSR operations centre. It could be staffed by military officials and diplomats of both nations, able to communicate with their own headquarters in respective capitals, and thus, in times of crisis, to explain ambiguous events or apparently threatening actions. They could share intelligence when it was decided by their superiors that doing so would reduce risks of war through misunderstanding.

But these actions could be taken only on higher authority. Such an arrangement could thus confuse matters by setting up a parallel chain of communication. Moreover, where would the centre be located? And what about problems or deception? These and other objections properly generate a degree of scepticism, and would have to be examined closely. So far the thought remains only an interesting speculation.

A less far-reaching step would be the establishment of regular consultations between senior defence officials of the US and USSR, both ministerial and professional military. This was proposed at the Vienna Summit in 1979 but Soviet actions in Afghanistan and the US failure to ratify SALT II aborted the prospects of such a development. Such consultations and exchanges are particularly needed when super-power relations are bad. It is precisely then that they are most difficult to establish. Therefore they should be initiated on a regular basis whenever a modest easing of the present state of affairs allows.

The US has given considerable attention to eliminating the possibility of the use of nuclear weapons through accident, unauthorized action, or mistaken perceptions of being under attack. Computer malfunctions have given false warnings, and individual sensors have given mistaken signals. But confirmation from separate sensors and circuits is required for substantial movement even toward recallable actions and no irreversible actions can be taken without human judgments at the highest political level. Past malfunctions are indeed reason enough for serious concern and system revisions have been made but in fact US nuclear forces have never begun to come at all close to being launched in a retaliatory mode.

Improvements can be made in other ways to reduce the chance of accident. Better security against conventional attack or hijacking of field-deployed tactical weapons are examples. Another is continuing improvement of mechanical controls that prevent firing without insertion of the correct code. Increasing the distance of stationing of ballistic missile submarines and intermediate range missiles from each other's capitals, to lengthen their flight time and increase warning time, has also been suggested. Verification poses difficulties, but the idea is worth exploring.

Ultimately, the West needs a policy for relations with the Soviet Union which, accepting the almost certain continuation of competition and risk of confrontation, includes political and economic incentives for constructive behaviour, as well as disincentives for disruptive behaviour. All of this is a very large order. And in the end, the adversary nature of the relations between the Soviet Union and the industrialized democracies, together with the existence of substantial numbers of nuclear weapons, means that the catastrophe of nuclear war will continue to remain a real possibility. The world will remain a correspondingly dangerous and frightening place. This limits what can be done by Western leadership in banishing the shadow of nuclear war. But publics are entitled to assurance that, insofar as it lies within the power of Western leadership, what can be done to reduce these dangers is being done.

Public Presentation
Political leaders will also need to discuss forthrightly with their publics both all the requirements and all the ambiguities of nuclear deterrence.

With respect to strategic nuclear doctrine and forces, the public must be persuaded, or repersuaded, about deterrence. Two propositions must be embodied in the case thus made. First, deterrence is, under any reasonably foreseeable circumstance, a necessary pillar of security. Moreover, it is also the only available strategy that carries reasonable confidence of success – even though it has elements of ambiguity and uncertainty, and includes contingency planning for morally repugnant behaviour. The ethical dilemma of threatening the destruction of a hundred million ordinary people in retaliation for a similar attack on the West as a way of deterring such an attack cannot be avoided: it has had to be lived with over the past quarter of a century. The practical dilemma created by nuclear weapons systems whose principal purpose is served only so long as they are not

used, indeed which will have succeeded as effective instruments of policy only so long as they are not used, will also remain.

It is not easy for publics to grasp the way in which a perceived 'overkill' in nuclear capability in the form of a very large stockpile could be transformed, through vulnerability to pre-emptive attack, poor command, control and communications, and loss of capability to penetrate defences, into an inadequate deterrent. Such analyses need to be better explained. Publics need to be educated as to why nuclear systems must be able to survive a surprise attack and be capable of control for scenarios other than a single spasmodic retaliatory strike. This can be done without Western planners succumbing to the delusion that protracted nuclear wars are likely, that a nuclear war can be planned with any confidence, or that limited nuclear wars, tactical or strategic, are likely to remain so.

Nuclear plans and credible nuclear response options should be explained to Western publics in terms of their intended purposes, along the following lines. These plans are to convince the USSR that she cannot hope to gain military or political advantage by having plans or capabilities for which the West has no appropriate response. Moreover, Western political leaders are more likely to make sensible decisions in a crisis or in case of an actual nuclear attack, of whatever nature and size, if such options exist beforehand and have been thought through and considered in exercises. Nothing could be more irresponsible than the creation of a situation in which a limited attack is detected as being in progress and Western political leaders are told that the only available choices are no response or an all-out nuclear retaliation, because it had previously been decided that such an attack was impossible.

Convincing publics along these lines is bound to be more difficult than the explanation of the simple deterrence of an all-out Soviet attack on the United States through the threat of all-out retaliation.

Most analysts, planners, parliamentarians, publics and political leaders have come to recognize the existence of a state of approximate equivalence in the Soviet–American strategic nuclear balance. Inevitably, the utility of US nuclear forces in deterring Soviet nuclear or conventional aggression in Europe or against Japan has correspondingly diminished. What de Gaulle said in the 1960s and Kissinger in 1979 may or may not have been true at the time, but has come increasingly to be so, perhaps in part because they said it. There remains, in my view, a penumbral area of extended deterrence. It makes both super-powers substantially more cautious in taking steps that they consider to have a substantial probability of causing their own conventional military forces to become engaged with the conventional military forces of the other. It rests on the belief that the coupling of conventional and nuclear (theatre and strategic) forces of the super-powers is sufficiently close that such conventional conflict would have a high risk of escalating into a nuclear war – but that is a rather far cry from the way in which extended deterrence was once declared to function, with conventional aggression in much of the world substantially deterred by the threat of US nuclear retaliation. Moreover, in a state of nuclear parity, when the balance of conventional forces is marginal or unsatisfactory, opportunities for political intimidation as well as for military attack will arise.

US nuclear forces deployed in Europe represent a special and intense case of public interest. Analysts, strategic thinkers and political leaders in Western countries – and this applies particularly in Europe – need to be able to present publics with a more clearly explained and believable rationale for their purpose, deployment and potential use. This will be particularly difficult because few if any scenarios for their employment are convincing. Such forces do, however, continue to function as a powder train, acting to assure whatever penumbral effect exists of extended deterrence. Battlefield or longer-range nuclear weapons have, by their very existence, had an effect on Warsaw Pact conventional forces, including their tactics and deployments. The Warsaw Pact must spread out these forces, thus reducing their ability to crack allied defensive lines by massing armour. The possibility of Soviet political intimidation based on a threat to confine a nuclear war to Western Europe is reduced through the existence of US intermediate-range nuclear missiles with the capability to strike targets in the Soviet Union. These US missiles also provide reassurance for Europeans who may believe that the US would be reluctant to use her strategic forces in an initial response to a nuclear attack on Europe.

Finally, political leaders need to pay more attention to the goal of increasing public confidence that US and allied policies are directed toward reducing the chance that a nuclear war will occur. NATO missed an opportunity in this regard when it gave little publicity to the decision made in 1979 to withdraw 1,000 nuclear warheads from Europe. As the United States implements her current plans for a further withdrawal of more than a thousand air defence and older missile warheads, she should emphasize the reduced NATO emphasis on nuclear defence. The public also needs to be made more aware of the widespread deployment, both in tactical and strategic forces, of Permissive Action Links (PAL), which mechanically prevent the launch of nuclear systems or their explosion in the absence of the receipt of the proper coded signal along with the authorization for their use.

Conclusion

In summary, Western publics consider themselves more secure insofar as they believe that Western military strength is adequate, that it is under responsible control, and that their leaders are informed, wise and sensitive to the concerns of their citizens. But the ambiguities and paradoxes of the nuclear age must be accepted and lived with along with the imperfections of leaders in democracies. Publics must come to understand that, although there may be some easing of, there is no escape from, the threat of nuclear annihilation so long as nuclear weapons exist in large numbers in an atmosphere of adversarial relationships between East and West. Neither of these circumstances is at all likely to change in the coming decades, even if there were a complete freeze on the production and deployment of nuclear weapons, a significant reduction in the nuclear stockpiles, and a sincere expression of an intent not to be first to use nuclear weapons.

Public officials responsible for national security will have to be prepared to address the entire complex of nuclear policy and related issues described above. Public debate will be necessary with those who have various concerns or contrary views. The thirty-year diffusion of nuclear policy consideration and formulation from official through academic and intellectual to journalistic and public circles is now irreversible. The debate will have to be carried out in public at a level comprehensible to publics and to conclusions they can afterwards support.

The declaratory policies of Western governments must mirror actual nuclear policies more closely than has been the case in the past. Nuances may separate the ways in which US nuclear doctrine and planning appears to or is described to various audiences. Indeed, the nuclear planners and political leaders themselves may not see their policies in exactly the same light as any of the parties at whom their declaratory policy is directed – domestic publics, allies, neutrals or potential adversaries. Blatant contradictions however are another matter. By presenting adversaries with unreal dangers or opportunities, they risk unintended crises. By confusing domestic publics, they lose the political support necessary to maintain realistic security policies.

Political leaders in the industrialized democracies will continue to confront enormously difficult issues in designing an effective nuclear posture. They will now face the additional task of re-establishing a domestic consensus about the role of nuclear weapons in their overall security policies. Creating a consensus to this end, unified beyond the domestic constituencies to encompass the whole of the global alliance, will be even more challenging. But the genie of public involvement and discussion, like the genie of nuclear weapons, is already out of the bottle. There is no alternative to living with both.

Domestic Concerns and Nuclear Doctrine: How Should the Nuclear Posture be Shaped?

JOHAN JØRGEN HOLST

Defence Policy and Consensus

In democratic societies, defence policy must be socially acceptable in order to remain viable and credible. Sharply controversial policies are prone to erosion by political opposition and therefore tend to be less credible and predictable than those which command broad support. Social acceptance does not imply unanimous support nor does it suggest a need for enthusiastic endorsement. Broad consensus on the basic features of national security policy and the assumptions on which it is predicated is necessary, however, for democracies to be able to maintain a steady course in a turbulent and uncertain world. Frequently, public attitudes to arms policies are volatile and harbour many inconsistencies. Nevertheless, governments must strive to fashion policies which are reasonably coherent, stable and consistent. Governments are, however, subject to constraints imposed by existing commitments, economics, technology and competing interests. They are invariably and justifiably concerned about re-election. They should ignore public concerns at their peril. But governments also have an obligation to lead, to choose a course of action under conditions of uncertainty, to focus on long term consequences and options rather than simply succumb to short-term expedience. However, if they lack public support they will fail. They must persuade and listen. Communication and dialogue between government and the governed, between state and society are keys to effective policy-making in democracies.

The complexity of modern weapons and the esoteric nature of nuclear strategy make real public dialogue about defence policy extremely difficult. Alienation and frustration often shape attitudes, demonstration tends to replace conversation. The dialogue tends to assume Chekhovian qualities as the participants talk past each other and stop listening. The problems are compounded by changes in Western society. The arrival of material plenty has shifted emphasis away from a primary concern with material well-being and physical security toward greater emphasis on less tangible qualities of life.

A mood of discontent has been stimulated by a waning belief in the idea of progress, in the blessings of technology and in man's ability to avoid catastrophe. War has become an abstract notion which has been delegated to experts. In terms of experience, war is something which happens to other people in distant lands. At the same time a subliminal fear of a repetition of the carnage of the Second World War permeates and shapes the European sense of vulnerability. Societies crave for reassurance against the perils of war as such. Nuclear war appears to be a greater danger than the political ambitions or misjudgments which could unleash it. The welfare state and discontent with it are transformed into fears about the possible emergence of a warfare state. A growing fear of war coincides with an economic crisis which exacerbates the choices between guns and butter, between social welfare and insurance against warfare, between deterrence and detente. At the same time the educational revolution has produced a larger section of society which is interested in national and international politics and which is seeking participation in decision-making at this level. It enables many to engage in what Ronald Inglehart calls 'elite-challenging' as opposed to 'elite-directed' activities.[1] Public oppos-

85

ition is spearheaded by 'counter-elites'. The intelligentsia is capable of challenging the details of policy-making, thus forcing governments to engage in esoteric discourse which is beyond the comprehension of the ordinary citizen. Basic purposes and irreducible dilemmas get lost in a cloud of technical ornaments of a baroque quality which increases the sense of alienation and anger.

The emergence of single issue political movements constitutes a challenge to the established institutions for the integration of competing interests and objectives in our societies, such as parliaments, political parties and governments. The 'peace movement' contains an institutional challenge in addition to questioning the premises and priorities of Western defence. It constitutes an example of expressive politics, enabling and encouraging citizens to express concerns and attitudes towards the policies of governments which must be moved by instrumental concerns about the consequences, costs and risks of specific courses of action, about the relationships between ends and means and the constraints on options imposed by competing interests and wills. Nevertheless expressive political movements are often needed in order to foster realignment of the priorities and calculations between society and the state. We are not confronted, however, by a simple phenomenon of the 'people' against 'establishments'. Popular movements are spearheaded by counter-elites, by the would-be establishments and sometimes by members of former establishment elites. The new intelligentsia appears to harbour a certain proclivity for 'conformist opposition'.

The public argument is shaped to some degree by a decline in the perceived legitimacy of hierarchical authority and reduced confidence in established institutions. The younger generations of Europe have never experienced invasion and war in their homelands. There is a discontinuity of experience across the generations in Europe. We should note also that class voting is declining in Western democracies. Support for parties of the left may increasingly be coming from the middle classes. Their claims to political participation will frequently derive from an issue-oriented approach rather than a desire to support a given group of leaders. The issues on which the counter-elites will mobilize are difficult to bargain over as they do not have the incremental nature of economic issues, but tend instead to assume a moralistic tone making compromise very difficult. The nuclear weapons issue is a key case in point.

This paper does not attempt to analyze the sociology of the peace movement nor its political basis and purposes. The movement encompasses a variety of views and prescriptions. Some ambiguity is necessary in order for the movement to stay together. The protest is to some extent inchoate. Nevertheless, it does represent and reflect a broadened concern in our societies about the dangers of nuclear war. The intensity of its expression may oscillate, but the basic concern is likely to persist and re-emerge in connection with specific decisions concerning nuclear weapons in the defence posture of the West. It is easy to attack the peace movement for being one-sided, for focussing on Western decisions and actions while being rather muted in its reaction to Soviet arms policy. However, we should accept that the peace movement is now part of the political culture of Western democracies. It is part of our political process and will direct its energies and attention towards affecting decisions to which it can obtain some access. (Incidentally, it should be noted that policy-makers and analysts in the West frequently approach defence problems with little attention to how the recommended actions may be perceived 'on the other side of the hill'. All evidence suggests that ethnocentric propensities are even more pronounced and pervasive on the Soviet side).

The defence postures in the West and their associated doctrines have evolved incrementally through the post-war era. It would be surprising if the accumulated results of a long and varied history were coherent and consistent, and we can claim no such surprises. It is difficult, moreover, to establish criteria and yardsticks for measuring effectiveness and consistency. Defence postures serve tasks beyond that of containing the aspirations of would be adversaries. In coalitions they become currencies for the management of political relations, for the marking of commitments, and preservation of options for future change. Particular weapons and deployments assume symbolic significance which affects the cost of whatever reconfiguration is necessary to enhance credible deterrence. Defence postures and doctrines are relevant, in other words, to shaping the conditions of the political order, present as well as future. Such impacts and relationships are, however, rather abstract and conjectural. Complexity, contingency and uncertainty are hard to convey and still harder for the concerned citizen to fathom. The physical realities and prospective horrors of nuclear devastation seem more tangible and real. In addition, political perspectives and priorities may differ within coalitions of states, as indeed they are likely to do within the Western Alliance in the years ahead. Continued domestic strife over the shaping of defence policy may amplify and exacerbate political differences within the West, particularly with regard to policies towards the East. There are strong reasons therefore to undertake a basic reconsideration of the whole structure of Western defence with a view to restoring broad domestic and inter-Alliance consensus. In addition there are important considerations of strategy which point towards the need for changes in the posture and doctrine of Western defence. Some of the key issues which relate to the structure and purposes of the nuclear posture will now be examined.

Shifts in the Nuclear Posture

The following discussion will lead to three normative propositions concerning the shifts which *ought* to take place in the Western nuclear posture as a result of restructuring and possibly by negotiated agreement with the East:

- The *size* of the nuclear arsenals (both in terms of warheads and delivery systems) should be markedly reduced.
- The *pressures for early use* of nuclear weapons should be markedly reduced.
- The *reliance* on nuclear weapons should be markedly reduced.

The basis for these propositions will be developed with regard to strategic nuclear forces, battlefield nuclear weapons and intermediate range nuclear weapons respectively. The changes needed derive from the evolution of the arsenals and deployments over the last twenty years, and particularly from the changes in the relative capabilities between East and West and in the present and prospective weapon technologies.

The issues will be dealt with conceptually rather than technically, although it must be recognized that technological and operational feasibility will constrain implementation of the basic reforms which are proposed. It is necessary, however, to create a conceptual framework for a consideration of the defence posture rather than having the latter be driven by available technology. Such an approach may suggest priorities also with respect to technological development. Furthermore, while declaratory policies serve important functions in projecting intentions and shaping expectations, they will be but empty shells unless they are buttressed by changes in the posture which emphasize the intentions conveyed. The discussions of a no first use of nuclear weapons policy has been unsatisfactory so far because, to the degree that it has focussed on changes in the existing posture, it has dealt almost exclusively with the perceived need to strengthen options for conventional defence and left out of consideration the changes which would be needed also in the nuclear posture.

In dealing with changes in the nuclear posture it is important to distinguish between three basic avenues of approach: negotiated agreements on arms reduction and limitation (arms control); national (and Alliance) defence policy; and confidence-building measures (CBM). A new balance has to be struck in order to develop a viable system of management which is able to exploit synergistic relationships among the three approaches.[2] Nations have been trying to do too much through arms-control negotiations, engaging in negotiations about the detailed shaping of defence postures. In future, negotiations should aim to establish broad parameters of constraints, primarily through agreements on force reductions and qualitative limitations rather than provisions for detailed regulation. The parties should be left free to mix forces within the negotiated parameters. Negotiations have tended to have a built-in political bias in favour of symmetry, and detailed regulation has implied symmetry in detail. Such agreements are difficult to negotiate and to verify and they tend to produce a great deal of controversy due to the variety of assessments which detailed regulation stimulates. The approach collides also with the different traditions, service interests, technological choices and geographical circumstances which shape the deterrent postures which states adopt. It tends also to increase pressures for matching the forces of the adversary and to aim for high ceilings. The detailed structuring of defence postures should be the task of prudent defence policy. Such policies should be enlightened by a practice of mutual restraint and by recognition of the perceptions and conditions of the other side. CBM may be viewed as the connecting link between national defence policies and negotiated arms-control agreements.[3]

The Strategic Nuclear Posture

The size of the American strategic missile force was essentially determined early in the Kennedy Administration. We do not know how the Soviet force levels were defined and to what extent those definitions were influenced by American decisions. The American levels were the result of political compromise rather than the derivation of 'an internally consistent strategy and compatible targeting plans'.[4] Doctrine, however, provided an *ex post facto* rationalization for prior decisions concerning size, and provided a framework for combating pressures for expansion.

It is commonly believed that the Soviet Union and the United States have been engaged in an accelerating strategic arms race. This particular belief is incompatible with the facts.[5] The size of the US strategic forces is smaller today than at the end of the 1950s when it included almost 1,500 medium bombers of the B-47 variety, a delivery vehicle which was MIRVed in the sense that each aircraft carried several nuclear bombs each of which could be directed to separate targets. The number of nuclear warheads in the American nuclear stockpile has actually decreased by twenty-five per cent over the last

fifteen years while the total megatonnage has dropped by a factor of four. While the US nuclear stockpile decreased by some 6,000 warheads, the Soviet stockpile reportedly grew by some 8,000, causing the overall Soviet stockpile to exceed the American. Still the size of the total stockpiles on both sides is awesome and it includes some 24,000 weapons on the American side alone. It can legitimately be asked if deterrence requires such enormous destructive potential or if it could not be assured at substantially lower levels.

The size of the strategic forces must reflect a variety of considerations, including such factors as expected reliability, survivability, penetrability, targeting policy and target structure. The basic considerations revolve around the concept of deterrence: how to relate the size and shape of strategic nuclear forces to the task of dissuading a would-be adversary from undertaking specific actions. Deterrence, as has often been noted, is basically a psychological phenomenon. It is not susceptible to precise calculation. Any quantified expressions of how much is enough for deterrence are at best tools for analysis in planning force postures. It is possible to calculate the marginal utility of additional forces for accomplishing a given mission. However, any quantified expression of the destruction which is postulated to deter is basically arbitrary. Deterrence must inevitably reduce to the question about who is to persuade whom not to do what in which set of circumstances.[6]

Technology will influence calculations about the relative effectiveness of weapon systems and identification of potential options for deployment or employment of weapons but the political calculus will remain intractable. The dilemmas are awesome and inescapable. It is very hard to imagine any American or Soviet leader being persuaded that a nuclear war could now be won with 'acceptable' damage. Political leaders know from experience and by instinct that something always goes wrong and, precisely because things may go wrong, they cannot commit the future of their nations to an unqualified presumption that deterrence will not break down. Here we confront the basic dilemma of choices between 'assured destruction', 'controlled response' and 'war-fighting capability', the choices that governments make and which influence the size of their forces.

The notion of assured destruction has a deceptive clarity and neatness. The problem of deterrence is reduced to being able to confront a would-be adversary with an ability to retaliate in an unacceptably destructive manner with high confidence after having been attacked. Admittedly the detailed questions of design and planning are not easy. The survival of sufficient forces for retaliation has to be assured, it cannot be assumed. Choices must be made concerning warning, dispersal, protection and command and control. However, basically it is not possible to determine how much assured destruction will assure deterrence. In most instances a reasonable chance of having to suffer but a fraction of the destruction which has been established as a planning objective would suffice. The problem is, however, that choices are unlikely to present themselves very neatly in terms of retaliating or not retaliating. Decisions are likely to be more incremental and cumulative than that. They could come at the end of a process which narrows the alternatives and creates almost irresistible momentum; accidents and miscalculation may trigger and channel the momentum. Governments therefore cannot ignore the question of what to do if deterrence fails. As a minimum they should invest in capabilities for reflection, negotiation and eventual termination short of absolute catastrophe. Responses have to be controlled and measured rather than constitute simply reflexive wrath. However, the ability to withhold action and to tailor the response to circumstances carries on its back the temptation to go further and develop capacities for conducting extensive limited nuclear war campaigns as a matter of deliberate policy, including first-strike options. The question is again one of deciding how much is enough and to be able to cut off at a level of ambition which is clearly on the side of prudential insurance against the breakdown of deterrence and not on the side of an open-ended chase of a war-winning posture. The dilemmas are real and troublesome. They must be resolved not only in the abstract through intellectual analysis; choices must be made which will have sufficient resilience against pressures for re-

duction and addition in the policy-making processes. They must be viewed also from the point of view of the perceptions of allies and adversaries.

Domestic Support for Strategic Deterrence
What choices are likely to command domestic support? Any answers to that question must necessarily be conjectural and value-loaded. One assessment may be summarized in the following way: a simple posture and doctrine of assured destruction is not a viable choice. Public confidence in the ability of governments to do their job has been declining and scepticism is likely to persist, even from that perspective which equates the avoidance of war with the promise of massive destruction and which seems risky in the extreme. If defence is associated with the purpose of effecting large-scale destruction, it will remain a highly controversial aspect of public policy. The deliberate targeting of cities, a posture which holds citizens as hostages for the good behaviour of their governments, will not and should not receive broad social support. There is a difference between accepting the possibility of large-scale destruction as a consequence of war and accepting its deliberate creation as a legitimate purpose of policy in the event of war.

The very idea of mutual assured destruction is abhorrent and inconsistent with even a rudimentary ethical perspective with respect to the purposes of statecraft and the international security dilemma in the nuclear age. It ignores the many ways in which wars may break out, ways which are beyond deterrence or on the margins thereof. One could agree with Fred C. Ikle who has observed: 'The jargon of American strategic analysis works like a narcotic. It dulls our sense of moral outrage about the tragic confrontation of nuclear arsenals, primed and constantly perfected to unleash widespread genocide. It fosters a current smug complacence regarding the soundness and stability of mutual deterrence. It blinds us to the fact that our method for preventing nuclear war rests on a form of warfare universally condemned since the Dark Ages – the mass killings of hostages'.[7]

The first order of business then is to move away from the distorted dogma that deterrence must be based on a threatened response involving the mass killing of people. Furthermore, there appears to be no reason why the response has to be prompt and instant. That presumption points towards the logical perversity of 'launch on warning', when enormous political decisions have in effect been delegated to machines. Instead I would argue for a doctrine of deterrence based on 'adequate retaliation' and 'assured reflection'. There is no absolute way to determine what measure of retaliation would be adequate. Therefore flexibility must be built into the strategic force posture, allowing the political authorities to make that judgment concretely. Clearly a capacity for adequate retaliation requires survivable and controllable forces but the absolute size of the forces could be substantially lower than at present.

The second element in a preferred doctrine is based on the notion that deterrence may fail in spite of the best attempts to assure it. In that event the military posture should be designed to support deliberate attempts to avoid and limit destruction. Therefore the concept of 'assured destruction' should be replaced by a concept of 'assured reflection', enabling governments to assess the situation *after* the outbreak of war and to hold and measure responses with a view to terminating the war. A posture of 'assured reflection' will include a highly reliable system of command, control and communication (C³) and a strategic nuclear force which is sufficiently invulnerable to pre-emptive immobilization to pose with high confidence the threat of second strike retaliation, and sufficiently accurate to be launched against military targets, but not necessarily against hardened missile silos. Such a force could be significantly smaller than existing forces but bringing down the levels requires agreement between the United States and the Soviet Union for reasons of domestic politics as well as because of the impact on survivability of substantial numerical disparities.

Strategic Posture and Force Levels
The current round of negotiations on the reduction and limitation of strategic nuclear forces should therefore try to shape a more stable balance at substantially reduced levels.

Deep cuts of some thirty to fifty per cent would amount to a salient reversal of the trends of the last decades and contribute to the recreation of public confidence in the commitment and ability of governments to avoid the trap of an open-ended competition leading to constantly changing and generally expanding arsenals of strategic weapons. Stability can be enhanced by a combination of explicit provisions and implicit incentives. Unfortunately, the 'MIRV genie' is out of the bottle. However, agreed limitations on the total number of warheads are likely to diminish incentives for the further fractionation of the payload of each missile out of concern for the ability of the delivery vehicles to survive a first strike. Limitations on the total number of delivery vehicles, combined with freedom-to-mix, are likely to increase incentives to move missiles to sea, particularly as such missiles acquire accuracies which enable them to threaten fixed land-based missiles. Dispersal in smaller submarines rather than increased concentration of missiles in large submarines may make sense, in operational as well as in economic terms. It is part of the established wisdom that strategic forces should not be concentrated in one basket; different systems should present an adversary with separate sets of uncertainties. However, the concept of a 'strategic triad' sometimes appears to be designed less with a view to enhance deterrence than in order to protect a multi-service solution to its maintenance. Apparent simplicity of design will improve the chances of gaining public confidence; conspicuous complexity is likely to stir concerns about malfunctions and fears of the tyranny by machines over man as has been shown by the controversies in the United States over successor systems to the *Minuteman* ICBM. Sea-based systems, however, pose particular problems of command and control which consequently require close examination.

The posture must be compatible, of course, with a strategic doctrine which is credible and supportable. In the past many have confused the *de facto* existence of an 'assured destruction posture' with the attainment of a desirable and stable conclusion of human endeavour. We may be temporarily trapped, but to elevate such entrapment to a permanent principle of international relations is short-sighted at best and seems certain to stimulate desperate attempts to escape. There are too many ways that things may go wrong. History does not warrant the placing of confidence in the indefinite functioning of particular arrangements for nuclear deterrence, even if these arrangements have proved themselves more robust than initially expected. An assured destruction posture tends to focus public attention on the destructive horror of nuclear war, causing rejection rather than viable proposals for modification. The state becomes associated with unacceptable destruction and governments must be concerned about the consequences of a break-down of deterrence. There must be a serious problem of credibility during crises if the only alternative to surrender is self-destruction. Immobility and fear are not likely to contribute to resolution or defusing of crises or permit gracious disengagement from confrontation.

A Seminar on Strategy

A posture of 'assured reflection' would certainly carry with it the danger of being extended to encompass a variety of limited nuclear war-fighting options. However, acceptance of rough parity and an active pursuit of force reductions should contribute to the containment of such impulses. In addition, mutual confidence between the United States and the Soviet Union could be enhanced by the institution of a systematic dialogue about strategic doctrine and postures. We are not arguing for the negotiation of common strategic doctrines but rather for the establishment of a Seminar on Strategy, with the appropriate acronym of SOS, which would enable the parties to explain the rationales behind their defence postures and to voice any apprehensions which may exist about the motives of the other party and the implications of its policies. Hence, the SOS could presumably serve to alleviate fears about the pernicious consequences of specific choice and make both sides more sensitive to the concerns and outlooks of each other. The SOS could take place within the framework of the Standing Consultative Commission (SCC) which has been established in connection with the SALT I Agreement.

Extended Deterrence

What would be the consequences of such an approach for extended deterrence? Threatening to blow up the cities of your adversary in order to protect your allies will always beg questions of credibility and proportionality. In future, deterrence is likely to be viewed less as a result of the certain prospects of unacceptable destruction than as a result of substantial residual uncertainties concerning the progress of events if the major nuclear powers should clash at points of vital interest.

Extended deterrence in its simple form was based on strategic superiority. Real strategic superiority is for all practical purposes now unattainable. Extended deterrence therefore must be based more on the projection of common political purposes and an ability to resist aggression at the point of challenge than on the threat to initiate strategic nuclear war. In order to maintain public support and confidence in Alliance defence in the years ahead, a viable conventional defence option is needed, permitting European societies to become real subjects with respect to their own protection rather than the objects for threats of nuclear destruction. Part of the reasons for the present malaise is the perception that control over the destinies of European society has been abdicated to Presidents of the United States and the Soviet Union whose political acumen and wisdom do not invariably inspire trust and confidence. Indeed the differences in political style and culture between the United States and Western Europe will constitute a heavy burden on an alliance relationship which makes defence depend primarily on decisions about nuclear response in Washington. Such an arrangement is likely to stimulate the propensity which General Bernard W. Rogers (currently Supreme Allied Commander, Europe) has warned against, that of placing the super-powers on the same moral plane and at the same time applying double standards to the two.[8]

Battlefield Nuclear Weapons

Nuclear weapons are not, of course, only deployed in the territories of the United States and the Soviet Union. In the present analysis, however, the French and British nuclear forces will be excluded. The analysis will concentrate on the nuclear force posture of the United States. The number of theatre nuclear weapons in Europe reached a maximum of 7,000 during the Kennedy Administration. It has recently been reduced by 1,000, primarily by the withdrawal of warheads for obsolete *Honest John* short-range missiles. The relationship between the present force posture and NATO defence doctrine is both tenuous and controversial. Even after the withdrawal of the *Honest John* warheads, more than half of NATO's theatre nuclear weapons are associated with systems which have a range of under 30 km, namely nuclear artillery and very short-range missiles. About one third are associated with medium-range (150–1,500 km) systems, primarily nuclear bombs for dual-capable aircraft. The balance is made up of nuclear munitions for air defence missiles, atomic demolition munitions (ADM) and anti-submarine warfare (ASW) weapons. The nuclear munitions are stored in Special Munition Sites (SMS) of which there are some 90 when the air defence sites are excluded. Some 20,000 US and Allied personnel are probably associated with the SMS. Most of the sites are rather vulnerable to attacks even with conventional munitions, and the short warning time which is likely to prevail makes dispersal of the nuclear munitions very difficult. Considerable attention has been devoted to improving the safety, security and survivability (S³) of the SMS. However, the measures are often mutually exclusive. For example, a particular measure designed to improve safety could result in reduced survivability.

The functions of NATO's theatre nuclear forces (TNF) have varied over time; some have been added and their relative importance has changed. They include: deterrence of large-scale conventional attack; compensation for inferiority in conventional forces; deterrence of the first use of nuclear weapons by the other side; and the provision of links to American strategic nuclear forces.

The Employment of Battlefield Weapons
The doctrine for nuclear employment is based on the strategy of flexible response as embodied in NATO document MC 14/3 encompassing the triple functions of direct defence, deliberate escalation and general nuclear response. Employment is constrained by agreed political guidelines beginning with the Athens Guidelines of 1962, the Guidelines Concerning Consultation Procedures of 1969, Guidelines for Initial Tactical Use of 1970, the ADM Guidelines from 1970, and the 1972 Guidelines Concerning the Theatre Nuclear Strike-Role Concept.[9] Nuclear release has to be authorized by the American President (and that applies to all nuclear weapons which are deployed to Europe under Programmes of Co-operation (POC), in consultation with Allies in the North Atlantic Council (NAC) according to agreed procedures. Once a 'package' of theatre nuclear weapons has been released, its tactical use is controlled by a corps commander, sub-package employment can be delegated to divisional level, but, generally, not further down.[10] A corps package reportedly could, but need not, consist of between 100–200 nuclear weapons and the time-frame for employment may be restricted to from several hours to a day.[11] According to American doctrine, five general categories of constrained theatre nuclear employment may be distinguished: demonstration; limited defensive use; restricted battle area use; extended battle area use; and theatrewide use.[12]

SACEUR's Nuclear Operation Policy (NOP) includes prepared selective employment plans as well as a general strike plan in co-ordination with the American Single Integrated Operation Plan (SIOP). Battlefield weapons are not included in the prepared attack options. It is significant to note, however, that NATO has not managed to agree on guidelines for follow-on use of nuclear weapons if a first attempt to communicate NATO's intentions through a controlled demonstrative detonation does not suceed in persuading the adversary to halt hostilities. Discussion on this topic has proceeded for more than ten years. The failure to agree reflects some of the basic political dilemmas and difficulties with the current nuclear posture in Europe. Operational plans for follow-on use do, however, exist.

The present posture gives cause for concern from the point of view of public acceptability as well as operational effectiveness and reliability. The heavy reliance on short-range battlefield weapons in forward areas is inconsistent with the objective of reducing pressures for early use of nuclear weapons. On the contrary, it is likely to generate precisely such pressures as the nuclear assets in forward locations may be in danger of being overrun by advancing enemy forces. Tactical situations may thus come to exercise strong pressures on the political decisions concerning the conduct of a war. Once the nuclear threshold has been crossed, the possibility of limiting a nuclear war in Europe with current arsenals seems remote in the extreme. Hence, it is arguable that current defence arrangements fail to provide plausible protection.

The dilemmas are many and complex. Generally speaking it is easier to employ theatre nuclear weapons early rather than late, due to the inevitable confusion on the battlefield. Command, control and communication will constitute formidable problems. Furthermore forward defence based on short-range battlefield weapons forces NATO into rapid reactions with imperfect knowledge against a very complex and dynamic target cycle. Rigid control may limit close-in use, generating pressures for delegation. Furthermore, it is going to be very difficult to slow the battle tempo and enemy advance by attrition only; such employment does not change the shape of the battlefield.

NATO's present reliance on nuclear weapons involves a serious danger of political immobilization in a crisis or in war. The problem has been graphically depicted by Fred C. Ikle:

In the context of a conventional war, it would take but one nuclear detonation somewhere – a 'warning shot' or an accident – to propel the horror of nuclear destruction into public consciousness in every Western country. And if a large-scale conventional war in Central Europe broke out, it might not even require the emotional impact of a nuclear detonation to bring into consciousness the terror of nuclear war. Enormous pressures would be mobilized and brought to bear on government leaders – through parliaments, the media and other channels – to avoid at almost any price the risk of large-scale nuclear war.[13]

It should be recalled here that it is NATO strategy to use nuclear weapons for demonstration in the event of a decision to use them first. It is not at all clear that such employment would demonstrate resolve as much as consternation, nor that the effect would be pressure on the enemy to halt rather than on NATO governments to seek accommodation. Again one could agree with Fred C. Ikle who observed that in a crisis 'the long-standing reliance of NATO governments on the nuclear back-up to a conventional defence would suddenly turn from an asset to a liability . . . Far from bolstering a full-scale conventional defence, NATO's nuclear threat of first use could turn inward to unravel the Alliance in the hour of crisis'.[14]

'No First Use'

The option of a 'no-first-use' pledge has recently received increased public attention. Such proposals clearly capture a mood and indicate a desirable direction of change but the changes which are needed in the nuclear posture for such declarations to be convincing have not been sufficiently examined.[15]

A 'no-first-use' commitment could serve to widen and strengthen the fire-break between conventional and nuclear weapons. It could reduce expectations that armed conflict would inevitably escalate to the nuclear level. It is arguable that such changed expectations would weaken deterrence. However, the impact need not be very significant. Residual uncertainties would be very large and no party could be confident that it could push the other against the wall without causing him to abrogate his commitment. The importance would lie in the direction of the change involved – reduced reliance on nuclear weapons, particularly on their early use.

As has been observed above, extended deterrence can no longer be based on the assumption of American strategic superiority. Hence coupling between theatre forces and strategic forces becomes more complex. It should be recalled also that, during the 1970s, the Soviet Union eliminated NATO's advantage in theatre nuclear forces. It is likely, as has been argued above, that a commitment to first use could unravel the Alliance in an extreme situation, irrespective of the coupling to

American strategic forces. Again one should avoid treating the issues in black and white, as 'either-or' questions, because residual uncertainties would be enormous and the continued existence of powerful nuclear forces would certainly affect the propensity to push to the limit.

The change in doctrine which is involved in a 'no-first-use' pledge is not in fact as large as all that. NATO has already moved away from a 'first-use' doctrine to a 'not-necessarily-first-use' doctrine. The difficulties in agreeing on guidelines for follow-on use after a demonstration shot indicate that it may be very difficult indeed for the Alliance to agree on first use in war. However, the posture in Europe is such as to exercise strong pressures for early, and possibly massive use, of nuclear weapons. Any change in declaratory policy should therefore be associated with some basic restructuring of the Alliance's theatre nuclear posture. It is probable that a restructuring of that posture should be associated with a further shift in doctrine to 'no early first use', recognizing that the definition of 'early' may be ambiguous but, more importantly, in order to allow more time for consideration of the changes needed in the conventional force posture in order to accommodate reduced reliance in nuclear response and lend credence to a 'no-first-use' intention. We are not arguing in favour of a negotiated agreement with the Soviet Union about 'no-first-use' of nuclear weapons. Such agreements could permit contentious claims of *droits de regard* in respect of the defence arrangements on both sides which are unlikely to contribute to East–West tranquillity or domestic harmony. Formal pledges could also stir up differences and tensions within the Alliance which could possibly be contained by moving instead towards an implicit pledge as a result of restructuring of the theatre nuclear posture so as to reduce the pressure for *early* use. In any event, a formal pledge must follow rather than precede a process of restructuring.

The changes in the theatre nuclear posture (intermediate-range nuclear forces will be treated separately) which should be implemented in order to permit a shift towards 'no-(early) first use' of nuclear weapons by NATO include the following:

- withdrawal of battlefield nuclear weapons from forward areas in Europe;[16]
- reduction by several thousand of the nuclear battlefield weapons in Europe;[17]
- cessation of nuclear air defence systems (the existence of such systems stimulates pressures for the early use of nuclear weapons and the pre-delegation of authority to fire them. NATO is currently in the process of reducing reliance on nuclear air defences. The successor system to *Nike-Hercules*, the *Patriot*, will be conventional only);
- withdrawal of ADM. While such weapons have not been 'prechambered' in Europe, their existence could involve pressures for early deployment in order to stop conventional offensives and, in addition, once they had been emplaced they would impose a rigidity on operations which could lead to rapid escalation;
- a stand-down of quick-reaction–alert forces. A small number of aircraft and *Pershing* I missiles are specifically withheld for rapid nuclear strike missions and are permanently loaded with nuclear munitions, ready for instant launching;
- re-evaluation of the commitment of dual-capable aircraft to nuclear roles. The ambiguity posed by dual-capable aircraft could provide incentives for extensive pre-emptive actions by the adversary. The need for enhanced conventional air-power combined with the vulnerability of tactical aircraft to nuclear or conventional pre-emption suggest that stability might improve with a reordering of missions, relying on missiles for nuclear strikes over medium ranges. More importantly, improved conventional munitions may substitute increasingly for nuclear munitions.

The Implication of Re-structuring
This proposed restructuring of NATO's theatre nuclear posture in Europe should be implemented unilaterally as part of an Alliance defence policy designed to bolster the firebreak between conventional and nuclear weapons and to reduce pressures for early use of nuclear weapons, including pre-emption by the adversary. Desirable changes in NATO's nuclear deployments should not become hostage to Soviet consent to reciprocation.

It should be emphasized that neither the purpose nor the result of the changes proposed would be to make Europe 'safe for conventional war'. Indeed the current discussion of nuclear weapons has reminded us that the overall European concern is that of preventing war of any kind in Europe. Modern warfare is enormously destructive; the pictures from Beirut in the summer of 1982 carried convincing proof of that assertion. Europeans have in part resisted building up their conventional defences to higher levels out of fear that it could indicate a readiness to accept the consequences of a major conventional war in Europe. However, the social circumstances in Western Europe as well as basic changes in the Soviet–American strategic nuclear balance necessitate a reconsideration of earlier positions. Credibility in the 1980s requires the initiation of changes involving reduced reliance on nuclear weapons.

Planning assumptions in NATO have been largely separated from assumptions about how a war might actually break out. It is difficult to discuss the possibilities for fragmentation in a crisis but the issues cannot be assumed away. A real crisis will test the ability of the Alliance to respond to ambiguous warning. The present posture is not well suited to provide the basis for unified responses, nor can heavy reliance on early use of nuclear weapons provide a basis for repeatable responses to ambiguous signals of heightened danger. In addition the present nuclear posture may prove destabilizing in wartime due to points of vulnerability which may invite Soviet pre-emption. Incentives for Soviet pre-emption may even increase with the expectation of a NATO resort to early use of nuclear weapons.

It makes little sense, of course, to consider the theatre nuclear problems in Europe separately from the conventional defence tasks. Somewhat different perceptions exist with respect to how much additional effort is needed in order to create a viable conventional defence option. However, its feasibility is not questioned provided the resources are made available.[18] That, of course, will always be a key problem, particularly in a period of economic difficulties. This Paper is limited to considering the nuclear posture. The threat of nuclear weapons has led the Soviet Union to disperse and deeply echelon their forces. The result is that greater time is required for second and third echelon forces to follow the initial thrust. We must consider therefore whether the threat of the first Alliance use of nuclear weapons is not needed in order to maintain a high risk of the massing of forces. Again the answer would seem to be that the Soviet Union could never rely on NATO's abstaining from resort to nuclear weapons if faced with a massive and unambiguous Soviet offensive. It should be recalled that this Paper has not argued for the denuclearization of NATO's defences, only for a major reduction in numbers and a restructuring which would involve the preferential withdrawal of battlefield systems. It should be considered whether any nuclear artillery is needed and if so how much is required simply in order to impose desirable constraints on the offensive operations of an adversary. The emphasis should probably be on a *small* force of highly survivable and controllable theatre nuclear systems of medium range, always recognizing that survivability for land-based systems in Europe is inherently difficult to attain. It is more attainable, however, if it is fixed as a characteristic in the design of the weapon system beforehand rather than treated simply as an additional requirement to be met after a decision has been taken in favour of deployment.

A shift in the direction of a 'no-first-use' posture is usually predicated on a commitment to improve conventional defences. Such improvements are clearly desirable and restructuring, redeployment and re-equipment of NATO's conventional forces should be considered and implemented. However it is less clear that reliance on 'early-first-use' of nuclear weapons makes sense under present conditions nor that early resort to nuclear weapons can compensate for conventional inferiority. In fact it has never been demonstrated how NATO could defeat an attack by nuclear weapons if it was not able to defeat it by conventional force.

The ambiguities which exist about the relationships between the deployment of theatre nuclear weapons in Europe and NATO's employment doctrine may have served to avoid damaging disagreements in the past but the nuclear posture and associated dilemmas have now become a source of public restiveness. Ambiguity can create a serious lack of confidence. In addition we have to be concerned about the ability of the Alliance to respond to a broad variety of possible contingencies in the complex world of the 1980s. Heavy reliance on early use of nuclear weapons is likely to increase tension and disagreements within the Alliance in the event of ambiguous warning and limited conflict of uncertain nature and scope. A viable conventional defence, on the other hand, should bolster the ability of the Alliance to cope with military challenges. If such an effort should not receive social support, our societies are even less likely to support decisions to initiate the use of nuclear weapons, from which they would suffer inconceivable destruction.

In order to enhance conventional defence more effort should go into improving the firepower of in-place forces, improving and diversifying the capacity for mobilization, expanding territorial defence forces and into developing an effective capacity for holding second and third echelon forces at risk. It should be noted here that there is a difference between improved conventional capabilities and a conventional defence option. Furthermore, improvements which are designed to fill gaps in the existing conventional force posture may not coincide with the measures which would be undertaken if the goal is that of shifting emphasis from reliance on nuclear to conventional means. It should be possible, however, to identify and exploit synergistic effects. Adoption of the 'Airland Battle' concept, with its heavier emphasis on mobility as opposed to a linear defence orientation with emphasis on attrition, may enable NATO to be more imaginative and effective in its defence but reduced reliance on nuclear weapons will tend to increase NATO's reliance on the safe passage of reinforcements across the Atlantic, which will in turn increase the interdependence of the Central Front and the NATO's Northern Flank.

Intermediate-range Nuclear Forces (INF)

The INF issue has occupied centre stage in East–West relations and in the domestic controversy over defence policy in Western Europe in the last few years[19]. It involves fundamental issues of political balance and equity in Europe.

It is true that the Soviet Union has 'traditionally' deployed a rather substanial continental-range nuclear strike capability against Western Europe. However, the SS-20 should not be considered solely as a replacement for obsolescent SS-4 and SS-5 missiles. It should be considered in the context in which its deployment was initiated. That context was essentially different from that of the 1950s and 1960s as the Soviet Union had achieved essential equivalence, or parity, in intercontinental-range nuclear strike systems during the 1970s. The arrival of parity was formally recorded in SALT. The SS-20 deployment coincided also with growing concerns about the relative vulnerability of land-based strategic missile forces. Moreover, the SS-20 did not fit into the previous context of a 'balance of imbalances' so it raised several basic questions with respect to Soviet long-range intentions in Europe, about the purposes of the Soviet Union's continued investment in special capabilities for holding Europe as a nuclear hostage. In other words, the role and position of the Soviet Union in the political order in Europe was at issue, as was the position of Europe in the context of super-power relations.

If the challenge inherent in the SS-20 deployment had not been met, it is arguable that the widening asymmetry between the Soviet Union and Western Europe in the broader context of super-power parity could have a stronger, more lasting and even more polarizing impact on the domestic politics of the states in Western Europe than that which followed in the wake of the dual-track decision in NATO in 1979. Almost all the states of Western Europe, it should be recalled, are *capable* of producing nuclear weapons. If unattended to, the SS-20 could also have given rise to new tensions within the Western Alliance concerning the credibility and efficacy of extended deterrence.

The political issues were compounded by the special characteristics of the SS-20 and by the coincidental deployment of a new generation of short- and medium-range nuclear systems by the Soviet Union. In addition to having improved accuracy and multiple war-heads (MIRV), the SS-20 maintains a much higher state of readiness than the SS-4/-5 (a set-up time of about an hour compared to more than a day). Hence, it provides options for rapid attack in support of military operations. The number of special munition sites and major airfields in Western Europe is not very large compared to the number of SS-20 warheads deployed. Moreover, the SS-20 seemed to fit into a broader process of force modernization designed to provide an enhanced warfighting capacity.

Fundamentally, the issue at stake in the NATO decision on INF modernization was that of creating some symmetry of territorial vulnerability in Europe by weakening the sanctuary position of the Soviet Union *vis-à-vis* Western Europe.

The Soviet Union has in fact been caught applying double standards. On the one hand the Soviet Union seeks co-equal status as a super-power with the United States (The Khrushchevian task of catching up with and surpassing (*dognat' i peregnat'*) the rival super-power may have blinded the Kremlin to the European implications of certain weapon decisions). On the other hand she seeks acceptance as a major power within the European political order. Such acceptance, however, depends critically on reassuring Western Europe that the USSR does not have hegemonic aspirations. The political balance in Europe cannot be reduced to a simple derivation from the balance of deterrence between the US and the USSR. It depends on acceptance of the principle of the equality of states and the need for reciprocal restraint. Soviet insistence on including US Forward-Based Systems (FBS) in Europe in the INF negotiations because some of them in principle could reach Soviet territory, while refusing to include similar Soviet systems which threaten targets in Western Europe, illustrates the duality. From the point of view of Western Europe, Soviet forward-based missiles and aircraft of medium range could provide functional threat equivalents to SS-20 missiles and *Backfire* aircraft deployed to the Soviet rear. American sea-launched cruise missiles (SLCM) could produce similar problems for the Soviet Union. Hence a treaty on INF limitations would probably have to include agreement on collateral constraints to protect the Treaty against circumvention.

The NATO decision on INF modernization was motivated also by considerations relating to Alliance cohesion, such as the need to couple American strategic power more closely to the direct defence of Europe in the context of strategic parity and a broad build-up of Soviet theatre nuclear forces. It could be viewed also as a means of providing capacities for threatening Soviet second and third echelon ground forces in the event of a major attack in Europe. Such tasks, however, may perhaps be accomplished more credibly by modern conventional weapons.

The Zero Option
The zero option proposal for reciprocal reductions which has been put forward at Geneva is consistent with the proposition that the issues posed by INF are primarily *political* issues which relate to the structure of the political order in Europe. The precise calibration of that option must, of course, be determined through negotiations. The important consideration will be that Soviet levels should be drawn down considerably below the 1979 level and fixed by mutual agreement. The NATO numbers were never designed to match Soviet INF numbers.

It is arguable, of course, that the Soviet Union lacks strong incentives to bargain on the basis of an agreement involving substantial reductions in existing forces in return for NATO's abstaining from a deployment which may in any case be prevented by domestic opinion in Western Europe. The stakes are very high, however. Failure to carry through with deployment in the absence of concrete results from negotiations would cause a major crisis of confidence within the Western Alliance. Governments have much at stake in the decision and Soviet intransigence is likely to affect attitudes among the Western publics. A lost opportunity to turn the tide could change the climate of East–West competition in a manner which would be a real burden on and bring real risks to the Soviet Union in a period of serious economic constraints and a still unsettled succession. The simplicity and salient fairness of the Western position also constituted an advantage. However, that advantage would evaporate quickly if it came to be seen as a piece of propaganda and gamesmanship rather than as providing a serious negotiating platform.

The composition and scale of the INF deployment which was decided by NATO was designed to communicate defensive intentions. Cruise missiles are too slow-moving to constitute a first-strike threat against the Soviet Union. 108 *Pershing* IIs hardly constitute a first strike potential against Soviet strategic and intermediate-range forces. The flight time is, however, short (comparable to that of the SS-20 against targets in Western Europe) and it could constitute a threat to Soviet command and control installations. Their vulnerability could be reduced by hardening and dispersal, and by a negotiated agreement which eliminates or bounds the threat. In any event the idea of instant retaliation is unsettling in the extreme. We have a dangerous situation if a difference in warning time of some twenty-five minutes has a major impact on the Soviet response. It is possible that an INF agreement has to be constructed in phases, starting perhaps with an agreement involving a reduction of SS-20 to levels below the 1979 levels and a commitment to forego the deployment of *Pershing* II coupled to an agreement on the parameters of the second phase negotiations about substantial reductions in cruise missiles and comparable aircraft on both sides as well as the residual force of SS-4/-5 and SS-20 missiles. The phasing of the negotiations and the shape of the agreements need to be considered in conjunction with the phasing and shaping of an agreement about strategic arms reductions (START). British and French submarine-launched missile forces may be taken into account in START and the (relatively few) French land-based intermediate-range missiles in the second phase of the INF negotiations.

We should therefore be looking towards a negotiated outcome which essentially eliminates intermediate-range nuclear forces as a major determinant of the political order in Europe by establishing very low ceilings. Negotiations, like deployments, should be phased in order to permit the two sides gradually to knit a web of reciprocal restraints

with regard to the deployment of intermediate-range nuclear forces capable of reaching targets on the continent of Europe. That web would clearly have to extend also to cover the forward and seaward deployment of nuclear systems of shorter or similar range. It would seem important too to protect options for enhancing conventional capacities, or at least to identify them so as to be able to assess the costs of their abrogation. At the same time particular attention should be devoted to enhancing the survivability of *Pershing* II and GLCM in the event that it should prove impossible to negotiate a 'zero' solution.

The Broader Perspective

There is no escaping from the dilemmas posed by nuclear weapons. They do not lend themselves to disinvention but nor should they be accepted as 'just another weapon'. They are different. That difference is an important consideration in any responsible approach to force planning and the development of doctrine. They will always inspire awe and revulsion. Hence, nuclear deterrence will never be a popular aspect of modern statecraft. Nor should it be. But it is a necessary part of the burden of responsibility in our times. It is to be hoped that it will be but a temporary expedient in the history of mankind. It should never be considered a desirable end-point. Political organization and technology should, in the long run, enable man to transcend the almost arcane logic of nuclear deterrence.

It has been argued here that residual uncertainty has a considerable impact on deterrence, on the threat which implicitly leaves much to chance due to the limits of prediction and control, and this is a general feature of the predicament in the age of nuclear weapons. In force planning, attention must be paid to the size of the uncertainty. Deterrence will not work automatically, nor will it work invariably.

Some would contend that even a conditional intention to use nuclear weapons is as immoral as the use itself but as Geoffrey Dunstan, a noted theologian, has observed: 'The intention in possessing a nuclear "deterrent" force is *not* to use it, but to restrain a potential enemy from the first, provocative use. The *intention* is, by maintaining, a credible threat, to prevent any occasion for its use – to deter the other side from the first immoral act, the nuclear strike'[20]. Here is another argument in favour of moving towards a 'no-first-use' posture and for the adoption of a doctrine of 'assured reflection'. For, if deterrence should fail, we may not choose to copy the immoral act.

NOTES

[1]Ronald Inglehart, *The Silent Revolution: Changing Values and Political Styles Among Western Publics* (Princeton, N.Y.: Princeton University Press, 1977).

[2]For further elaboration see Johan Jørgen Holst, *Arms Control Revisited: An Exploratory Essay*, NUPI/R–63 (Oslo: Norwegian Institute of International Affairs, December 1981).

[3]For a discussion of CBM see Johan Jørgen Holst, *Confidence Building Measures: A Conceptual Framework* NUPI/N–253, Oslo, Norwegian Institute of International Affairs, September 1982.

[4]See Desmond Ball, *Politics and Force Levels: The Strategic Missile Program of the Kennedy Administration* (Berkeley, Los Angeles, London: University of California Press, 1980), p. 209.

[5]See Albert Wohlstetter, 'Racing Forward or Ambling Back?', *Survey*, (314) Summer/Autumn, 1976, pp. 163–217.

[6]The best discussion is still Ithiel de Sola Pool, *Deterrence as an Influence Process* (Cambridge, Mass: Center for International Studies, Massachusetts Institute of Technology, 1963).

[7]Fred Charles Ikle, *Can Nuclear Deterrence Last Out the Century?*, California Arms Control and Foreign Policy Seminar, January 1973, p.14.

[8]Speech by General Bernard W. Rogers, Supreme Allied Commander Europe, to the 35th Congress of the Inter-Allied Confederation of Reserve Officers in Washington, 9 August 1982.

[9]See *The North Atlantic Treaty Organization. Facts and Figures*, Tenth Edition, Brussels, NATO Information Service, Chapter 13, pp.152–4.

[10]John P. Rose, *The Evolution of U.S. Army Nuclear Doctrine, 1945–1980*, (Boulder, Colorado: Westview Press, 1980), p.175.

[11]*Ibid.*, p.172.

[12]*Ibid.*, p.170.

[13]Fred Charles Ikle, 'NATO's Nuclear Use: A Deepening Trap?' *Strategic Review*, Winter 1980, p.20.

[14]*Ibid.*

[15]For an early and systematic analysis see Richard H. Ullman, 'No First Use of Nuclear Weapons', *Foreign Affairs*, 50 (4) Spring 1972, pp. 669–83. The present debate was initiated with the publication of McGeorge Bundy, George F. Kennan, Robert S. McNamara and Gerard Smith, 'Nuclear Weapons and the Atlantic Alliance', *Foreign Affairs*, 60 (4) Spring 1982, pp. 735–68. A German response was presented in Karl Kaiser, George Leber, Alois Mertes and Franz-Josef Schulze, 'Nuclear Weapons and the Preservation of Peace', *Foreign Affairs*, 60 (5) Summer 1982, pp. 1,157–70. See also various exchanges in 'The Debate over No First Use', *Foreign Affairs*, 60 (5) Summer 1982, pp. 1,171–80. The most rigorous analysis to date is probably that by Fred C. Ikle, *op. cit.* in note 13.

[16]This recommendation was made by the 'Independent Commission on Disarmament and Security Issues'. See *Common Security: A Programme for Disarmament* (London: Pan Books, 1982), pp.146–9.

[17]This recommendation parallels that of Senator Sam Nunn (although his is explicitly predicated on prior agreement and the start of implementing measures to create a viable conventional defence). See *NATO: Can the Alliance be Saved?* Report of Senator Sam Nunn to the Committee on Armed Services, United States Senate, 97th Congress, 2nd Session, 13 May 1982, p.13.

[18]E.g., General Bernard W. Rogers, 'The Atlantic Alliance: Prescriptions for a Difficult Decade', *Foreign Affairs*, 60 (5) Summer 1982, pp. 1,145–56; 'Do you sincerely want to be non-nuclear?', *The Economist*, 284 (7248) 31 July 1982, pp. 30–32. John J. Mearsheimer, 'Why the Soviets Can't Win Quickly in Central Europe', *International Security*, 7 (1) Summer 1982, pp. 3–39, and Robert W. Komer, 'Is Conventional Defense of Europe Feasible?', Unpublished paper (Second draft 13 May 1982).

[19]This section is adapted from the author's article 'Arms Control in Europe: Towards a New Political Order', *Bulletin of Peace Proposals* 13 (2) 1982, pp. 81–9. See also Johan Jørgen Holst, 'The Future of East-West Relations: Some Policy Perspectives', *Naval War College Review*, (Forthcoming).

[20]G. R. Dunstan, 'Theological Method in the Deterrence Debate', In Geoffrey Goodwin (ed.), *Ethics and Nuclear Deterrence* (London: Croom Helm, 1982), p. 50.

Domestic Priorities and the Demands of Alliance:
An American Perspective

DAVID CALLEO

Vietnam and Watergate revived the old question of whether US domestic politics and priorities are compatible with her international role. Worsening economic conditions and rising military costs have kept the topic alive.

The subject remains many-sided and hard to grasp. Analytically, the distinction between foreign and domestic goals is often elusive. Many domestic aims depend closely upon a certain kind of international order. Alliances are almost inevitably enfeebled when principal members suffer from deteriorating and neglected domestic economic and social conditions. Prescribing the appropriate sum and balance of foreign and domestic claims, even when such claims are distinguishable, depends upon answering numerous complex questions: abroad, what are the nation's appropriate commitments and acceptable ways of meeting them? At home, what level of prosperity and welfare is needed to sustain a stable social and political system solidly committed to democratic values? At what point does diverting resources from civilian purposes undermine growth and long-range strength? Can the burden of external commitments be shared through the international economy? What are the consequences for economic and political stability? Analysing why policy reaches the answers that it does requires an understanding of the perspectives and dynamics of US mass and elite opinion, the political process with all of its structures and mobilized groups, the economic trends and expectations, and the role of foreign pressures. Analyses of such matters are highly controversial in themselves, let alone in conjunction.

The Traditional View
The issue of domestic versus external goals is not only inherently complex, but difficult for students of international relations to approach without distorting preconceptions. Those who study and practice foreign policy are strongly inclined to regard interfering domestic priorities like psychosomatic causes of bad health – unfortunate and unnecessary. Their natural inclinations towards the primacy of foreign policy are strongly reinforced by certain widely-prevailing views about recent history. The Second World War is blamed on Europe's 'appeasement' of Hitler a policy traced to the domestic self-indulgence of democracies with provincial leaders.

Alongside this common view of European appeasement is an equally traditional picture of American isolationism and its international consequences. In this traditional historical view, the United States should have taken up the indispensable role of world manager as Britain grew progressively enfeebled. The *Pax Britannica* should, it is said, have been sustained by being transformed into a *Pax Americana*. Instead, the isolationist inclinations of its masses kept America aloof. The disintegrating world balance led to two world wars, neither of which could be resolved until internationalist-minded elites manoeuvered the United States out of her domestic self-preoccupation. Thanks to the Cold War after World War II, America's elites, with transatlantic help, were able to keep the country's attention on international responsibilities. The post-war *Pax Americana*, NATO in particular, was a sort of benevolent and successful conspiracy of transatlantic elites against an erratic American public. Populist isolationism revived, however, with Vietnam. America's policy, and the world's stability, have been seriously undermined ever since.

However valid this isolationist paradigm may seem for the past, it is irrelevant to the Alliance's current problems. The American public is not opposed to foreign commitments, least of all to America's European commitments. The current quarrel is not between the public and its elites but among the transatlantic elites themselves. Those in charge of foreign policy in Europe and America do not agree over the shape of the future world system. Increasingly, they do not agree on how to deal with the Soviet Union, or with the Third World, or with their own relationship. On the American side, at least, the springs of this conflict are not to be found in the popular heartland, but in elitist Washington. If American foreign policies are more and more 'unilateral', by which it is usually meant that Europe does not approve of them, the blame should not be laid on the American public's domestic preferences.

Public Opinion and the Alliance

Measurements of public opinion over the past few years confirm the continuing mass support for using American troops against a Soviet attack in Europe. According to one set of data,[1] a post-Vietnam bottom of 48% in favour was reached in 1974–5, with 34% opposed. Support began rising by 1976, with a temporary post-war high of 74% in favour with only 19% opposed in July 1980, following the invasion of Afghanistan by the USSR and the seizing of American hostages in Iran. Polls in 1982 show support down to a more normal 56% in favour and 25% opposed. Logically enough, the public also supports keeping troops in Europe. A Gallup poll in February 1982, showed half the American public favouring American European forces at their present level, and 16% wanting an increase, while 10% favoured a reduction and 11% wanted the troops out altogether.[2] But even in 1974, with anti-Vietnam feeling still running high, 52% favoured retaining the same troop levels, with 3% wanting an increase, while 25% favoured reduction and 12% elimination.

Rising support for the European commitment after the mid-1970s was paralleled by sharper increases in support for defence spending. In various polls from the late 1960s to the mid-1970s, one third to one half the respondents regularly found US defence spending excessive, whereas those who found it insufficient ranged 9% to 17%. By 1975, an NBC poll recorded 41% who still found spending excessive, but 25% who believed it

insufficient. The trend thereafter changed the ratio dramatically. By 1980, various polls showed only 5–14% who found spending excessive and 46–76% who found it insufficient.[3] By March 1982 the huge Reagan defence proposals seemed finally to have produced a public reaction. A CBS/*New York Times* poll showed 49% favouring defence cuts against 41% who did not.[4]

Such surveys hardly reveal an American mass opinion chronically disposed to place domestic goals above military needs and obligations. On the contrary, even in the wake of Vietnam and the more sanguine view of Soviet-American relations prevailing in the heyday of Kissingerian detente, public support for NATO remained strong, with a near majority even at its lowest point in the mid-1970s.

Today's revived public support for external commitments is, however, selective. The strong majority found to favour NATO in Europe in 1982 diminishes slightly for the American commitment to Japan (54% in favour to 30% opposed) and dwindles into a minority of one-third (with 51% opposed) for South Korea.[5] Support for Central American interventions is almost non-existent. The public also seems increasingly wary that the Reagan Administration's foreign policy is too belligerent and undiscriminating. A Harris poll of 17 June 1982 shows 52% worried about Reagan 'getting the country into a war', with 45% not worried, and 53% giving the President 'negative marks on his nuclear weapons negotiations with the Soviets', with only 41% positive.[6]

When nuclear weapons are mentioned, even public support for European defence looks more ambivalent. An NBC poll in October 1981, showed 52% opposed to America's using nuclear weapons in reply to a Soviet nuclear attack on Western Europe. Only 29% favoured either a limited or an all-out American nuclear response; 78% felt neither side could win a nuclear war.[7]

Even if public support for the Alliance has always remained strong, it has nevertheless varied considerably over the years but other issues of foreign and defence policy have seen even wider swings. What mechanism governs changes in public opinion?[8] On foreign policy issues, public opinion as a whole generally appears less volatile than the opinion of what might be called its 'upper stratum', those occupying high occupational, economic and educational status. Mass opinion tends to follow this upper stratum but with a smaller fluctuation. The upper stratum, for example, turned against the Vietnam War and defence spending earlier and more sharply than the general public. It also seems to have grown fearful of declining American strength earlier than the public at large.

Opinion in this upper stratum is said to be particularly sensitive to the treatment of foreign policy events in the media. The media themselves reflect the foreign policy elites – Administration leaders and other politicians, bureaucratic 'experts', vigorous interest groups, as well as a sizeable band of private pundits and research centres.

At the present time, criticism of the Alliance in foreign policy circles has grown intense and is already amply represented in the media. Upper-stratum and ultimately mass opinion may thus be affected. Mass opinion seems already well aware of the current transatlantic friction. An NBC poll in early 1982 revealed 72% who saw Western European allies not supporting US sanctions against Poland sufficiently and 80% who saw insufficient support for American policies in general.[9] Should such disappointments and irritations ultimately disintegrate popular support for the European commitment, however, the shift would not fit the traditional isolationist paradigm. An autonomous and fickle mass drift to neo-isolationism would not overpower the internationalist elites. Instead the mutation in public support would follow debates initiated among elite policy-makers and private experts in which the Alliance lost ground and the consequences gradually filtered into mass opinion.

Cultural Community

Transatlantic recrimination among foreign policy elites has, of course, been frequent since the NATO Treaty was signed in 1949. Yet the public has remained faithful. An intense cultural community, close economic inter-action and a myriad of personal connections are thought to form a community of identity and perception that shields military and political ties from the inevitable collisions of national interest. The political benefits of cultural interpenetration may, of course, be exaggerated. Intense inter-dependence has characterized relations among European states throughout much of their history without preventing innumerable European wars. Post-war Europe and America, however, have had the crucial advantage of being able to define their common values and interests in relation to an obvious common enemy. Yet detente has now made European-American-Soviet relations more ambiguous and, in addition, many people perceive a corresponding attenuation of transatlantic cultural ties.

Factors like cultural sympathy and mutual identity are difficult to define or measure. Relationships that can be counted do not in fact reveal diminishing transatlantic interactions. From 1962 to 1977, for example, the number of Europeans studying in America in any year increased nearly four times, while nearly twice as many Americans were studying in Europe. From 1960 to 1977, the annual number of European visitors to the United States increased almost tenfold, while the number of Americans visiting Europe more than doubled.[10]

The quality of relations may deteriorate, of course, even as the frequency increases. Changes in education can make Europeans and Americans know each other less well even as they see each other more often. American elite education, once heavily oriented toward European history and culture, has entered into a time of relative proliferation and disarray, with greater sensitivity to non-European aspects of America's heritage.[11] Education in Europe, too, has undergone a democratic revolution of its own. Serious knowledge or interest about America seems less common. Many young Europeans, moreover, are intrigued by a Third World where, in the Leftist perspectives that dominate much of European education, America has been cast in a heavy and unsympathetic role – a part the Reagan Administration seems ready to play. As a result, what was close identity in the last generation threatens to become only ritualized nostalgia in the next. If so, the problem is not the quantity of communication but its substance. Present uneasiness over the quality of cultural bonds suggests both the need for careful thought on how they may be reinforced and less complacency about their capacity to compensate for deep political differences.

Domestic Pressure Groups:
The Anti-Nuclear Movement
To affect policy, public opinion needs to be mobilized. In political systems as open and unstructured as the American, well-organized interest groups can give minority views greater weight than the widespread but inert predispositions of the broader public. Apart from the essentially economic pressure groups discussed below, two groups seem particularly relevant to America's external commitments: the renascent anti-nuclear movement and the long-standing Israeli Lobby.

The recent rise of a militant mass movement against nuclear weapons seems to belie the stability of popular support for America's external commitments, particularly in Western Europe, where a nuclear deterrent is widely thought essential to compensate for an imbalance in conventional forces.

America's mass anti-nuclear movement is sufficiently recent, sudden and diffuse to resist easy generalizations. Its rise can be most plausibly explained, not as a spontaneous defection from old commitments, but as a popular reaction to the Reagan Administration's massive arms build-up and bellicose rhetoric.[12] Not unreasonably, the public fears not only nuclear war but men in power who appear to anticipate it with complacency.[13] Logically, an American fear of nuclear war could easily turn into hostility toward the Atlantic Alliance. Renewed American interest in European conventional defence, for example, is driven by fears not only that regional deterrence in Europe may be inadequate, but also that the United States may thereby be drawn into a nuclear war.[14] As more radical experts occasionally suggest, America's nuclear risks would greatly diminish without her NATO commitment.

Whether the anti-nuclear group's momentum will carry it from condemning nuclear war to advocating withdrawal from nuclear commitments remains to be seen. European agitation over the dangers of American missiles on European soil may, of course, resonate to America but assuming a link between the anti-nuclear movement and isolationism seems premature. The logical affinities, however, suggest the importance of making public sense out of military strategies and official positions on arms control. An intemperate and insensitive official posture risks provoking an organized wave of public mistrust that may greatly inhibit external commitments in the future. No doubt experts will then blame neo-isolationism.

Ethnic Lobbies
Of America's lobbies claiming to represent ethnic groups and pressing particular foreign policy goals, the Israeli Lobby is the most ambitious and effective. Not only American Jews but a large part of the general public feels a special sympathy and obligation towards Israel. For several decades a coalition of diverse agencies and individuals has effectively mobilized and brought this support to bear on Congress and the Administration. Pro-Israeli influence has been felt not only on American policy toward the Middle East but also toward the Soviet Union. Soviet persecution of dissenters, plus support for Syria and the PLO, have in recent years encouraged a certain coalescence between pro-Israeli and anti-Soviet perspectives. This coalescence has played its part in the deterioration of Soviet–American detente. In particular, the Jackson–Vanik Amendment, hoping to constrain the Soviet Union to permit more emigration, became a serious obstacle to building up Soviet–American trade.

Some of Israel's American supporters have also grown increasingly critical of Europe. In an American perspective combining support for Israel with loathing for the Soviet Union, European states can easily be criticized for 'Finlandization' at home, a pro-Arab bias in the Middle East, and a generally fatuous complacency about revolutionary movements in the Third World. European inclinations to appease this criticism have declined and European disapproval of current Israeli policy has grown more vehement. With most European states increasingly alienated from Israel, how significant for American–European relations is this coalescence of pro-Israeli, anti-Soviet and anti-European perspectives?

An American foreign policy opposing detente in Europe while condoning Israeli militancy in the Middle East clearly was not formulated with European sensibilities in mind but, if popular antipathy against the Soviet Union remains strong in America, support for Israel's present militant course seems on the wane, not least in the American Jewish Community itself. Even Americans deeply attached to Israel and sympathetic to the dilemmas involved in 'appeasing' the Arabs must wonder at the cost to the United States of a policy that progressively alienates not only the Arab states but also the European Allies. Such sentiments are widespread among foreign policy elites and surface more and more frequently in the media.[15] If the American public is unlikely to renounce concern for Israel, the escalation of the diplomatic costs should make future support less unconditional and sweeping. Logically, a certain coalescence of American and European views on the Middle East is more imaginable than formerly. At least one source of transatlantic friction shows some possibility of diminishing.

Economic Constraints on Foreign Policy
Every Western state has a multitude of powerful economic interest groups. Deteriorating economic conditions intensify their vigour and competitiveness. Greater competitiveness between domestic economic goals and foreign commitments seems logical, even if the distinction is often elusive.

Examining tensions between domestic interests and foreign obligations involves looking at both macro-economic and commercial policy. In macro-economic policy, the size of the defence budget is the most self-evident foreign policy issue. Defence spending obviously has its domestic beneficiaries but since the state's resources are not infinite, a bigger defence budget appears to mean a smaller civilian budget. Whether a particular defence budget seems adequate obviously depends upon estimates of the foreign commitments that national security requires, the forces needed to meet the commitments adequately, and the reasonable cost of such

forces. Someone who believes that the United States should be the 'world's policeman', with a secure first-strike capability against the Soviet Union and the capacity to fight two or three major conventional wars simultaneously, requires a different sum and balance of domestic and foreign spending from someone with more limited external requirements.

Comparing American with Soviet, or NATO with Warsaw Pact military spending is one obvious, if misleading, index of military adequacy. The difficulties of such comparisons are well known. Straightforward comparisons do not, however, show an overall imbalance unfavourable to NATO. In 1980, before Reagan's major build-up, the US defence budget was $142.6 billion. Published CIA calculations have the Soviet Union spending the equivalent of around $185 billion. The rest of NATO, however, spent well over $98.2 billion, as opposed to roughly $16.7 billion for the rest of the Warsaw Pact. The West also has slightly more men under arms in peacetime (4.93 million as opposed to 4.78 million).[16] Such comparisons, obviously crude, nevertheless help to put into perspective the widespread notion of the Warsaw Pact's superior military resources. That NATO should be able to outspend and outnumber the Warsaw Pact should not be surprising. The West is far superior in population, industrial infrastructure and technology.

Despite its inherent superiority in resources and its explicit superiority in spending and manpower, many analysts find the West's effective combat strength markedly inferior, particularly for conventional war. Logically enough, some trace this putative inferiority to a misallocation of resources. Its critics, for example, often find American defence planning without an adequate military doctrine to link commitments, tactics, weapons and forces. In this view, official planners, bemused by technology, know more about weapons than about fighting. Reagan's build-up is seen merely as an extravagant shopping list of new weapons, in many cases without serious military justification. The United States lacks not money and men but the brains and imagination needed for adequate doctrine and organization. Even if critics are more convincing when pointing to defects rather than to alter-

104

natives, America's low ratio of combat forces makes the criticism plausible.[17]

The inability to formulate coherent and efficient military doctrines does not in itself indicate a scarcity of material resources. Rather the opposite is true. Nor do budgetary politics in recent years suggest a squeezing of defence spending. From 1960 to 1980, American military outlays increased 7% at constant prices. The rate, to be sure, was uneven. A compound annual growth rate from 1960 to 1970 of 2.7% was followed by a 1.9% compounded annual decline from 1970 to 1979. The American decline in the 1970s, however, was more than matched by compound annual increases of 1.8%, 3.3%, 2.8% and 3.5% for Britain, France, Germany and Italy, respectively.[18] In any event, the Carter Administration had already reversed the American decline. The Reagan plans announced in 1981 called for defence expenditures to rise from $161 billion in fiscal year 1981 to $343 billion in fiscal year 1986 – a gradual increase to an annual level $181 billion higher.[19]

Despite the straitened economic circumstances and prolonged congressional budgetary struggle of 1982, the new defence programme emerged virtually unscathed. In the end, Congress abandoned not the military build-up, but any prospect of moving toward budgetary equilibrium. Despite all the rhetoric about fiscal responsibility, the Administration proposed and the Congress accepted an overall budget that would predictably lead to a deficit of well over $100 billion.[20]

The 1982 budget battle was simply a more theatrical version of an annual American performance.[21] Once more, Congress proved unable to reconcile domestic and foreign claims within the resources it was willing to make available. True, in the face of a tax cut and substantial military increases, the annual rise in civilian expenditures was slowed; it nevertheless continued to grow and a record deficit became unavoidable. Resolving the budgetary dilemma through a large deficit has, by now, become the normal state of affairs. Except for 1969, the US Federal Budget has been in deficit every year since 1960.

Deficits are not cost-free. Depending on whether monetary policy is generous or tight, perpetual and substantial fiscal deficits generally mean either inflation or else a shortage of capital for private investment. The United States has now experienced both forms of cost. Until recently, Congress's traditional aversion to high interest rates meant financing deficits with easy money. Hence we have seen a steady rise of inflation along with a weak and often depreciating dollar. Given the dollar's international role, much of the inflation was exported, adding significantly to the inflationary problems of most advanced capitalist countries. The cost of America's deficit was thus shared throughout the Alliance.

Tighter American monetary policy since 1979 has meant more financing from real savings borrowed in the capital markets. Unfortunately, this shift to tight money has coincided with a severe cyclical recession and Reagan's greatly increased fiscal deficits. Unprecedented interest rates and a dramatically appreciated dollar have made it difficult for either the American or other economies to recover. Unemployment and bankruptcy have reached levels unknown in the post-war era. Few predict a sustained recovery under present circumstances. In short, the deficits once paid through inflation are now being paid through deflation.

The political distress of prolonged recession could easily force either a new round of excessive monetary creation, and hence renewed inflation, or else a new drive toward fiscal equilibrium, and hence a serious battle for fiscal priority. Either course poses real difficulties for the Reagan Administration.

Renewing inflation is the traditional and perhaps the easiest tactic. Some analysts believe the Federal Reserve and Treasury, fearful of world-wide depression, financial collapse and protectionism, were already following such a course by the autumn of 1982. If so, a new and even more exaggerated cycle of 'boom and bust' may be expected to follow. Whether this traditional stop-go pattern can be continued through another round without a major breakdown may be doubted. The alternative of trying seriously to move toward fiscal equilibrium means either raising taxes or cutting spending. Congress did impose considerable tax increases during the early autumn of 1982, but increasing taxes sufficiently to restore some semblance of fiscal balance would threaten the Administration's basic 'supply-side' economic strategy and might well prove self-defeating in a recession. Moving toward balance by cutting expenditures, on the other hand, means a heightened confrontation between civilian and military spending. With the recession boosting welfare costs and draining the Administration's political support, success in cutting civilian budgets grows increasingly improbable. Since American defence expenditures are already much higher than Western Europe's, and US welfare expenditures are relatively meagre, a budgetary squeeze risks a backlash not only against the expanded military budget, but against the NATO commitment itself.[22] Such a reaction, logical and widely feared, might sorely test the public's long-standing devotion to the Alliance. In 1982, it bears repeating, it is still the foreign-policy elites and not the general public who are most exercised over the 'free-riding' allies.

Whatever else may be said, the Reagan Administration's economic policies cannot be construed as domestic priorities over-riding foreign commitments. Wisely or not, the Administration, supported by the public, has refused to cut back its ambitious plans for the increased defence spending it believes vital for national security and world obligations. In effect, economic policy has been sacrificed to defence policy. If some of the consequences have been as unpopular abroad as unfortunate at home, they must be blamed on an excess of internationalist zeal rather than a rebirth of isolationist domesticity.

Protectionism and the Alliance

Whereas the international significance of America's domestic fiscal and monetary policy has only gradually been recognized, commercial policy has always seemed crucial to Alliance relations. Liberal trade has long been thought essential to foreign political and military ties. Liberal trade, of course, is not a foreign obligation necessarily honoured at the expense of domestic priorities. Many domestic interests depend on foreign markets for their prosperity. Among these are the farmers – with many of the industries tied to agriculture – and the multinationals in general – including the big banks.

The notable economic disruptions of the 1970s were widely expected to threaten liberal trade with a rebirth of protectionism. Rich Western economies would seek to insulate themselves, it was thought, against an increasingly erratic and unfavourable international environment. Even internationally-minded economic firms would limit their horizons to more predictable home or regional markets. But, despite inflation, oil shocks, competition from newly industrializing countries and increasingly severe business cycles, trade remained remarkably open in the 1970s. In the 1980s, however, with unprecedented recession and unemployment in both Europe and America, and several basic industries in deep structural difficulty, commercial barriers have been proliferating. As the recent transatlantic conflict over steel imports illustrates, the American Government has great trouble controlling protectionist forces.

The change is less abrupt than it seems. The liberalism of commercial exchange in the 1970s was to a considerable extent illusory. Generous monetary policy, unbalanced fiscal policy and the dismantling of capital controls meant a periodically declining dollar, which the Government refused to defend.[23] Demands for trade barriers were thus appeased by a regularly depreciating dollar. The combination of policies gratified both the nationalist and the internationalist wings of the American economy. Unprecedented freedom to export capital was a boon to internationally-oriented business, banks in particular, while a steadily depreciating dollar helped to keep home-based manufacturers competitive, despite their inflating costs. Such a policy was as 'mercantilist' as formal protectionism. But it did make direct trade barriers unnecessary and, one way or another, concealed and diffused the costs of America's inflation to her partners. When the accumulating costs of inflation finally forced a tightening of American monetary policy, and the dollar thereby began to appreciate sharply, American products lost their continually renewed competitive advantage. In a depressed economic climate, pressure for direct protection was bound to increase. In this perspective, the new American protectionism of the 1980s is not a shift toward mercantilism but merely a change in its form. American manufacturers and workers now expect tariffs to export the domestics costs of deflation as formerly they expected a declining currency to export the domestic costs of inflation.

A return to genuine liberalism seems improbable so long as American monetary policy is condemned to oscillate from exaggerated inflation to exaggerated constraint. A more stable monetary policy would require re-establishing control over fiscal policy, an unlikely achievement without some reconciliation between the American Government's resources and the domestic and foreign goals it pursues. Until this elementary equilibrium is achieved, the West can look forward to mounting economic disorder. Like some deep inner sickness, America's fiscal imbalance may be expected to generate a shifting and accumulating variety of noxious symptoms.

The significance of the military budget in the overall American budget, and the weight of the NATO commitment in that military budget, together link the Alliance directly to America's fiscal problem. Any serious attempt to achieve American budgetary equilibrium may well involve a showdown in NATO over respective defence costs.[24] For obvious reasons, such a confrontation would constitute a major political challenge. Understandably, European governments would prefer to avoid it. From a broader perspective, however, significant adjustments in the responsibilities and costs of European defence may seem not only beneficial but essential. For the United States, to achieve fiscal equilibrium, and hence monetary stability, cannot be counted a selfish domestic goal pursued at the expense of foreign obligations. America's fiscal disorder has contributed heavily to the World's inflation, unemployment, financial over-extension and general economic disarray of the past few years. Those 'burdens' have been shared in a way that military costs have not. Economic conditions that steadily sap the West's productive vitality and undermine its social peace are no less real a threat than a Soviet invasion of Western Europe. Americans may certainly be criticized for failing to tax themselves adequately. Such criticism, however, does not sit well from rich allies whose own territory is directly menaced but whose defence spending is disproportionately less.

Democracy and Foreign Policy

What broad conclusions can be drawn about the relationship between America's domestic priorities and her Alliance obligations? In direct military and political obligations the traditional isolationist paradigm does not seem to apply. Isolationism is not deeply rooted in the masses, nor does internationalism depend upon the elites. The general public has supported America's European commitment and the military budgets demanded to sustain America's external role, a willingness no doubt made easier by America's relatively underdeveloped civilian demands and compulsive fiscal deficits. Present US dissatisfaction with Europe stems, if anything, from the foreign-policy elite itself. The issue, moreover, is not priority of domestic over foreign goals but a different international strategy.

In economic relations, a different picture emerges. Rising American protectionism clearly suggests a conflict for priority between domestic and foreign claims – between preventing further unemployment in home-based industry and sustaining an open international economy. This growing protectionist pressure is not a populist mutation, but results logically from present economic policies carried out under present circumstances. The chain of causes that ends with turning away from internationalism in trade passes through a macro-economic policy of perpetual fiscal imbalance. For over twenty years, the American political system has failed to reconcile the sum of the resources it is willing to raise with the civilian and military budgetary claims it insists upon meeting. The accumulating consequences have seriously undermined Western economic prosperity and progressively soured transatlantic political relations. The resulting pressure to end American fiscal instability also feeds a quarrel within the Alliance over military budgets. A long-standing structural imbalance between respective national resources and military responsibilities has itself played a considerable role in that American fiscal imbalance which lies at the heart of the economic deterioration. From this perspective, the Alliance might be better off today if the American public had long ago insisted more firmly on its domestic priorities and been less fond of its foreign obligations.

The analysis may perhaps be put in more general terms. Over the past two decades, neither the United States nor the states of Western Europe have come to terms with their changed situation. American wealth and power, the initial foundation of the post-war system, has inevitably diminished in relation to both America's adversaries and her allies. America's relative decline represents not a failure of long-standing policy, but its logical consequence. Under the circumstances, preserving the highly integrated and relatively stable post-war order, of which the Atlantic Alliance has been the keystone, requires a more plural sharing of cost and control. This means a substantial adaptation of roles and general perspectives within the Alliance itself.

To ask whether American public opinion would comprehend and support such an evolution seems premature. American leaders have never presented the public with a realistic view of the country's changing world posi-tion. Nor, it must be confessed, have its foreign policy and political elites been fertile sources of appropriate new policies. Instead, official America has been bemused first by unrealistic notions of detente and now by an unrealistic nostalgia for hegemony. The result has been a progressive renunciation of serious efforts at accommodation with the Soviet Union, followed by a progressive alienation from Western Europe. As more sensitive poll-sters suggest, it is not the public that is demanding unilateral world hegemony. Unfortunately, failures in American leader-ship are not without their analogue in West-ern Europe. If American policy may be accused of wanting detente or hegemony 'on the cheap', present European policy might be dubbed 'self-determination on the cheap'.

In America, at least, it is the elite and not the public that has failed. At the moment, public education in foreign policy falters for lack of a suitable curriculum. Blaming the bankruptcy of elite policies on the domestic constraints of democracy seems a judgment mistaken in its analysis, evasive in its pres-criptions, and dangerous in its implications.

NOTES

[1] Surveys for Potomac Associates kindly provided, along with much good advice, by William Watts. See his 'The United States and Japan: How We See Each Other', speech delivered on 28 May 1982 in Tokyo, p.14. Also Lloyd Free and William Watts, 'Internationalism Comes of Age . . .Again', *Public Opinion*, April/May 1980, p.46. For interpretations I take to be along the broad lines developed here, see also Daniel Yankelovich, 'Cautious Internationalism: A Changing Mood Toward U.S. For-eign Policy', *Public Opinion*, March/April 1978, p.12; Daniel Yankelovich and Larry Kaagan, 'Assertive Ameri-ca', *Foreign Affairs, America and the World*, 1980, Vol-ume 59, Number 3, pp.696–713; Bruce Russett and Donald R. DeLuca, 'Don't Tread on Me: Public Opinion and Foreign Policy in the Eighties', *Political Science Quarterly*, 96, Number 3, Fall 1981, pp.381–401; a broad view which has influenced my thinking is John Lewis Gaddis, 'Containment: Its Past and Future', *International Security*, Volume 5, Number 4, Spring 1981, pp.74–102.

[2] International Poll by Gallup-Affiliated Institutions dur-ing February 1982, for *Newsweek International*, and other European news organizations.

[3] Various CBS/*NY Times*, NBC and AIPO surveys as summarized in Table 1 in Russett and DeLuca, *op.cit.* in note 1.

[4] CBS/*NY Times* Poll, 18 March 1982.

[5] William Watts, *op.cit.* in note 1.

[6] Harris Poll, 17 June 1982.

[7] NBC Poll, 10 November 1981 (taken in October 1981).

[8] Bruce Russett and Donald R. DeLuca, *op.cit.* in note 1.

[9] NBC Poll, 5 February 1982.

[10] Derived from various years of *UN Statistical Yearbook* and UNESCO, *Statistics of Students Abroad*.

[11] See David P. Calleo. 'The Alliance: An Enduring Relationship?', *SAIS Review*, Number 4, Summer 1982.

[12] For a comprehensive recent survey, see Fox Butter-worth, 'Anatomy of the Nuclear Protest', *New York Times Magazine*, 11 July 1982, p. A13. For public opinion on whether the Reagan Administration is too bellicose, see note 6.

[13] See, for example, two articles by Robert Sheer, 'Civil Defense Program to be Revised: Reagan Seeks to Counter Possible Attack by Soviets', *Los Angeles Times*, 15 Jan-uary 1982, Section I, p.1; and 'U.S. Could Survive War in Administration's View', *Los Angeles Times*, 16 January 1982, Section I, p.1; also Judith Miller, 'Panel Angered by Failure of Aide to Testify on Civil Defense Plans', *New York Times*, 17 March 1982, p. A16, and her 'Civil Defense Notions Change but the Skepticism Remains', *New York Times*, 4 April 1982, p. 6E.

[14] See McGeorge Bundy, George F. Kennan, Robert S. McNamara and Gerard Smith, 'Nuclear Weapons and the Atlantic Alliance', *Foreign Affairs*, Spring 1982.

[15] Polls in early July 1982, assessing public reactions to

Israel's Lebanon invasion varied widely. For a sensitive analysis of growing anti-Israeli sentiment, see Stephen S. Rosenfeld, 'Anti-Semitism and U.S. Foreign Policy', *Foreign Policy*, 47, Summer 1982, pp. 172*ff.*

[16] International Institute for Strategic Studies, *The Military Balance 1981–1982, passim.*

[17] For a survey of Congressional and other critics of military budgeting, see Richard Halloran, 'Criticism Rises on Reagan's Plan for 5–Year Growth of the Military', *New York Times*, 22 March 1982, p. 1; James Fallows, *National Defense* (New York: Random House, 1981) mounts a comprehensive attack on the defence budget. Concern about NATO's effectiveness among Congressional leaders generally worried about defence can be found in Senator Sam Nunn, *NATO: Can the Alliance Be Saved?*, Report to the Committee on Armed Services, United States Senate, 13 May 1982 (Washington DC: USGPO, 1982). For a recent newspaper survey of NATO's deficiencies, see Neil Ulman. 'An Out-gunned NATO has Much to Discuss at its Summit in June', *Wall Street Journal*, 26 May 1982, p. 1. Specialist literature on military issues is extensive. Representative American critiques of present doctrines and force structures are Steven L. Canby, 'Territorial Defense in Central Europe', *Armed Forces and Society*, Volume 7, Number 1, Fall 1980, pp. 51–67; or William S. Lind, 'Some Doctrinal Questions for the United States Army', *Military Review*, Volume 17, Number 3, March 1977, pp. 54–65. For sharp critique of the critics, see John J. Mearsheimer, 'Maneuver, Mobile Defense, and the NATO Central Front', *International Security*, Winter 1981–82, pp. 104–122. A survey assessing and synthesizing contrasting positions is Colonel T. N. Dupuy, U. S. Army, retired, 'The Nondebate Over How Army Should Fight', *Army*, June 1982, pp. 35*ff.*

[18] IISS, *op. cit.* in note 16, p.110.

[19] *New York Times*, 5 March 1981, p.A1. An updated request can be found in Department of Defense, *Annual Report to the Congress: Fiscal Year 1983*, January 1982.

[20] For a detailed account of the Senate debate, see Pat Towell, 'Defense Authorization Bill Passed by the Senate after Trims Made to Meet Budget Goals', *Congressional Quarterly, Special Report*, 15 May 1982, pp. 1,155*ff.* For the flavour of the House debate, see Margot Hornblower, 'House Backs Reagan on Military Spending', *International Herald Tribune*, 31 July–1 August 1982, p.1. For various estimates of the deficit, see 'U.S. Aides Downplay Report on Economy', *Ibid.*

[21] For an extended version of this argument, see David P. Calleo, *The Imperious Economy* (Cambridge and London: Harvard University Press, 1982), chapter 9.

[22] In 1980, defence expenditure as a percentage of GNP for Britain, France, Germany and the US were 5.1%, 3.9%, 3.2% and 5.5% respectively. American social security expenditures are, in proportion to GNP, about two-thirds those of Britain and roughly half those of France and Germany. IISS, *op.cit.* in note 16, p.112. Social security figures are from the Comparative Studies Staff, Office of International Policy, Social Security Administration, and are spelled out in Calleo, *op. cit.* in note 21, p.96.

[23] Calleo, *ibid.*, chapters 4 and 8.

[24] David P. Calleo, 'Inflation and American Power', *Foreign Affairs*, 59, Spring 1981, pp.781–812.

Domestic Priorities and the Demands of Alliance: A European Perspective

DOMINIQUE MOÏSI

Introduction

In his memoirs, 'Die Welt von Gestem', the Austrian writer Stefan Zweig described the period before World War I as the 'Golden Age' of security. The guns of August 1914 were to destroy that age, maybe forever. Yet, thanks to the protection of the American nuclear umbrella and to the logic of nuclear deterrence during a period of US nuclear superiority, the Europeans were able to enjoy for more than twenty years – from the death of Stalin to the Yom Kippur War – a feeling of relative security. They had the illusion that Europe, no longer at the centre of World History, could live in a prosperous and comfortable cocoon, in relative isolation from the sound and fury of a violent world. Crises did of course occur, such as over Berlin and Cuba, but their resolution simply confirmed a climate of security that gave birth to the word detente. The crises that did develop inside the Alliance were reflections of its success. The aim of security achieved, however, many in the US now consider the price of the Alliance economically too high, while many in Europe feel the political cost too heavy.

It has been the disappearance since 1979 of that feeling of security that gives a new significance to the troubles of the Alliance, and makes some observers question its very survival in its present form. Since the Soviet invasion of Afghanistan there has been the sensation of living in a state of permanent crisis; the use of military force to impose political solutions is becoming the rule and is no longer the exception. The past is now evoked to stress the danger of the present and the fear of the future. Analogies with 1914 and 1939 recreate a link with history of the kinds of crisis and wars that the existence of nuclear weapons seemed at one time to render impossible. The evolution of the balance of forces of

the Soviet Union, the multiplication of opportunities for crises and the dual revolution of nuclear technology (precision added to miniaturization) has seemed to add rationality to these new fears.

The divisive impact on alliances of the logic of nuclear war, denounced in the 1960s by de Gaulle and his followers, has now taken on a new validity. How can the Americans, who are not even sure of having enough weapons to defend themselves, protect Western Europe? European fears over the inadequacy of US military capabilities are reinforced by frustrations with US political behaviour.

The Nature of the Crisis

The present crisis of the Alliance is preoccupying not only because it takes place within the context of a different balance of forces but also because it translates into the conflicting interests of the respective governments and the divergent evolutions of societies' historical and national emotions. These two evolutions meet and reinforce each other. The constellation of values that constituted the basis of the Atlantic Alliance is slowly eroding. The 'troubled partnership' no longer places France in opposition to the United States, as it did in the 1960s, but now it opposes all of Western Europe against America, something which could only be interpreted positively if it were to lead to real European solidarity.

Nor is the current crisis of the Alliance any longer limited either to quarrels over its internal fabric (as under de Gaulle) or to crises occurring beyond its geographical boundaries. As demonstrated by the 'pipeline' issue, the very essence of the origins of the Alliance and its justification has come under fire in the debate over the type of relation the West should have with the East.

Both in Western Europe and in the United States, the present crisis could be summarized as the tendency to give priority to domestic considerations over international ones, to national interests over the concerns of the Alliance. From a gallocentric perspective one could smugly describe this phase as a posthumous triumph of a *Gaulliste* view of the world. When the German Director of the IISS refers to attitudes of the Federal Republic of Germany as '*Gaullisme* in a minor key' and when a well-known French commentator accuses the present US Administration of 'Californian *Gaullisme*', they describe the growth of what can only be called a 'new nationalism' in the Western World. This new nationalism is assertive in the US and in France. It is an inward-turning nationalism in most nations of Northern Europe including the FRG. The French and the Americans want to carry out what they consider their historical mission. The rest wish rather to be left alone, out of the limelight and tempest.

The return to nationalistic attitudes is understandable in a world rediscovering such 'classical' concepts as the use of military force, and the predominance of national actor states over transnational groupings. We may be witnessing a progressive divorce between the economic and political realms. Yet, even if it exists as a temptation, real protectionism is no longer a possibility in a truly interdependent world economy.

This rediscovery of nationalism erodes the Alliance's solidarity not only at the political and economic level but, more seriously, at the level also of culture and society. This is not the place to discuss the issue but one could here evoke in parallel the erosion of the ideals of the European Community.

To analyse the political and psychological dimensions of what I here call a crisis and the growing conflict between domestic priorities and the demands of Alliance, it is necessary to examine the roots of anti-nuclear, pacifist and neutralist forces in Western Europe. The words used to describe them are either too simplistic or too ambiguous. Moreover, it is difficult to make generalizations for historical, geographical, religious and cultural differences render any such attempts treacherous but it is nevertheless a necessary exercise.

The Peace Movements in Western Europe
The peace movements that have emerged with various success in Western Europe have three characteristics: they seriously question the logic of nuclear deterrence; they correspond to the growth of a new brand of anti-Americanism, different from the old brand practised by France; and they are also the consequences of an identity crisis diversely affecting some Western European countries, partly as a result of the adverse effects that NATO has had on the development of a national defence effort. The peace movements are strongest in those countries where these three factors are present and can reinforce each other.

Nuclear Deterrence
The evolution of the balance of the forces in favour of the Soviet Union, linked to a technological revolution that makes limited nuclear war less impossible to imagine (at least in abstract terms), have exposed the political weaknesses of the 'flexible response' doctrine and therefore its relative inadequacy. One may even wonder whether this doctrine did not always presuppose psychologically that the United States enjoyed superiority and that the prospects of war in Europe were so remote as to be a complete abstraction. The moment the risks of war appear somewhat conceivable, and the extent of US protection doubtful, the entire logic of nuclear deterrence rebounds. Its rationality is questioned in the name of 'civilization'. The fear of nuclear holocaust in the name of civilization is what ultimately unifies such different messages as the 'no-first-use' proposal presented in *Foreign Affairs* by four well-established experts or the extremism of unilateralist nuclear disarmers such as E. P. Thompson in Britain

Until and including World War II, one could sacrifice one's life for the freedom of one's country. Now it may appear moral to sacrifice one's freedom for the survival of the planet. The anti-nuclear movement is particularly strong in countries where moralism is reinforced by religious or ecological concerns. Nuclear forces tend to atomize the spirit of defence. Debates among experts, once they are exposed to the public by the media in demand of explanation and sensation, can only have a negative impact on populations, which understand very little and are rightly shocked by the often barbaric nature of these debates. In this context America's protection is increasingly seen as more a threat than a guarantee, and the Soviet Union less frightening than the prospect of war.

It is easy for Soviet propaganda to play on these morally if not politically justifiable fears and to denounce in particular the danger represented for the Europeans by the installation of medium-range nuclear missiles on their soil. In that sense, one can say that Chancellor Schmidt in his 1977 speech in London, Kissinger in 1979 in Brussels or President Reagan lately on many occasions, were the best Soviet propagandists. It is as if the nuclear horrors of tomorrow are obliterating the conventional horrors of yesterday both for Europe and for many non-European countries. Many people conveniently forget that Europe has been shielded from these bloody conflicts by the existence of the nuclear weapon.

Anti-Americanism
The second factor that accounts for the growth of nuclear pacifism is the birth of a new anti-Americanism. For many Europeans, the United States today combines negatively the imperial tradition of *Pax Americana* (as reawakened by the Reagan Administration) and the continuation of the incoherence of the Carter period. America appears as authoritarian and bent on pursuing its self-interest and it is the European countries that have traditionally expected the most from the United States that are the most disappointed. But anti-Americanism goes beyond the mere denunciation of American political style and political choices. There is also a rebellion against American values and models and this translates into an anti-establishment trend. By rejecting America, one refuses the model of one's parent. Ironically this rejection corresponds to an American type of radicalism. Reagan's present policy towards Central and South America conveniently rekindles the old anti-imperialist cause. Denunciation of American imperialism acts as a common denominator for both the old (political) and new (cultural) brand of anti-Americanism. Jack Lang's denunciation in Mexico of the American cultural imperialism is a perfect illustration of this new symbiosis.

The Crisis of Identity
Third, the growth of self-styled peace movements corresponds to an identity crisis that is affecting the countries of Northern Europe in various ways, nowhere with greater consequences than in West Germany.

The long-term impact of NATO's protection over countries with weak military traditions (like the Netherlands), or too strong military traditions (like the Federal Republic) could only be adverse. It is difficult in the long run to act responsibly when one does not exercise responsibilities. The fact that the US protection is above all nuclear can only accentuate that trend. What is the meaning of a conventional defence effort whose value seems mainly complementary to nuclear weapons and whose use is either linked to marginal or catastrophic scenarios?

In this context, a country like the Netherlands could easily be tempted to return to its historical tradition of quasi-neutralism and countries in the middle of a serious national crisis (such as Belgium) are also affected. But the main problem of course arises over the evolution of the Federal Republic of Germany. Symbolic demonstrations against the United States in Berlin, where Kennedy had been greeted ecstatically, and concrete governmental decisions in defiance of the American wishes on East–West matters are evidence of a change that is undeniable. This evolution evokes so much passion that it must be treated with great care and restraint. 'Peace movement' activists are only a small minority in the Federal Republic, 5–6% of the population at most. Even if the number of their sympathizers is added, they still represent as a fraction no more than the Communist (PCF) voters in France, i.e. less than 20%. If one can derive truth from polls, America is far more popular in the Federal Republic than in Britain for example – 73% against 46% (*Newsweek* poll, 15 March 1982). But the Federal Republic of Germany is not Britain. It is at the heart of Europe and it remains a divided country with a unique past. Any shift of public opinion and governmental attitudes there is significant.

The evolution of the Federal Republic is both normal and inevitable but that does not mean that it should not worry us. Integration within the West was achieved by Adenauer. Normalization with the East (and with the German Democratic Republic in particular) was achieved by Chancellor Willy Brandt. Under Chancellor Schmidt, the Federal Republic has been engaged in a policy of normalization *vis-à-vis* itself. Such a policy, while maintaining the dual heritage of Adenauer and Brandt, takes into account the interests of a middle-size power who wants to be recognized as such throughout the world.

In taking this road, the Federal Republic has been encouraged by the example of a neighbouring country that places self-interest above all. But once *Gaullisme* started to cross the Rhine, it contained within it at least the seeds of problems. Normalization in the German case means confronting a division which is bound to appear artificial. It is not the German State that is the problem but the German Nation. With the passage of years and the maturing of new generations, it was simply natural for Germany to rediscover and confront both her immediate and her remote past. In her efforts to place herself firmly in the West, the Federal Republic had to accept as normal an abnormal relation with herself. That simply could not last for ever. In a world of crises, both economic and international, leading to a rediscovery of the 'virtues' of nationalism, the problem of Germany was bound to surface. It is not simply a political or partisan problem. There ought not to be anything reassuring about scenarios that shift party politics towards the right and envisage the return of the CDU to power. It was more or less inevitable that, once the vision of an integrated Western Europe faded in the 1950s, the Federal Republic should start looking towards East Germany and towards a definition of self-interest that was more German and less Atlanticist or European. Inevitable or not, the French, by providing the example of *Gaullisme*, and the US, by disappointing the Federal Republic, have accelerated the tempo of this evolution. It is our common responsibility to limit the consequences of these changes by making the Germans feel that they are an integral part of the West and of Europe. In this task, the French (for geographic and historic reasons) have a special responsibility.

Why France is Different

That rejection of the logic of nuclear deterrence, and identity crisis and anti-Americanism are at the roots of the developments of the peace movements in Europe, can be further demonstrated by the counter-proof of France. If France appears as an island of stability and firmness confronted by the growing waves of European pacifism it is partly because the peace movement in France is largely controlled by the Communist Party and this tends to repel the majority. But it is mainly because the three factors just described above do not apply to the French case. *Gaullisme* may have made France a nuisance to her Allies in the 1960s, but it is now largely responsible for its steadfastness. The principle of an independent *force de frappe* is no longer a matter of political debate in France since, by the middle of the 1970s, the Communists and the Socialists had accepted its logic. Nor does anyone question that France should remain outside the integrated military body of NATO. This consensus – some would say on the value of bluff – has protected France from disturbing debates. Together with a fortunate geography that places Germany between France and the Soviet threat and the fact that France is not concerned with the TNF modernization decision, this lack of contentious issues explains France's relative immunity to pacifism. *Gaullisme* has helped France on two more counts. It has provided France – exaggeratedly may be – with the sense of a special mission in the world, most recently emphasized by President Mitterrand. This conviction, linked with the control France has over her defence policy, has protected her existential interrogation. France does not face a crisis of identity. Nor does anti-Americanism, as a symbol of a rebellion against the values of the establishment, apply to France as it does to Northern Europe. Thanks largely to *Gaullisme*, a certain kind of anti-Americanism has been a value shared for many years by the political establishment itself and therefore anti-Americanism cannot represent for Frenchman a way of defining oneself by opposition to one's parent. The intelligentsia which might have acted as a focus for dissent, discovered the *gulag* in the early 1970s and this confirmed their dislike of the Soviet Union. When one puts all these factors together, they account for the appearance of France as a pillar of stability in the Western Alliance. This optimism should however, be tempered by four considerations. If France is not affected by neutralism it is because her strategic doctrine is largely one of neutrality. If anti-nuclear movements were to see their influence spreading in the West it would be difficult for France to remain for long unaffected. Moreover, there has been an indirect price to pay for that earlier victory of *Gaullisme*; it may – as mentioned earlier – be taking its toll in Germany today. Finally the French Government has lately been using an old brand of anti-Americanism in a new third-world guise and condemnation of US cultural imperialism may prove as detrimental to the demands of the Alliance as the anti-establishment rebellion of the Northern part of Europe.

Conclusions

The tendency of our societies to drift apart is reinforced by government policies and by the democratic nature of our political system The Reagan Administration, in its search for a policy that would weaken the Soviet Union, has so far succeeded mainly in weakening the Alliance. The European Governments in a desperate attempt to preserve what can be saved of detente, have moved dangerously towards dissociating their economic exchanges with the East from their political and military implications, thus reinforcing both the Soviet Union and the advocates of a different kind of unilateralism in the United States.

Family analogies are fashionable these days to describe the troubles of the Alliance. What is happening clearly surpasses a family quarrel but it is our common duty to prevent a progressive divorce that would be catastrophic both for the United States and Western Europe. Pacifism should not be the only highly visible force that the Americans and the Europeans have in common.

The domestic nature of our societies and the weight of electoral considerations when given priority over international concerns are aggravating the seriousness of the crisis. Anti-Americanism or anti-Europeanism cannot be allowed to compensate, in the eyes of the electorate, for the competitive failure of the French and American economic programmes.

The erosion of the Alliance and the crisis of the logic of nuclear deterrence reinforce the advocates of a conventional defence for Western Europe. Europe can no longer remain a 'civilian power'. But, the reasons that have prevented the creation of a European defence system yesterday are still present today. France, comforted in her tranquil selfishness by the way the international system has evolved, is not ready to modify her strategic doctrine. The Federal Republic cannot become a nuclear power and is neither ready nor willing to exchange an American nuclear guarantee for a French one. Moreover, the economic crisis makes *any* further defence effort a very difficult proposition. On each side of the Atlantic, there are growing frustrations with the state of the Alliance but no-one can think of serious alternatives. It is highly symbolic that, in spite of the fertile imagination of those who work in the field of international relations, we have found no word to describe the post-cold war post-detente era. It may very well be that for more than 30 years we have lived through an exceptional period. There was in the West a generous and powerful giant, there was apparently a stable balance of forces, there were prosperous economies and nationalism, as a result of two world wars, was weak. All these ingredients are slowly disappearing. European pacifism and American unilateralism are both symptoms of the resurgence of new nationalistic trends in the Western World. Shakespeare was making a prudent meteorological judgment when he observed that: 'So foul a sky will not clear without a storm'. Let us hope, at least in the case of the Western Alliance, that Shakespeare was wrong.

Deterrence, Consensus and Reassurance in the Defence of Europe

MICHAEL HOWARD

To ask a historian to look into and prescribe for the future is to invite a presentation consisting of as much past history as the author thinks he can get away with and as little prophecy and prescription as he thinks his audience will accept. Historians have seen too many confident prophets fall flat on their faces to lay themselves open to more humiliation than they can help. We know that all we can do is to help diagnose the problem or, better, expose false diagnoses. We also believe that in doing this it is helpful to consider how a situation has developed. I make no apology therefore for spending a few moments in casting a backward look over the origins and development of the Western Alliance to see how we have got to where we are now. There is little point in considering where we should be going if we do not first decide where we are starting from.

Let us go back thirty-five years, a third of a century, to the immediate aftermath of the Second World War. After the 'Battle of the Books' between the revisionist and counter-revisionist schools, a picture has now emerged over which most historians now agree. It is one of wartime understandings between the Soviet Union and her Western Allies – understandings based largely on Western illusions or at best the most fragile of hopes – breaking down within a few months of the end of hostilities. The Soviet Union moved in to consolidate, as part of her Empire, the territories already occupied by her armed forces – economically, politically and militarily. Simultaneously the United States was liquidating her wartime commitments to her European allies as quickly as – some might say more quickly than – she decently could. As a result, Western Europe in 1946–7 trembled on the verge of economic collapse, a collapse which its Moscow-orientated Communist par-

ties were fully prepared to exploit. In Germany, and especially in Berlin, democratic political parties fought what seemed to be a losing battle against strong, well-organized and confident Communist opponents who, for the past fifteen years, had been preparing for just such an opportunity. There was a widespread fear, not so much of Soviet military attack on Western Europe, but of a disintegration of the whole political and economic structure that would make any such attack unnecessary.

It was to prevent such a disintegration that the United States initiated, in 1947, the European Recovery Programme. This programme may have had an unforeseen escalatory effect in that it was perceived by the Soviet Union as a threat to their own control of Eastern Europe, and so precipitated those actions in Prague and Berlin in 1948 that were read by many in the West as clear evidence of Soviet aggressive intentions. If the Russians were thwarted in their use of political means for attaining their objectives (so the argument went) might they not use military ones – unless they were deterred from doing so by the clear perception that any such move would bring them up against the enormous latent power of the United States?

Strategic Reassurance

This was the thinking that led to the creation of the North Atlantic Treaty Organization in 1949. In Western Europe serious expectation of Soviet armed attack was still not high. It was to increase dramatically for a few months at the time of the Korean War, but even then the Europeans were less conscious of any imminent 'Soviet Threat' than they were of their own weakness, disunity and inability to cope with such a threat if one emerged. The American military presence was wanted in

Western Europe, not just in the negative role of a *deterrent* to Soviet aggression, but in the positive role of a *reassurance* to West Europe, the kind of reassurance a child needs from its parents or an invalid from his doctors against dangers which, however remote, cannot be entirely discounted. This concept of *reassurance* has not, so far as I know, hitherto been a term of art in strategic analysis, but it should be, and so far as I am concerned it is now.

Whether the North Atlantic Treaty and the steps taken to implement it were really necessary to deter the Soviet Union from a military onslaught on Western Europe we cannot tell until the Soviet Union is as generous with access to her official documents as we are in the West. It is, however, improbable, given both her historical record and her political philosophy, that she would have seriously contemplated such an action unless and until a recognizable 'revolutionary situation' had developed in the West in which they could plausibly intervene to give fraternal support to the toiling masses and to a powerful indigenous Communist Party that would act as their agent in controllling the region after its conquest. These requirements seemed, in the 1940s, to be developing quite nicely. Within a decade they had disappeared. Whatever the effectiveness of *deterrence, reassurance* had worked. The economy of Western Europe recovered, and with it the political self-confidence of the West Europeans. The Communist Parties withdrew from the centre of the political stage to the periphery, and increasingly distanced themselves from Moscow. Serious fears of Soviet attack dwindled and, after Stalin's death, they almost disappeared from the public consciousness. The outbreaks in Eastern Europe from 1953 onwards showed that it was the Soviet Union that was now on the political defensive. Its treatment of the Hungarian rising in 1956 led to massive defections from, and splits within, the Communist Parties in the West. In West Germany the economic miracle sucked out of the Eastern Zone by the hundreds of thousands precisely those well-qualified young people that the DDR needed to reconstruct her own economy. By the end of the 1950s Western Europe was an economic power-house that would have dominated Eastern Europe if the Soviet Union had let it. A decade later it was beginning to rival its own protector.

During this period the success of *reassurance* was, in some respects, an obstacle to *deterrence*. The peoples of Western Europe were so effectively reassured that they were prepared to run those military risks that have given their military leaders nightmares for the past thirty years. In 1950 there may have been serious fears of Soviet attack. Three years later, when the European statesmen came to consider the price which their military advisers had calculated, at the Lisbon Meeting in 1952, that they would have to pay for a credible deterrent military posture, such fears had almost disappeared. The re-establishment of economic stability was considered to demand overriding priority and the 'Lisbon Force Goals' went out of the window. In the judgment of the political leaders of Western Europe the danger of Soviet military attack did not appear great enough to warrant the costs involved in building up the kind of defensive forces that, on a purely military calculus, would be needed to deter it.

The Nuclear Alternative: Defence on the Cheap

It was then that thermo-nuclear weapons came to the rescue of soldiers and politicians alike, providing a deterrent that appeared militarily credible at a socially acceptable cost. The long-term implications of depending on weapons of mass destruction for national security worried only a politically insignificant minority. Governments, and the majorities on which they relied, found in nuclear weapons so convenient a solution to their budgetary problems that they were adopted almost without question. 'Conventional forces', with all their heavy social costs, could be reduced to the status of trip-wires, or at most, of shields to repel an enemy assault for the brief time needed for the Strategic Air Command to strike decisively at targets within the Soviet Union. The critiques both of the moralists and of the military specialists made no impact on those real centres of power in Western governments, the Treasuries, centres which owe their power to their capacity to reflect and enforce broadly accepted social priorities. Whatever their defence specialists might tell them about the balance of military forces, the peoples of Western Europe, so long as they remained prosperous, saw little danger of Soviet attack and wanted defence on the cheap. They remained *reassured*, though whether this reassurance came from shrewdness or from self-delusion, from confidence in American nuclear supremacy or basic disbelief in the reality of any Soviet threat, it would probably be impossible to say. In any case throughout the 1950s and the 1960s deterrence and reassurance both worked. The Europeans did get defence on the cheap, as they were getting energy on the cheap, and, thanks to the benevolent Keynesianism of the ruling economic pundits, everything else on the cheap. As one European leader remarked of his own nation, they had never had it so good.

Pleasant as this condition was so long as it lasted, it had two characteristics which in historical perspective emerge very clearly. One was that the credibility of the *deterrent* posture depended on a continuing American nuclear ascendancy over the Soviet Union, something about which I shall have more to say in a moment. The second, and perhaps more significant, was that the peoples of Western Europe effectively abandoned responsibility for their own defence. Their own armed forces, forces which have always had the social role of embodying national self-consciousness and will to independent existence, became almost peripheral, part of a mechanism of nuclear deterrence the ultimate control of which lay elsewhere. The reluctance of the British and French Governments to accept this situation and their development of strategic nuclear capabilities of their own has to be understood in these psychological terms, rather than those of the somewhat tortuous rationales which French and British officials now advance to justify their existence.

And even if these nuclear strike forces do, however marginally, enhance national independence, they are not 'popular' forces. That is, they are not forces with whose fortunes the nation can identify itself, as the British people identified themselves with the fortunes of their forces in the recent Falkland Islands campaign. To show the significance of

this fact, permit me a brief excursion into history. Popular involvement in war, as all readers of Clausewitz will know, is a matter of comparatively recent origin. In the eighteenth century, wars in Europe were fought by specialists responsive only to the requirements of absolute governments, and the less the population was involved in them the better. The role of the good citizen was to pay the taxes needed for the upkeep of these specialists, to acquiesce philosophically in any incidental hardships that their operations might cause him, and to keep his mouth shut. It was the French Revolution that (after the American Revolution) made popular involvement an intrinsic factor in war, a factor that was to become of growing importance until, in the First World War, it overshadowed everything else. In that conflict popular passion rather than military skill, much less political wisdom, determined the course of the war and ultimately its outcome. In the Second World War popular participation was still an essential element, although the contribution of scientific and technical specialists was increasingly decisive. But in the nuclear age those specialists have again reduced peoples to the passive roles they played, or were supposed to play, in the eighteenth century. It is assumed that war, if it comes, will be fought for them by experts, over (if they are lucky) their heads.

The Experts and the Public
The extent to which this has occurred can be seen by considering the debates over NATO strategy that have taken place, whether in official circles or in centres for strategic studies during the past twenty years. Increasingly the defence of Western Europe has been considered simply as a problem of 'extended deterrence' involving calculations of possibilities and probabilities as abstract as those of a chess game; as a problem to be solved by various combinations and deployments of delivery systems, strategic, intermediate or tactical, land-based, sea-based or air-based, but all under American control. The expertise needed to make these calculations is shared only by small groups of specialists and officials in European defence ministries, who have seldom seen it as their duty to expound these calculations to a wider public. The efforts of

such bodies as the International Institute for Strategic Studies and its associates elsewhere in Europe to educate public opinion in these matters has had at best limited success. They are too abstract, too arcane. Whatever the merits of the argument, for example, that the Soviet deployment of SS–20 missiles had to be countered by the emplacement of cruise missiles and *Pershing* IIs, it did not arise out of any profound and widely held anxiety among the peoples of Western Europe. It was a debate between specialists – and specialists who did not have the political antennae to foresee that such emplacement might make people feel more vulnerable rather than less. Such specialists are like theologians. When they lose touch with the springs of popular belief, when their analysis becomes too complex and remote, their authority becomes attenuated. New teachers will arise, Martin Luthers, John Wesleys, pastors whose beliefs may be simplistic to the point of lunacy, but whose message is responsive to popular needs and who can speak in a language that everyone can understand.

This is not to say that the specialists are to blame for this failure in communication. In defence questions as in any other area of government – economic policy, for example, or finance – the layman does not expect to have to master the technical details. He employs the expert to handle them for him. In defence as in these other fields there is always likely to be a difference between expert and lay perceptions, and it is the job of political leadership to reconcile them. In the field of defence this difference appears nowhere more clearly than in the distinction I have made between *reassurance* and *deterrence*. For the expert the two are indistinguishable. He will not believe his country to be safe unless he is satisfied that provision has been made to counter every option open to every likely adversary. The layman may be less demanding, but sometimes he is more. In certain moods, for example, the Congress of the United States has refused to be reassured by the deterrent posture that its military specialists have pronounced to be adequate. In Europe, on the other hand, the peoples of the Western democracies have accepted as amply reassuring a deterrent posture that their experts have

repeatedly told them is dangerously inadequate, and if the events of the past thirty years are anything to go by, popular instinct has proved more reliable than expert fears. In spite of the repeated warnings of its military specialists, no threat has materialized. Instead, the prosperity of the West has reached unheard of heights. It is the Communist societies, those which thirty years ago seemed so psychologically as well as militarily menacing, that now appear to be on the verge of economic and political disintegration.

Changes in the International Structure
Since the system that we have adopted has proved so successful for so long, is there really anything for us to worry about? Is there any need to reassess the requirements for defence, deterrence or reassurance for the 1980s and 1990s. I must admit once more to a historian's bias, which predisposes me to assume the obsolescence of any international structure with the passage of time. The Vienna Settlement of 1814–15, for example, lasted for about forty years. So did the Bismarckian Settlement of the 1870s. The structure is bound to be transformed by the dynamics of social change, by the altered perspectives and beliefs of a new generation sceptical, and usually rightly so, about the settled assumptions of its predecessors. We must ask not only whether the existing solutions are still valid for the problems that evoked them, but whether the problems themselves remain unchanged, and whether attitudes stereotyped in the late 1940s will still be relevant half a century later.

There can be little doubt that since 1949 changes have occurred, both objective and subjective, on a scale comparable to those between 1815 and 1854, or between 1870 and 1914: changes in the relationship between Western Europe and the United States; and changes in the military balance between the United States and the Soviet Union. These have been on a scale quite sufficient to compel a reappraisal of requirements for deterrence and reassurance established a generation ago.

The various causes and symptoms of transatlantic tension have been discussed so generally and so repeatedly that I propose to focus only on that most relevant to our immediate problem, that is the degree of anti-American sentiment now so evident in so many countries of Western Europe, to say nothing of the understandable resentment this has created in the United States. Opinion polls have revealed this anti-Americanism to be far less widespread than its more dramatic manifestations may sometimes suggest but, whatever its strength and incidence, it is disturbing enough to demand an explanation and to be taken seriously into account. It indicates that, for an appreciable number of Europeans, what was once seen as the prime requirement for *deterrence*, that is the commitment of American power to the defence of Western Europe, no longer provides the political *reassurance* that once it did; in some respects indeed it provides the exact opposite. So far from the Americans being in Europe to help the West Europeans defend themselves, they are seen in some quarters as being here in order to prosecute *their* war, a war in which the Europeans have no interest and from which they will be the first to suffer.

How has such a widespread and grotesque misunderstanding come about? Obviously there is a whole complex of reasons, in which simple cultural friction plays its part. But it is at least in part the outcome of the process I have described, by which the defence of Europe has become perceived not as the responsibility of the Europeans themselves but increasingly in terms of a system of 'extended nuclear deterrence' manipulated from the United States in accordance with strategic concepts with which few Europeans are familiar. If I may return to my historical discourse, in the eighteenth century the European bourgeoisie was well content to leave the conduct of war to its specialists and enjoy the improved quality of life made possible by that division of labour. But it was precisely this divorce of the bourgeoisie and their intelligentsia from the whole business of national defence that gave rise to the first 'Peace Movements', comprising intellectuals who maintained that, because wars were conducted by monarchical states with aristocratic-led professional soldiers, it was this war-making mechanism that actually *produced* wars, and that all that was needed to abolish war would be to abolish monarchs, aristocrats and the

military profession. After that it could be assumed that the peoples of Europe would live together in peace and harmony. The wars of the French Revolution were to disillusion them, as the First World War was to disillusion another generation of peace-bred intellectuals and the Second World War yet a third. But it takes only one generation of successful peacekeeping to engender the belief, among those not concerned with its mechanisms, that peace is a natural condition threatened only by those professionally involved in preparations for war. The military become the natural target for the idealistic young. And how much more will this be the case if those military are predominantly foreign? If the decision for peace or war appears to lie with a group of remote and uncontrollable decision-makers whose values and interests do not necessarily coincide with one's own? And if war is going to involve slaughter on so unimaginable a scale? Is it not these foreigners who are actually provoking the war? Are not the bases they have established in our territories a standing provocation to attack, eroding rather than enhancing our security? So the growth of pacifism, always endemic in a society that delegates defence questions to specialists, has in contemporary Europe become associated with anti-Americanism, and derives from that a populist veneer that otherwise it might lack.

It is here that the change in the military balance comes in. I would not like to judge how far the effectiveness of American *reassurance* in the 1950s and 1960s was due to any general perception in Western Europe of American nuclear predominance. Certainly neither European nor American defence experts habitually cited this as evidence for the credibility of nuclear deterrence. One can only say that expectations of the damage Western Europe might suffer as a result of Soviet response to that American 'first use' on which NATO strategy explicitly depended led to no widespread questioning among Europeans of the validity of that strategy. It was the Americans, under Mr McNamara, who were unhappy about it, but they could find few people in Europe, outside our tiny defence community, to share their doubts. The fact that the 'Peace Movement' has become active

119

in Western Europe at the precise moment that the United States has publicly admitted Soviet nuclear parity may or may not be co-incidental. It does mean however that the 'Peace Movement' can now support its arguments with some fairly tough strategic analysis, and find more sympathy within the defence community than would have been the case twenty years ago. It is no longer only a minority of anti-militarist intelligentsia who question the validity and credibility of a deterrent posture which would, if activated, destroy everything it is concerned to defend.

The result of these developments has been a serious disjunction between *deterrence* and *reassurance*. The object of *deterrence* is to persuade an adversary that the costs to him of seeking a military solution to his political problems will far outweigh the benefits. The object of *reassurance* is to persuade one's own people, and those of one's allies, that the benefits of military action, or preparation for it, will outweigh the costs. It is true that the Europeans were reassured in the 1950s not by any careful calculation of what they would lose or gain by war, but by their perception of the reverse – of how much the USSR would have to lose and how little to gain. She could threaten, or rather her allies could threaten, such cataclysmic damage to the enemy, at such low *immediate* social cost to herself, that the risk of any comparable damage to herself was seen as remote enough to be tolerable.

This is the situation that has been changed by nuclear parity, and it is a change of which all Europeans and an increasing number of Americans have now become conscious. Defence specialists may be puzzled and scornful that people who have been under threat of nuclear attack for at least twenty years should only now be beginning to take the problem seriously, but that they have now begun to do so is a new political fact that governments will have to take into account. It is also apparent, at least in Europe, that *reassurance* cannot be re-established by any improvement in the mechanism of *deterrence*, certainly not of nuclear deterrence. Perhaps the people of Western Europe ought to feel safer when the installation of *Pershing* II and cruise missiles has made clear our capacity to counter an SS–20 first strike, but I doubt whether they

really will. Perhaps we should all feel safer if the United States did develop the capacity to carry on, and 'prevail' in, a prolonged nuclear exchange with the Soviet Union but in fact public opinion in Europe is terrified by the prospect – and so is much of it in the United States. In the calculus of nuclear deterrence both developments may appear appropriate, even essential, but such a calculus does not translate easily into the language of political reassurance and certainly not in a Europe where any nuclear exchange, on however limited a scale, spells almost inconceivable disaster. Limited nuclear options do not look very attractive if we are likely to be one of them ourselves.

The Fear of Nuclear War
Any consideration of domestic consensus on defence questions must therefore begin with the realization that in Europe the Soviet Union is very widely seen as less of a danger than is the prospect of nuclear war. I state this dogmatically and can support the statement with no evidence from opinion polls. It is an impression gained from a wide study of the press, the media, and discussion with friends and colleagues outside the defence community. It is also important to realize that the nuclear war anticipated is not seen as one arising out of a Soviet attack on Western Europe, but rather from some self-sustaining process of escalation, perhaps originating in an extra-European conflict, but essentially caused by the whole apparatus of nuclear weapons in some way 'getting out of control'. Nuclear war is seen as a *Ding an Sich* (thing of itself), unrelated to the existing political situation or to any security requirements likely to arise out of it. It is therefore against the prospect of nuclear war itself, rather than that of Soviet attack, that Europeans now require *reassurance*, and any measures taken to deal with the latter that make the former seem more likely will continue to be deeply disruptive. The explanation that any measures effective in deterring Soviet attack make nuclear war *less* likely is no longer, for many Europeans, altogether persuasive. As fears of nuclear war become detached from fears of Soviet attack, so reassurance becomes divorced from deterrence. And it must be admit-

ted that those calculations of nuclear strategy so distressingly prevalent in the United States, which take place in a kind of empyrean realm remote from the political realities of Europe or anywhere else, have powerfully contributed to this divorce.

Reconciling Deterrence and Reassurance

How are we to deal with this problem? How are deterrence and reassurance to be once more reconciled? This is the task that will confront statesmen and strategists for the rest of this century.

The task is complicated by differing perspectives on either side of the Atlantic as to what it is that we have to deter. The difference between European and American readings of Soviet power and intentions, to which we could and perhaps should devote an entire conference, have here to be accepted as given. As European fears of Soviet aggression have waned over the past thirty years, so American fears have grown. We have too the curious phenomenon that the countries most directly threatened by Soviet military power – West Germany and France – are those most confident in their ability to handle the Soviet Union through the normal machinery of diplomatic and political intercourse, while for the most remote, the most powerful and the least threatened of the allies – the United States – the Soviet Union still bulks as a figure of almost cosmic evil with whom no real dialogue is possible. Whether the European attitude is the result of greater wisdom or merely of wishful thinking is a matter that we could debate endlessly but I believe that a significant element in this difference of view lies in the degree to which the Europeans have abandoned the primary responsibility for their defence to the United States. Europeans have come to take the deterrence provided by others for granted and now assume that the dangers against which they once demanded reassurance only now exist in the fevered imagination of their protectors. A certain American tendency to hyperbole, an attachment to worst-case analysis and some unfortunate attempts to make our flesh creep with official publications in gorgeous technicolour whose statistics have been questioned even by European defence specialists,

have not helped improve matters. Such propagandistic efforts are widely discounted, and even when they are believed they are likely to engender not so much resolution as despair.

Our first task must therefore be to get Soviet power and intentions into perspective. The exaggerated melodrama implied in the term 'The Soviet Threat' seems and has always seemed to me unnecessary and counter-productive. There is a major problem of ideological hostility, and a major problem (though one not to be exaggerated) of military imbalance between a power the size of the Soviet Union and the smaller, even if richer and more dynamic, states of Western Europe. One does not have to attribute to the Soviet Union either predatory intentions or ambitions for global conquest to persuade all but a stubborn minority that the states of Western Europe have a problem of military security that must be solved if normal intercourse with the Soviet Union is to be sustained on a basis of equality. The Soviet Union has shown herself to be no more reluctant to use military means to solve political problems, when she can get away with it, than anyone else. It is not difficult to reach consensus within most groups of West Europeans that West Europe needs defences against the Soviet Union. Where consensus breaks down is over the question whether Europe can possibly be defended by nuclear war.

The second task therefore is to show that Europe *can* be defended, and that the costs of doing so would not outweigh the benefits. These costs must be seen as twofold: the prospective costs of nuclear war, with which public opinion is chiefly concerned; and the immediate costs of an economic kind, which are what worry governments. It is easy enough to say that no price is too high for the preservation of our independence, but it does not quite work out like that. Governments are concerned with independence, but they are also concerned with social stability. Even in the darkest days of the Cold War 'the soviet threat' was seen as ancillary to, and only given credibility by, the danger of social disintegration in the West. It is still a reasonable assumption that a stable and prosperous Western Europe will not present an attractive target to Soviet ambitions. Defence expenditure has therefore to be fitted in to a general framework of economic policy in which the maintenance of an industrious economy and a high level of social welfare (so far as these can be reconciled) must enjoy an overriding priority. This assumption has not altered over the past thirty years, nor is it likely to change much over the next thirty.

During the past thirty years this problem of costs was, as we have seen, taken care of by nuclear deterrence. The immediate costs were kept acceptably low, the risk of incurring the ultimate costs seemed acceptably slight. Now, although there is a far greater reluctance to incur those long-term risks, there is no greater readiness to accept any increase in immediate costs, especially during a period of recession when the danger of social instability seems greater than at any time since the 1940s. Again, it is easy to say that no price should be too high for the avoidance of nuclear war but, for governments concerned with their everyday tasks, nuclear war still remains a remote if terrifying hypotheses, while mass unemployment, commercial bankruptcies and industrial discontent are an imminent reality. A society where domestic consensus has collapsed is in no position to fight a war, nuclear or otherwise.

So where does this leave us? First, the requirement for effective deterrence remains, if only because the Soviet Union cannot be expected to observe a higher standard of conduct towards weaker neighbours than other states, whatever their political complexion, have shown in the past. Second, deterrence can no longer depend on the threat of a nuclear war, the costs of which would be grotesquely out of proportion to any conceivable benefits to be derived from engaging in it. Third, proposals to make nuclear war 'fightable', let alone 'winnable' by attempting to limit its targets and control its course, however much sense this may make in the military grammar of *deterrence*, are not persuasive in the political language of *reassurance*. And finally the problem cannot be solved by any massive transferral of resources to conventional capabilities. The immediate social costs of doing so, whether one likes it or not, are unacceptably high.

Reducing Dependence on US Deterrence

Whatever the solution may be, I do not believe that it can be found at the macro-level of nuclear deterrence. There is a point beyond which the elaboration of nuclear arsenals ceases to bear any evident relation to the real problems faced by political communities and, so far as Europe is concerned, we passed that point long ago. It must be sought at the micro-level of the peoples, the societies that have to be defended, and for whose political cohesion, moral resolution and military preparedness nuclear weapons can no longer provide a credible substitute. There has been for many years what I can only describe as a morally debilitating tendency among European defence specialists to argue that, if the reassurance provided by the American nuclear guarantee were to be in any way diminished, European morale would collapse. I do not believe this to be true and, in so far as it is true, it is as a self-fulfilling prophecy, and one that American defence analysts have taken altogether too seriously. The reassurance on which most Europeans rely is the presence among them of American troops, a presence that makes the defence of West European territory appear a feasbile proposition and has encouraged us to make greater provision for our own defence. What is needed today is a reversal of that process whereby European Governments have sought greater security by demanding an ever greater intensification of the American nuclear commitment, demands that are as divisive within their own countries as they are irritating for the people of the United States. Instead we should be doing all that we can to reduce our dependence on American nuclear weapons by enhancing, so far as it is militarily, socially and economically possible, our capacity to defend ourselves.

By 'defend ourselves' I mean defend ourselves in the conventional sense with conventional weapons. I know that this view will not be universally popular. It is often argued that no such defence is possible unless we are prepared to turn West Europe into an armed camp but that proposition would be true only if we intended to fight a total war aiming at the destruction of the Soviet armed forces and the dictation of peace in Moscow. It is also argued that, whatever effort we made, the Soviet armed forces would ultimately overwhelm us. Of course they could, if they were prepared to pay a very high price, which is why I for one would be unwilling explicitly to renounce under any circumstances the use of nuclear weapons. It has been argued that, for those exposed to it, conventional war is no less terrible than nuclear war, and indeed events in the Lebanon have shown us just how terrible it can be – especially for those who have no means of defending themselves. But terrible as conventional war would be in Europe, nuclear war would be unimaginably, unendurably worse. Modern societies recover from conventional war within a generation. Whether humanity would ever recover from nuclear war is a matter for legitimate doubt.

Let us remember what we are trying to do. It is to deter the Soviet Union from using military force to solve its political differences with the West and to deter them in a way that will be credible to their leaders and acceptable – *reassuring* – to our own peoples. It is to make clear to the Soviet Union that in any attack on the West the costs will hugely outweigh the benefits, and to our own people that the benefits of such a defence will outweigh the costs. We have to make it clear to our potential adversaries that there can be no easy military solution to their political problems, no 'quick fix'. And this is best done by showing that any attack would be met by lethally efficient armed forces, backed up and where necessary, assisted by a resolute and prepared population, with the distinct possibility that the conflict might escalate to nuclear war and the certainty that, *even if it did not*, their armed forces would suffer casualties out of all proportion to any likely gains. The object of such defence would not be just the denial of territory. It would be the infliction of damage on the attacking forces on a scale incommensurate with any political objective they could conceivably gain by their attack. The image that the West Europeans need to present is that of a hedgehog – painful to devour and impossible to digest.

This is no doubt an ideal model but I defy anyone to think of a better. The probable alternative is one of inadequate, ill-equipped and undertrained forces, fighting on behalf of a divided or an indifferent population and dependent on an American President being prepared to sanction a nuclear release that would certainly destroy all they were fighting to defend and that might very well unleash a global holocaust into the bargain. That is the prospect that worries so many of us today, and the 'Peace Movement' is only articulating, in extreme form, many widespread and legitimate doubts. To escape from this situation and move towards the goal I have suggested would mean a change of emphasis from nuclear deterrence to conventional, or even unconventional defence. It would mean a shifting of primary responsibility to the Europeans for the defence of our own continent. It should also involve a greater degree of popular participation in defensive preparations, participation the more likely to be forthcoming if it is clear that such preparations were predominantly if not wholly non-nuclear. An invitation to participate in such preparations would indeed be the acid test for the 'Peace Movement', sorting out those who were interested only in making moral gestures and those whose sympathies lie on the other side of the Iron Curtain from the great majority of thoughtful citizens seriously concerned with questions of defence.

Progress along these lines, however modest, would do much to resolve the difficulties within the Alliance and create what Professor Lawrence Freedman has called 'a more mature relationship'. It would create a defence posture acceptable to our own peoples as well as credible to our potential adversaries. It would not solve the problem of deterring a first nuclear strike by the opposition. For that, as for much else, the Europeans must continue to depend on the United States, and few Americans would wish it otherwise. But this reliance must be placed in perspective. A Soviet nuclear attack on Western Europe, or the plausible threat of one, is perhaps not utterly inconceivable. It is certainly an option that we need to deter. But it does not rank high on the list of political probabilities, and the measures taken to counter it should not be regarded or depicted as being basic to the defence of Western Europe. The necessity for such counter-measures should be fully and publicly explained, but they should be put in the context of the fundamental task which only non-nuclear forces can effectively carry out, the defence of territory. Nuclear deterrence needs to be subordinated to this primary task of territorial defence, and not *vice versa*.

It is the reassertion of this order of priorities, this reuniting of deterrence and re-assurance, that seems to me basic for the creation of consensus within the Alliance over the requirements for the defence of the West in the 1980s, or indeed for however long it may take to establish such intimate and friendly relations with the Soviet Union that defence becomes a pure formality. And in order to maintain consensus, the achievement of this relationship must be seen to be our long-term goal. I hope it goes without saying that any developments along the lines I have proposed should go hand in hand with arms-control initiatives, both to eliminate unnecessary causes of tension and to keep the costs of defence on both sides down to socially acceptable levels. But we should not allow ourselves to expect any miraculous breakthroughs as a result of such initiatives, or be unduly depressed or bitter if they fail. 'The Dual Track' is essential to effective reassurance: peoples expect their governments to provide them with adequate protection, but they also expect them to seek peace and, if they are not seen to be doing so, consensus over defence will crumble away.

Above all we must stop being frightened, and trying to frighten each other, with spectres either of Soviet 'windows of opportunity' or of the prospect of inevitable, self-generating nuclear war. Defence will continue to be a necessity in a world of sovereign states. Nuclear war is a terrible possibility that nothing can now eradicate, but of whose horrors we must never lose sight. To deal with the dilemma arising from these twin evils we need clear heads, moral courage, human compassion, and above all a sense of proportion. The main condition for consensus in the 1980s is in fact that we should all grow up. This, unfortunately, may be the most difficult requirement of all.

Broadening the Strategic Focus: Comments on Michael Howard's Paper

SAMUEL P. HUNTINGTON

On rare occasions in the history of any subject, a thinker has an insight and articulates a new concept or idea, after which everyone says 'How brilliant! How obvious! How did we ever get along before without it?' Such is the case with the concept of 'reassurance' that Michael Howard develops in his Paper. How *did* we ever get along without it? We surely will get along in the future only by making good use of it. It is the central contribution of an absolutely first-rate Paper, which is throughout original in thought, elegant in phrasing, and penetrating in analysis.

As a result, strategy must now be explicitly directed to not one but two problems: deterrence and reassurance. The solutions to these problems are related, sometimes positively, sometimes negatively. One major source of our current strategic difficulties, Michael Howard argues, is that the needs of deterrence now conflict with the needs of reassurance. That may be true. But it is also necessary to recognize that the current intensity of both problems stems from a common source. That source is the change during the 1970s in the military balance of power between the United States and the Soviet Union, particularly in the area of nuclear weapons. Perceptions of this changing balance and of the resulting relative weakness of the West are, as the public opinion polls demonstrate, widespread in both Europe and America. Weakness, in turn, generates fear. With some people the fear is of the Soviet Union, and of intensified Soviet aggression or pressure on the West. That is one version of the 'present danger', and those with this concern lobby for a greatly expanded military effort to restore a more satisfactory balance. With other people, however, the fear generated by weakness is of nuclear war and the awesome destruction that would be entailed by almost any use of nuclear weapons.

That is their 'present danger', and they debouch into the streets with 'peace' marches and demonstrations against nuclear deployments and in favour of nuclear freezes.

The current situation in the West thus bears marked similarities to that which existed in the late 1950s and early 1960s. As a result of *Sputnik* and Soviet missile developments and the apparently confident (but false) claims of Khrushchev about Soviet military prowess, feelings of weakness permeated Western societies. These resulted, on the one hand, in the Campaign for Nuclear Disarmament (CND), 'Ban the Bomb' marches, 'peace' candidates for public office, and the like. On the other hand, they also produced intense concern in the United States about the Soviet Union moving ahead in space technology and weapons, the Gaither Committee report, a 'missile gap' scare, and major efforts to push the US nuclear build-up, which took off dramatically following the advent of the Kennedy Administration in 1961. Fear of nuclear war and fear of the Soviet Union, in short, rose together from perceptions of Western weakness. In the event, some of the perceptions turned out to be misperceptions and the Kennedy Administration's efforts to expand US military power rapidly corrected the balance. The true nature of the balance was dramatically underlined by the Cuban missile crisis, after which fears of both nuclear war and of Soviet aggression declined markedly. Reassurance was re-established when it was shown that deterrence worked.

A somewhat comparable situation exists now. Reassurance will only be achieved when the credibility of deterrence is no longer in doubt. The conflict at present is consequently not so much between reassurance and deterrence as it is between short-term reassurance and long-term reassurance. Those whom weakness has made afraid of nuclear war want to be reassured that nuclear war will not happen; they seek that reassurance through nuclear freezes, 'no-first-use' pledges, nuclear-free zones, and the like. Insofar as these actions impede the re-establishment of Western military strength, as well as possibly encourage Soviet adventurism, however, they directly obstruct long-term reassurance. They treat the symptoms but not the cause of the present uneasiness in the West. That cause can only be removed by the massive reconstruction of Western – primarily US – military power to correct the effects of the eight successive years when the US consistently reduced her military strength. The first imperative, therefore both to enhance deterrence and to enhance reassurance is to rectify the military balance – particularly in the nuclear area – along the lines initiated by the Carter Administration and carried forward and intensified by the Reagan Administration.

In saying this, it must also be recognized, however, that we will never be able to recreate the levels of assurance against the Soviet threat that some right-wing extremists would like, nor the levels of assurance against the possibility of nuclear war that some street demonstrators would find comforting. We cannot escape the presences of a hostile power and of nuclear weapons, and while the appropriate military build-up can raise the levels of both deterrence and reassurance, nothing can be done to make the world reassuringly safe. We have no choice but to live with a certain level of anxiety with respect to both the Kremlin and the bomb.

Removing any doubt as to the equivalence – particularly in terms of survivability and flexible retaliatory capability – of US strategic weapons is a first priority. As has been recognized for years, however, and as was forcefully delineated by Henry Kissinger in his speech in Brussels in 1979, no attainable US nuclear capability can restore the older pattern of extended deterrence for Europe. Deterrence and reassurance in Europe require other approaches. There may be many possible ones; let me mention four.

First, it is conceivable that the existing and planned NATO military capabilities will suffice for deterrence. John Mearsheimer, among others, has made a powerful case that the conventional balance on the Central Front is nowhere near as precarious as it is often made out to be and that Soviet commanders could only see great losses and high risks in an offensive campaign in Central Europe.[1] In the discussions of this Conference, François de Rose argued that deterrence in Europe rests not on an American *nuclear* guarantee but on an American *security* guarantee which results from the fact that the independence and security of Europe are of vital concern and interest to the United States. Consequently, any attempt to destroy them would imply the risk of a major conflict with the United States which is probably what the USSR wants to avoid at all cost. Furthermore, any prospect that conventional hostilities in Europe could not bring immediate Soviet victory would be fraught with political and military dangers for the Soviet Union in Eastern Europe. This argument parallels the stress that the Reagan Administration has placed on protracted conventional war, horizontal escalation, force sustainability, and industrial mobilization.

There is therefore some reason to think that what we have (and will have) may be enough. Yet there remain powerful arguments on the other side as to the vulnerability of NATO, particularly to a quick offensive, and uneasy doubts as to whether, even with appropriate warning, NATO would in fact be able to mobilize its forces for an effective defence in Germany. Uncertainty as to the possible outcome of a war involving the current order of battle could be enough to deter the Soviet Union but it is not enough to reassure the Allies. The current balance and current policy are precisely the sources of the feeling that we are unassured and that, hence, the Soviet Union may be undeterred.

If the existing balance is inadequate for reassurance and possibly inadequate for deterrence, what are the alternatives? That which is most widely proposed is, of course, a significant increase in NATO conventional strength. Michael Howard makes an eloquent case for such a strategy. 'We (Europeans)', he says, 'should be doing all that we can to reduce our dependence on American nuclear weapons by enhancing, so far as is militarily, socially and economically possible, our capacity to defend ourselves,' that is, 'to defend ourselves in the conventional sense with conventional weapons.' This will, he notes, require a greater European military effort. He suggests that such an effort should not be beyond the realm of possibility if its purpose is not to be able to dictate peace in Moscow but to create a situation where, if they invaded Western Europe, the USSR 'would suffer casualties out of all proportion to any likely gains,' even if nuclear weapons were not used.

Deterrence by conventional defence has a certain appeal. It has, indeed, been set forth by a variety of committees, experts and conferences, at least since the noted Lisbon NATO Meeting of 1952. After thirty years, it remains appealing, but it also remains an unreality. Michael Howard himself calls his prescription an 'ideal model', and European Governments and peoples have never been willing to implement it in practice. For years this attitude was justified on the very practical grounds that it made more sense to rely on the American nuclear deterrent. Now that the latter is no longer what it used to be, perhaps a credible European conventional defence force will begin to materialize. But the attitudes of European publics and governments are no more favourable than they have been in the past, and economic conditions are far less propitious than they ever have been in the past. The burden of proof that conventional defence is a feasible option lies on its proponents and clearly has not been met.

There are further problems with the concept itself. Michael Howard speaks of a European conventional force that would impose unacceptable casualties on the Soviet Union. What would the level of such casualties have to be? A successful invasion of Western Europe could bring the Soviet Union a total change in the 1945 settlement and in the global balance of power, the projection of their power and influence to the Atlantic coast, the subordination of the industrial heartland of Europe in the Rhine and Ruhr valleys to Soviet purposes, the dissolution of the First OECD) World as we know it and its relegation to North America, Australia and New Zealand, since Japan would inevitably have to accommodate herself to the new power the Soviet Union would be able to wield in Asia.

How many casualties would a Soviet Government be willing to pay to achieve these results? A few hundred thousand? Certainly. A million? Very probably. Two or three million? Quite possibly. What forces would Western Europe have to have to impose such casualties? What European cabinets would vote the resources to maintain such forces? Even if one assumes three or four Soviet casualties for every European casualty (ignoring, for the moment, the fact that the war would be fought in the midst of European populations), how long would European Governments and armies be willing to suffer the hundreds of thousands and probably millions of casualties that would be necessary to convince the Soviet Union to back off?

There is yet a further problem. The purpose of NATO strategy is deterrence. A purely defensive strategy is inherently a weaker deterrent than one which promises retaliation against valued assets of the aggressor. This has long been recognized to be the case at the strategic nuclear level. It is also true at the conventional level. Given the nature of modern conventional weapons and current NATO forward defence strategy, a Soviet offensive is almost inevitably going to be a partial success. Even if it does not reach the North Sea or Frankfurt or the Rhine, it will still penetrate some distance into West Germany. Once it is stopped, the Allies may attempt to pull together forces for a counter-offensive. Such would be a difficult political and logistical undertaking. Inevitably the pressures will be on all parties to attempt to negotiate a cease-fire and a resolution of the conflict. With their armies ensconced in Bavaria and Saxony, the Soviet Union will clearly have the upper hand in such a negotiation. Although they may not have gained everything they wanted, they are certainly likely to come out of the conflict in a better position than they were before they started hostilities.

On the record to date, then, a conventional defence strategy has been unfeasible politically; if it could be implemented, it would be of dubious value militarily.

Are there other alternatives? In his Paper Michael Howard points out that the Congress of Vienna Settlement and the Bismarckian Settlement of the 1870s each lasted about forty years. The fortieth anniversary of the end of the 1939–45 war is only a short time away, and hence we should ask 'whether attitudes stereotyped in the late 1940s will still be relevant half a century later'. Discussion of NATO strategy has in large part accepted the constraints of the post-1945 settlement. This is particularly marked in the extent to which the alternatives debated have been spread along a single continuum from total reliance on the American nuclear deterrent, at one end, to total reliance on a European conventional defence force, at the other. Forty years later perhaps it is time to get off that continuum and to consider other possibilities that may be more appropriate for the changed conditions of the 1980s. Many such 'off-continuum' strategic alternatives may exist. Let me mention two, which perhaps deserve more serious consideration than they have received.

First, given the problems involved in a conventional defence of Europe, is there any way in which a credible nuclear deterrent can be recreated? The answer is that there is an obvious way, if Europeans are willing to pursue it. The threat to use nuclear weapons in response to a conventional attack is most credible – and, indeed, may only be credible – when the national existence of the state attacked is at risk. No one seriously doubts that an Israeli Government, for example, would use nuclear weapons if massed Arab armies threatened to swarm across its borders and into Tel Aviv. Although it is certainly not NATO's only problem, NATO's central problem is the possibility of Soviet aggression in Central Europe. One relatively certain way to deter that aggression would be to create a reasonable-sized, invulnerable German nuclear force capable of retaliating against the Soviet Union. Such a force could be based both at sea (in submarines and on surface ships) and in a mobile form on land. It could conceivably develop out of the deployment of US *Pershing* II and GLCM (ground launched cruise missiles) to Germany. It is planned to have these weapons under purely US control. Conceivably, they could be shifted first to dual control and then to purely German control. As it developed, the German nuclear force might or might not join French and British

nuclear forces as part of a broader European multilateral (if one dares use that word in this context) nuclear deterrence consortium. The *sine qua non*, however, is that one finger on the nuclear trigger should be in Bonn; nothing less would provide a sufficiently credible deterrent against a conventional attack by the Soviet Union.

Movement in this direction would mean discarding several assumptions of the late-1940s settlement, particularly that which saw Germany as an inherently aggressive power which consequently had to forgo defence measures permitted other states. But the Federal Republic has accepted the division of Europe and of Germany. However much she may wish for a peaceful reunification, she clearly is not a *revanchiste* power. (Even if she were, it is not clear how a modest-sized nuclear force would help her to achieve her objectives.) The unassailable logic which President de Gaulle applied to the development of the French *Force de Frappe* in the early 1960s is even more relevant to Germany now, which is, after all, in the front line. While the Soviet Union might well be willing to sacrifice a million soldiers to control Western Europe, they are not likely to be willing to sacrifice Moscow, Leningrad, Kiev, Stalingrad, and much else besides to achieve that end. The damage that could be inflicted by even a modest size nuclear force would be devastating; the certainty that it would be inflicted would be as close to one hundred percent as anything can be in the uncertain world of politics and war. Deterrence would operate.

What about reassurance? Paradoxically such a strategy would probably provide a great deal of reassurance for Germans and would quite likely cut the ground from under the German anti-nuclear movements. As Michael Howard points out, the debilitating aspect of current strategy is the extent to which it makes Europeans dependent upon Americans for their security. That is not a healthy situation. A minority of the German public is intensely opposed to the deployment of American theatre nuclear weapons in their country. It is highly unlikely that the same opposition would manifest itself to German nuclear weapons. People become reassured when they feel they have some control over the critical decisions affecting their future. It is also hardly coincidental, as many have pointed out, that pacifism and anti-nuclearism have been much weaker in France, which proudly accepts responsibility for her own nuclear and conventional defence, than in other European countries which are more dependent on American protection. A German nuclear deterrent would put responsibility for the key decisions affecting German security in German hands, although it would not necessarily mean that Germany would opt out of NATO or forego the security guarantees of the United States and the other European powers. It might well, however, facilitate the withdrawal of some American troops from Germany.

A German nuclear deterrent might be somewhat less than reassuring for at least parts of the publics in other European countries. World War II, however, is now almost two generations in the past, and on this issue the successor generation may well have greater tolerance and understanding than its predecessors. In the late twentieth century it is difficult to see why France and Britain can be trusted with nuclear weapons but not Germany. One person expressed to me the fear that Germany would target Paris; if that is the basis on which opposition to a German nuclear deterrent rests, it should be brought out into the open for the ridicule it deserves. A German nuclear force could, however, raise deterrence concerns elsewhere in Europe. The certainty of increased costs to the Soviet Union for aggression in Central Europe could enhance the relative attractiveness to them of aggression on the flanks of Europe. The price of the more assured deterrence in Germany for the Alliance, could, in short, be a greater external commitment of men and resources to the defence of Norway and Turkey. I do not now recommend the creation of a German nuclear force. I do suggest, however, that the issue deserves a far fuller and more serious consideration than it has received for some while.

A much preferable alternative to such a move would be for NATO generally to adopt a conventional retaliatory strategy. Such a strategy would capitalize on the developments during the past decade in Eastern Europe and the changed relationships between Eastern and Western Europe. Next to a nuclear attack on the Soviet Union herself, the contingency that the Soviet Union fears most must be an Allied conventional offensive into Eastern Europe. The arguments in favour of a shift in NATO strategy from flexible response to conventional retaliation are overwhelming, and I have enumerated them elsewhere.[2] Suffice it here simply to make three points.

– A politically-diplomatic defensive stance in favour of the maintenance of the *status quo* need not imply a militarily defensive strategy once the *status quo* has been attacked. This is simple common sense. In addition, of course, for two decades NATO has contemplated nuclear retaliation against the Soviet Union, in the event of an attack on Western Europe. The concept of conventional retaliation into Eastern Europe is morally far preferable and hence should be far more acceptable than one which relies on early recourse to nuclear weapons.
– A strategy of conventional retaliation would not require the massive conventional build-up needed for a strategy of conventional defence. The widely quoted axioms that the offence requires a 3–1 or 4–1 or 5–1 superiority applies not across the front as a whole but rather at the point of attack. A Soviet offensive is a real threat not because they have that a 3–1 superiority in the overall balance of forces in Europe, which they do not, but because they can concentrate their forces to achieve it at the critical point or points. NATO can do exactly the same in reverse, and the new US army 'Air-Land Battle' tactical doctrine is precisely suited to this purpose.
– The virtual certainty of the immediate movement of West German divisions into East Germany and of American divisions into Czechoslovakia and Hungary would be a major deterrent to Soviet attack on Western Europe. The Soviet Union would not and could not count on the loyalty of Eastern European forces and populations. Most importantly, neither could Eastern European governments, do so and they are likely to do everything they could to dissuade the Soviet Union from attacking the

West. NATO strategy has for too long relied on the diminished credibility of the threat to go up the escalation ladder. A conventional retaliatory strategy would make deterrence rest not on the threat to go up but on the threat to go East.

How much reassurance would a strategy of conventional retaliation provide? It would certainly provide more than a strategy that places major reliance on American nuclear guarantees, but it would also clearly require a substantial American conventional capability in Central Europe. It would be a strategy to which the Europeans could make major contributions, either to the offensive forces required for prompt movement to the East or to the holding forces required to slow down the Soviet movement to the West. To a large extent the latter should be militia and reserves derived from Michael Howard's 'resolute and angry population'. Indeed his emphasis on a more popularly-based defence of Western Europe becomes feasible and militarily useful *only* when it is combined with the threat of a rapid eastward movement by NATO regular forces. In effect, the Soviet Union would be told: 'if you go West, you will confront an organized, armed and trained population ready to make you pay a price, bearable but still heavy, for every kilometer, while we go East to encounter unreliable armies and to arouse the sullen and rebellious populations which you remember so well from 1953, 1956, 1968 and 1980–81.'

While there may be other strategic alternatives for NATO, there are, then, at least these four:

- continuation of the existing strategy and forces;
- creation of a massive conventional defensive force;
- creation of a German nuclear deterrent force;
- adoption of a strategy of conventional retaliation.

To put it mildly, there is unlikely to be an immediate consensus forming in support of either of the latter two possibilities. People will say that both ideas are unsettling and dangerous. New ideas are, however, always unsettling; that is their virtue. They are also always labelled dangerous; that is their burden. In the 1980s, however, NATO is unlikely to achieve the desirable minimum levels of deterrence or reassurance either with the current strategy, which has been found wanting because it is incredible, or with the conventional build-up strategy, which is lacking because it is unfeasible. The post-war era is over. A new strategic environment demands new strategic policies. Deterrence, reassurance and consensus require a broadening of the strategic focus and a consideration of the new strategic alternatives which are more appropriate for the conditions of the 1980s than the outworn options that have figured so long in strategic debate.

NOTES

[1] John J. Mearsheimer, 'Why Soviets Can't Win Quickly in Central Europe', *International Security*, Vol. 7 (Summer 1982), pp. 5–39.

[2] See my 'The Renewal of Strategy', in *The Strategic Imperative: New Policies for American Security*, (Cambridge, Mass.: Ballinger, 1982), pp. 21–32.

Index

135